PRAISE FOR
Confirmation Bias

"[An] entertaining and shrewd book. . . . As a longtime Washington correspondent, Hulse is an expert guide through the machinations on Capitol Hill."

—*New York Times Book Review*

"The book is an absorbing, if dispiriting, look at the maneuverings of inside players like [Mitch] McConnell and Donald McGahn, Trump's first White House counsel, and outside advocates like Leonard Leo of the Federalist Society, who appears to have steered judicial selection as much as anyone at the White House. Hulse, a *New York Times* correspondent, probes moments of escalation over the years and the backroom machinations of the Trump strategy now transforming the courts and the law. Inevitably, he covers previously reported ground, but *Confirmation Bias* is an important guide at this crucial time for the stature of America's judiciary."

—*Washington Post*

"Carl Hulse has produced an engrossing take on America's judicial wars. . . . Essential reading. . . . [Hulse] fills his book with interviews and history, which people readily share. . . . *Confirmation Bias* . . . gets the story right, however disconcerting it may be."

—*The Guardian*

"A gripping tale of insider Washington with implications far beyond the capital and far beyond our own time."

—*Boston Globe*

"The book sheds light on the events of the past two years."

—*San Francisco Chronicle*

Confirmation Bias

Confirmation Bias

Inside Washington's War Over
the Supreme Court, from Scalia's Death
to Justice Kavanaugh

Carl Hulse

HARPER

NEW YORK · LONDON · TORONTO · SYDNEY

HARPER

A hardcover edition of this book was published in 2019 by HarperCollins Publishers.

CONFIRMATION BIAS. Copyright © 2019, 2020 by Carl Hulse. All rights reserved. Printed in the United States of America. No part of this book may be used or reproduced in any manner whatsoever without written permission except in the case of brief quotations embodied in critical articles and reviews. For information, address HarperCollins Publishers, 195 Broadway, New York, NY 10007.

HarperCollins books may be purchased for educational, business, or sales promotional use. For information, please email the Special Markets Department at SPsales@harpercollins.com.

FIRST HARPER PAPERBACKS EDITION PUBLISHED 2020.

Library of Congress Cataloging-in-Publication Data has been applied for.

ISBN 978-0-06-286292-1 (pbk.)

20 21 22 23 24   LSC   10 9 8 7 6 5 4 3 2 1

To my parents, Jane and Toppy Hulse

It is not easy to conceive a plan better calculated than this to promote a judicious choice of men for filling the offices of the Union.

—ALEXANDER HAMILTON, *Federalist* no. 76, on the Senate's role of advice and consent

Contents

Confirmation Bias

1

Calling the Play

On January 5, 2017, two weeks before Donald J. Trump would be sworn in following his astonishing election as president, a select group of the incoming administration's most senior officials gathered in a secure room in the presidential transition headquarters in an office building not far from the White House Trump would soon occupy. They were casually going about their business to avoid attracting too much attention.

On hand were the vice president elect, Mike Pence, and his counsel Mark Paoletta; Trump's strategist Steve Bannon; the incoming chief of staff, Reince Priebus; and the incoming White House counsel, Donald F. McGahn II. They would spend much of that day interviewing the finalists for a Supreme Court vacancy that had been instrumental in Trump's victory over Hillary Clinton, an outcome few saw coming. It was time to cash in on that stunning win and fill the empty seat as quickly as possible once the administration took office on January 20.

The court opening had given conservative Christian voters and other skeptical Republicans a reason to back Trump despite his well-documented character flaws and their own doubts about him. With the seat in mind, they had sent to the White House an inexperienced and unpredictable man whom most of the country and world knew as a brash reality television celebrity. Now his presidency was about to become a reality, and the Supreme Court would be among the first institutions to feel the impact.

Picking a Supreme Court nominee is usually a complicated, time-consuming process that involves a close review of the nominee's record and writings, along with background checks, interviews, consultations with advocacy groups, and intense internal debate. But the Trump team had been weighing this vacancy for some time—the seat had been open for nearly a year because of an extraordinary campaign mounted by Senate Republicans, led by Mitch McConnell, the majority leader, to prevent President Barack Obama from placing his own nominee, Merrick Garland, on the court.

What's more, in May 2016 candidate Trump had taken the unprecedented step of disclosing a list of his potential Supreme Court nominees and then pledged to choose from only that list. It was another first in a campaign full of them. So the Trump insiders already had a good idea of whom they would recommend to the new president.

Five top-tier conservative judges were interviewed that day. But as the final candidate entered the room, everyone present was nearly certain that they were about to question the next justice of the US Supreme Court, Neil M. Gorsuch, age forty-nine, a federal appeals court judge in Colorado. To them, he had emerged as the right man to fill the seat—if not the shoes—of the revered Antonin G. Scalia, the justice whose death in early 2016 had touched off the whole political drama.

What not everyone in that nondescript room knew was that a few of them saw this as the initial step in filling not one Supreme Court seat, but two. They believed that Justice Anthony M. Kennedy, the eighty-year-old swing vote on the court, could soon be encouraged to step down, creating a second vacancy. McGahn was among them, and he had already made up his mind about the pick for the Kennedy opening and confided in Bannon. It would be Brett M. Kavanaugh, fifty-one, a member of the highly influential US Court of Appeals for the District of Columbia Circuit and a fixture in Washington's Republican political and legal circles. "It was Gorsuch and Kavanaugh, back-to-back," one top Trump official at the meeting remembered. "The play was called."

McGahn had the clout with Trump to make it happen. His work for Trump and his handling of the campaign's judicial list, which had shored up conservative support and acclaim for Trump, gave the incoming president tremendous confidence in McGahn and earned him wide latitude when it came to judges.

Others would be evaluated and interviewed, their names circulated in media leaks. During the screening, someone else might conceivably rise to the top and supplant Gorsuch or Kavanaugh. Trump would have the final say on his picks—though he was certain to be heavily swayed by the recommendations of McGahn and Leonard Leo, the executive vice president of the Federalist Society, an influential organization of conservative lawyers. Leo was a major force in conservative judicial politics and had helped McGahn with compiling Trump's judicial list during the campaign.

But McGahn knew whom he favored, and his motivation was clear. Gorsuch and Kavanaugh were known for writing powerful opinions aimed at diluting the influence of government bureaucrats—the "administrative state," as it is derisively known to conservatives like McGahn, Leo, and Bannon. In elite conservative legal circles, the two judges were considered thought leaders for interpreting the law as a means to strip power from the state.

McGahn himself was an unusual mix of conventional Washington Republican and formerly long-haired radical libertarian who was an excellent guitar player in a beach bar cover band on the side. He may have been a card-carrying conservative, but he still carried a musicians union card. His selection as White House counsel had thrust him into a rarified legal world.

Obsessed with the composition of the federal courts, he would now have tremendous authority over the selection and confirmation of judicial nominees—and not just for the Supreme Court. In negotiating his agreement to join the Trump administration, McGahn had won unparalleled power from Trump to select nominees for the federal bench.

Inflamed and inspired by the fight over Robert Bork's nomination to the high court in 1987, McGahn had received law degrees at Widener University and Georgetown after doing his undergraduate work at Notre Dame. He had been a campaign finance attorney, working for the National Republican Congressional Committee and a host of name-brand conservative clients. He was eventually nominated to the Federal Election Commission by President George W. Bush and was confirmed by the Senate with an eager assist from Senator Mitch McConnell, the Republican leader and longtime foe of campaign finance restrictions.

After his Senate confirmation in 2008, he was sworn in by a former Bush administration operative sitting on the US Court of Appeals for the District of Columbia Circuit—Brett M. Kavanaugh. McGahn still had the picture taken in Kavanaugh's chambers after the swearing-in stored with his memorabilia at home. "That guy's going to be on the Supreme Court someday," he told Shannon Flaherty, his future wife, as they left the ceremony.

As chairman of the FEC, McGahn set out to weaken the regulatory role of the agency, just as McConnell had counted on. McGahn was considered a holy terror there by Democrats and campaign finance watchdogs. By persuading the other two Republican appointees to consistently vote with him, he brought the FEC's work to a halt and sought to disrupt the agency and limit its investigatory power. He left the agency in 2013 to join a private practice.

In late 2014, McGahn began casting about for a Republican presidential campaign to join. He was steered to Trump by his friend David Bossie, head of the Citizens United group, whose landmark Supreme Court victory in 2010 had helped usher in the era of dark campaign money. As he assessed the political landscape, McGahn liked the idea of an unconventional candidate like Trump, calculating that a run-of-the-mill Republican would not be able to upend Hillary Clinton.

Bossie smoothed an introduction, and Trump and McGahn hit it off. At the end of their get-acquainted session at Trump Tower, Trump made his usual offer to pose for a photo. McGahn declined, a rare refusal for what Trump considered a coveted keepsake.

Instead, he asked Trump to sign a book to McGahn's son—Don III. Trump rustled up a copy of *The Art of the Deal*. "You've got a great dad," Donald Trump inscribed the book to Don III. A relationship was born.

When it came to judges, McGahn, Bannon, and other conservative thinkers in the Trump circle cared about the touchstone conservative cultural and social issues such as abortion, gay rights, and religious freedom that often dominated the public conversation surrounding Supreme Court confirmation conflicts. But they were even more consumed with "deconstructing the administrative state"—tearing down the federal government's regulatory structure, which had grown up over decades. To them, that bureaucracy represented a major threat to individual freedom by exerting enormous influence over American lives through edicts issued by agency personnel. Conservatives argued that those unelected and unaccountable governors had been freed by the courts to go far beyond policy enacted by Congress and were essentially making law on their own. The willingness of the courts to bow to agencies' decisions in instances in which legislation was ambiguous was known as the "Chevron deference," since it had grown out of a 1984 Supreme Court ruling on air pollution rules challenged by an environmental group but later upheld on an appeal by the oil company.

To Democrats, environmentalists, government watchdogs, and others alarmed about the influence of corporate America, the whole "administrative state" argument was bogus, simply a ruse to limit government regulation and let businesses and industry trample the environment and consumers. But weakening bureaucratic power was fast becoming a central pillar of conservative thought when it came to the judiciary, and the Trump team was lining up its court picks to pursue its goal of unraveling the federal apparatus.

"It was going to be around the writing," said one top Trump official about the credentials for nomination. "Who can drive the court intellectually in this new era of taking apart the Leviathan. It was always Gorsuch *and* Kavanaugh."

Gorsuch had attracted the interest of conservative legal scholars for his call to challenge federal agencies' power, saying in one decision issued just a few months earlier in 2016 that existing Supreme Court precedents "permit executive bureaucracies to swallow huge amounts of core judicial and legislative power and concentrate federal power in a way that seems more than a little difficult to square with the Constitution of the framers' design. Maybe the time has come to face the behemoth."

Gorsuch had practically grown up with the Chevron decision. His mother, Anne, was the head of the Environmental Protection Agency (EPA) during the Reagan administration and approved the rule that was upheld in the landmark finding on deference. She was the victor in a decision her son believed had invested too much authority in the bureaucracy. Now he was intent on undoing it. He also had memories of his mother's ugly ouster from Washington in an agency scandal.

Kavanaugh, who served in both Bush presidencies, was also recognized in the legal world for a record that was aimed at limiting the discretion that federal agencies have in setting policy. He wasn't in the running for the Scalia vacancy; he hadn't even yet made it onto Trump's list of judicial candidates. That would come later at McGahn's direction. He was a nominee in waiting.

Gorsuch, the current top contender, got help from his rivals for the nomination. Asked who they would pick if they weren't the nominee for the Scalia vacancy, all named Gorsuch. Only Gorsuch didn't offer an alternative, saying he would need to review all the opinions of the others before making his choice. It was a shrewd response, and it only underscored how strongly the others rated Gorsuch, considering their willingness to volunteer his name.

There was a long way to go, but in less than two years from the day of the meeting, both Gorsuch and Kavanaugh would be Supreme

Court justices, creating a new conservative power center built around two Trump-nominated newcomers who could be on the court for decades. The outcome would have grave implications for the court. With the Trump campaign benefitting from what US intelligence agencies agreed was Russian interference in the 2016 election, Democrats and others hostile to Trump considered his appointees essentially illegitimate. They would always have the unique circumstances of their confirmations hanging over them, not to mention the Republican obstruction that had prevented Obama from filling the Scalia seat.

The conflict also focused new attention on the politics surrounding the high court and stirred interest on the left in making significant changes such as expanding its size or establishing term limits to prevent one decision by a president from having such an enduring effect on the nation long after that president was gone.

The Republican success in the 2016 election also ignited a furious effort by the Trump administration and Senate Republicans to place like-minded conservatives on lower courts around the country, filling scores of vacancies that Republican senators had held open by refusing to act on Obama's nominations. To Republicans, changing the ideological makeup of the courts was paramount, since they increasingly saw federal judges as their best defense against the march of progressive policies on health care, the environment, immigration, voting rights, gender identity, and much more.

Given the demographic changes occurring in the country, the influx of conservatives holding lifetime appointments on the bench raised the prospect of a widening ideological gulf between much of the public and the federal judiciary, a divide that could threaten the public trust underpinning the courts.

The Senate, the presidential partner in confirming nominees, was also in turmoil, badly torn by decades of bitter judicial wars. The institution had been engaged in a destructive running battle over the courts since the mid-1980s, a conflict escalated to an entirely new and divisive level during the Obama administration.

Trump was taking office thanks to an open Supreme Court seat, and with a Senate majority, Republicans had the means and motivation to bulldoze through lifetime judicial appointees over the objections of Democrats. Washington was in for a shock, and the consequences could roil leading government institutions for generations.

None of this would have been possible but for a single decision made by a single member of the Senate on a holiday weekend in February 2016.

2

A Death in Texas

CIBOLO CREEK RANCH is a remote luxury resort in West Texas that has for years attracted celebrities and the affluent looking for well-appointed seclusion and a bit of high-end hunting, fishing, and hiking. Located just under forty miles south of Marfa, a small but picturesque city that has often represented Texas in popular film, the resort has its own landing strip, able to accommodate most private jets. Two men from Washington were among those who landed there in a private aircraft on Friday, February 12, 2016.

The ranch was owned by John Poindexter, a wealthy entrepreneur, a decorated Vietnam War veteran, and a leader of the International Order of Saint Hubertus, a semiprivate social club for well-heeled Catholic outdoorsmen. At Poindexter's invitation, a group of about thirty-five people gathered to enjoy a weekend quail hunt and dinner on Friday at the thirty-thousand-acre ranch. On Saturday morning, Poindexter noticed that one of his very distinguished guests from Washington had missed breakfast. He wasn't overly concerned. His visitor was older, and over supper the night before had said he was feeling fatigued.

It was only later in the morning that he became alarmed enough to go check on the still-absent occupant of the El Presidente suite. When a knock at the door went unanswered, Poindexter decided to enter the room. Inside he found Antonin Gregory Scalia, associate justice of the US Supreme Court and an icon to the nation's conservative community, still in bed. He was dead, three pillows stacked under his head, apparently to aid his breathing. A pillowcase had slipped down over his eyes, but the scene was peaceful enough that no autopsy was performed and the FBI declined an invitation to investigate, despite Scalia's national standing.

At seventy-nine and overweight, with a host of other medical troubles, Scalia was not in great health, and his passing was not a great surprise. Still, his death was a shock both to those at the Cibolo Creek Ranch and to the nation. He had been a larger-than-life figure on the court for three decades, casting an expansive shadow over its deliberations as the embodiment of American conservative thought and jurisprudence.

His passing was certain to precipitate a pitched political fight, given that the vacancy could tip the ideological balance of the court and came with just less than a year remaining in President Obama's second term. Within hours, an epic political clash would be touched off that would not only significantly change the court but arguably the very course of American history. It would help decide a presidential election, fundamentally alter the nature of the US Senate, and accelerate the transformation of the Supreme Court itself into a politicized body that serves as an extension of our bitter partisanship rather than a neutral arbiter rising above it.

Mitch McConnell was no one's idea of a beach bum. Casual, sand-between-the-toes moments seemed far beyond his comfort zone. Official Washington would find it impossible to imagine the painfully reserved, buttoned-down seventy-three-year-old Senate Republican leader from Kentucky frolicking in the warm Caribbean Sea or lazing in the island sun while sipping a piña colada. On occasions when he tried to strike an informal pose by dressing in jeans, he still looked like he was wearing a suit.

Yet on the day Scalia was found dead in remote West Texas, McConnell arrived on tropical Saint Thomas to spend the Senate's President's

Day break relaxing with his wife, then-former cabinet secretary Elaine Chao, on their annual beach jaunt. His vacation was about to be interrupted in a most unanticipated way.

Upon arriving in the Virgin Islands, McConnell received the shocking news of Scalia's death from his staff and television accounts. It was a hugely disorienting and upsetting development for McConnell. Scalia embodied conservativism on the court. To the Right, he was the erudite bulwark against creeping liberal progressivism, a movement McConnell viewed as a genuine threat to America. He believed the left turn personified by the election of Obama was capable of converting the United States into a version of socialistic western Europe. Scalia was also a personal hero of the Kentucky Republican, and a man he idolized. McConnell had served with Scalia as a junior staffer at the Justice Department in the mid-1970s, when some of the top legal minds of the conservative movement roamed the hallways of Main Justice: Scalia as head of the Office of Legal Counsel, Robert Bork as solicitor general, and Laurence Silberman as deputy attorney general.

As he sat in his hotel room transfixed by reports of Scalia's odd death at the luxury hunting lodge in Texas, McConnell's first thoughts were of his own dealings over the years with "Nino" Scalia, beginning with his days as a lowly staffer in the shadow of those three impressive officials. "I remember just being completely intimidated by the intelligence and wit of those guys interacting with each other every morning," recalled McConnell.

Ten years later, McConnell was in the Senate and able to enthusiastically support Scalia's nomination to the Supreme Court by Ronald Reagan. The two developed a warm personal relationship and would dine together occasionally. For McConnell, the death of Scalia represented a huge loss. "Clearly this was somebody of the Oliver Wendell Holmes, John Marshall class," he said. "A big, big deal."

This being Mitch McConnell, a political animal through and through, he quickly put aside personal emotion so he could pragmatically zero in on what really mattered—who and what would come next. "My second thought was to immediately turn to the politics of this situation," he said. "The first thing that came into my mind was that I knew if the shoe was on the other foot they wouldn't fill this vacancy. I knew it for sure."

"They," of course, meant the Democrats. To McConnell's way of thinking, if the situation were reversed and a Republican president were given the sudden and unexpected opportunity to name a new Supreme Court justice to the court and flip its ideological balance in the final year of his term, a Democratic Senate would balk and find some excuse to block the confirmation. He couldn't know for sure, of course, but McConnell figured that since it was what he would do, no doubt the Democrats would do the same thing. It made perfect political sense to him.

This was not just any vacancy; this was a vacancy that had the potential to throw the ideological balance of the right-leaning court to the left if President Obama was allowed the third Supreme Court confirmation of his presidency. Scalia, the conservative lion, could be succeeded by a justice named by a progressive president for whom McConnell had little regard. He had already done all he could to impede Obama during the previous seven years, and thwarting him on the Supreme Court would be one more phase of that strategy—though a hugely visible and risky one. But the prospect of a new Obama justice was a monumental threat in the eyes of McConnell, who could imagine the reconfigured court upholding the liberal health care and environmental policies pushed through by the Obama administration and perhaps even reversing the steady weakening of the campaign finance laws and labor union protections that McConnell so detested.

In addition, he saw Obama as a neophyte, a man who had not distinguished himself during his four years in the Senate (two of which were largely devoted to his presidential campaign)—a drive-by tenure under the standards of the institution—and someone who succeeded on the strength of charisma and a gift for rousing speeches. Charisma was one character trait that almost everyone, even McConnell himself, would admit was lacking in the Senate majority leader. The president also had a regrettable tendency to lecture much more senior and experienced congressional leaders during their regular phone calls and visits to the White House, and it thoroughly aggravated McConnell.

During one set of budget talks between Republicans and the White House, McConnell remembered a phone call with the president in which he watched an uninterrupted inning of baseball on television while Obama first laid out his view of the problem. "He talks down to people, whether in a meeting among colleagues in the White House or addressing the nation," McConnell complained about Obama in his memoir, *The Long Game*.

Mitch McConnell did not appreciate being talked down to by anyone, let alone Barack Obama.

He took to referring to the president as "Professor Obama" and said once in an interview with *Business Insider* that he found Obama's tendency to lecture a "grating and irritating characteristic that many of us had to endure." McConnell much preferred to do business with Obama's vice president, Joseph R. Biden Jr., his old dealmaking pal from their Senate years.

Usually with a death like Scalia's, politicians will give lip service to focusing first on the loss and the deceased, saying in somber, respectful tones that politics will have to wait a suitable mourning period. Those protestations are usually false, with the political wheels spinning furiously behind the scenes, but honored for reasons of good taste.

In this case, with its momentous implications, no one would wait for the political fight to kick in, certainly not McConnell. Over the next few hours, in consultation with only a handful of staff (his wife had headed to the beach), he made a bold and brazen decision that would change the history of three institutions—the Senate, the presidency, and the Supreme Court—in ways that Mitch McConnell could have never foreseen.

3

"Business to Attend To"

McConnell was not the only figure invested in Supreme Court politics confronting the shocking loss of Scalia. Across Washington and the country, members of both parties and the judiciary were learning of the death and quickly assessing the situation. Top officials and influential members of the legal community were drawn away from their holiday weekend gatherings and into the political fray. Washington, which had felt left out of the developing presidential race, had a crisis and rushed to embrace it.

One of the first called into action was Leonard Leo, the executive vice president of the Federalist Society, the conservative group that was a breeding ground for judicial nominees and had played a significant role both in promoting judges for Republican presidents and fighting the nominees of Democrats. A devout Catholic with seven children, Leo had served as an intern for Senator Orrin Hatch in the 1980s. He was a big man with a taste for good food and good wine, appetites acquired under Scalia's tutelage. He also possessed a healthy ego and was never shy about promoting his own influence and role in the byzantine judicial politics of Washington—a proclivity that even some of his allies found irritating.

He was a major figure among conservatives and was personally close to Justice Scalia, bound by their ideologies and strong Catholic faith. He was so close to Scalia in fact that he got a phone message that Saturday afternoon from one of Scalia's family members alerting him to an emergency. Leo knew the unexpected call on a weekend was not good news. He feared his friend the justice was sick or had been hospitalized.

Upon learning that his friend and judicial hero was dead, a reeling Leo sought to process the information. He hoped that Scalia had been prepared for death in the Catholic sense of reconciling with God and being in a state of grace. The family member told Leo that he should be discreet and not widely disseminate the news until all the members of the immediate Scalia family had been informed.

But, the family member also said, Justice Scalia himself would "understand you have some business to attend to." Leo was being given permission to put his grief aside and focus on court politics. To him, that plainly meant taking steps to ensure an acceptable successor to the mighty justice and cement Scalia's legacy. He knew what he was supposed to do and how to do it.

Leo, who was home alone, tried to compose himself even as he went into action. He called John Abegg, McConnell's key judicial staffer, so that he could pass the word about Scalia's death to McConnell and give him a head start on plotting a strategy for how to approach the vacancy. The two men had talked about how they might handle it in the past, but those discussions were more in the context of a planned retirement, not a sudden death.

"My biggest concern was that there was going to be a cacophony of voices," said Leo, noting that the Senate was on recess. He worried that the dispersed senators would offer a mixed message and, in their rush to sound somber and statesmanlike, give Democrats a political opening. McConnell, on the phone in the Caribbean, shared that same fear.

"It was very important to me that there be real discipline, and the only way that was going to happen was if Mitch came out very quickly, and he understood this," Leo recalled.

As the news sunk in, Leo also gave thought to his friend. "He lived a great life," Leo said, "and I'm pretty confident on where he is."

McConnell was now confident as well, suddenly certain of exactly what he was going to do about the court seat from his hotel suite in the tropics.

Having decided that there was no way he was going to allow Obama to fill the vacancy, McConnell knew he would have to get his fellow Republicans to go along with his strategy. That was no sure thing with elections looming in November. Republicans running in swing states such as Iowa, Ohio, and New Hampshire might not be willing to challenge the president on such a politically charged matter and potentially alienate independents, not to mention infuriating Democrats. Supreme Court nominees almost always got hearings and votes, even if they were rejected.

McConnell recognized that with eleven months remaining in the second term of a president who remained popular despite some stumbles, erecting an unbreachable blockade was not going to be easy. It would elicit a ferocious response from Democrats and their allies, aware, like McConnell, of the unexpected but incredible opportunity before them to gain the upper hand on the court.

McConnell began communicating with staff and advisers scattered for the recess, touching base with Abegg, his highly trusted assistant on judicial confirmations, as well as his chief of staff, Sharon Soderstrom, and Don Stewart, his communications director. They developed a plan of attack and began to execute it.

Another political factor that would propel the decision-making for McConnell and others was at work that night. The remaining six Republican presidential candidates were to meet for a nationally televised primary debate beginning at nine p.m. in Greenville, South Carolina. Scalia's death and what it meant for the court would certainly be a main topic of discussion.

In a phone conversation with McConnell, Josh Holmes, the senator's politically astute former chief of staff and top campaign aide, reminded McConnell of the debate. They agreed that if Senator Ted Cruz, the Texas Republican and presidential candidate widely disliked by his fellow senators, were to use the debate to be the first to call for Senate Republicans to block Obama's nominee, it would be a disaster for McConnell. Republican senators would not want to appear to be doing Cruz's bidding.

"I simply made mention to him that the debate was going to be that evening," recalled Holmes, now a top Washington strategist as founder of the consulting firm Cavalry. "I was absolutely sure that Cruz was going to take the furthest position, and if that was McConnell's view, he should get out in front of him. If it was branded as a Ted Cruz idea, he could lose half of his conference."

McConnell might have preferred to hold off before injecting politics into the moment, but time was of the essence. So within hours of Scalia's death, the majority leader's office issued a statement that arrived just after six p.m. in the email in-boxes of busy reporters who were still digesting the news while wondering if it would be bad form to begin raising the obvious political issues surrounding the jurist's passing.

The majority leader's statement first praised Scalia as a champion of the Constitution before ending with this startling edict: "The American people should have a voice in the selection of their next Supreme Court Justice. Therefore, this vacancy should not be filled until we have a new President."

On his own, McConnell was creating a new standard. No rule or language in the Constitution prohibited a court appointment in a presidential election year. Supreme Court vacancies are rare, and justices often time their retirements to when a president of their political preference can name a replacement. Scalia would not have willingly left his seat for Obama to fill, even though the Senate was in Republican hands.

Within the Senate, there was something whispered about as the "Thurmond rule," an informal understanding that said the Senate would quit considering judicial candidates at some point in a presidential election year given a potential change at the White House. Named for Strom Thurmond, the conservative South Carolina senator who had chaired the Judiciary Committee, it was not any formalized practice. To the extent it existed at all, it was a moving target, as judges were routinely confirmed in presidential election years. It definitely was not meant to go into force in February with nearly a year left in a presidential term.

Nothing said a president shouldn't act or that the Senate should rebuff him if he did. Plenty of time remained to make and win approval of a nominee in the more than 340 days remaining in Obama's term at the time of Scalia's death. The entire process typically took a little more than two months from nomination to confirmation vote.

Democrats had raised the prospect of holding off in a presidential election year in the past during Republican presidencies, but the idea was hypothetical, since a vacancy never materialized. McConnell was establishing new rules.

It was an act of outrageous audacity. Virtually on his own, without consulting a single elected Senate colleague, Mitch McConnell had decided to deny the Democratic president his right to fill an open Supreme Court seat. But he knew he had to act fast to hold Senate Republicans together. GOP senators were dispersed around the country and the world and were certainly going to be pressed by reporters on what to do about the court opening. He wanted to send clear signals about what they should say—and what they should not say about eagerly awaiting the president's choice or some other senatorial boilerplate that would typically be spouted after a high court vacancy.

"I had members all over the world, all over the country," McConnell recalled. "Normally if I had a recommendation to make, I would make it to the group and hope I could sell it sort of contemporaneously. Obviously, that was not possible. What I didn't want was, you know, fifty-three opinions about what to do by the time we got back. People having done interviews and taken positions, and here I was trying to unwind it all. I wanted to give them something to look at quickly."

Republican senators got little explanation for McConnell's move beyond what had been issued publicly. In a group email to Republican senators, McConnell added a short preface to his bold pronouncement: "Attached is my statement on the sad news about Justice Scalia. Please note the fact that It has been more than 80 years since a new justice was confirmed in an election year."

That was McConnell, short and to the point. And more than a little misleading, since Ronald Reagan's nomination of Anthony M. Kennedy had been confirmed by a Democratic Senate in the presidential election year of 1988, though Kennedy had been nominated in 1987. Such distinctions were about to become a regular facet of the nation's political discourse. The history of Supreme Court appointments in presidential election years could be spun multiple ways. The basic fact was that the situation just didn't occur very often.

McConnell was not the only influential Republican to quickly dispel any notion that the Senate would confirm an Obama nominee.

Shoveling snow back home in Iowa, Senator Charles E. Grassley, the chairman of the Judiciary Committee, which would normally review any nomination, first got the news of Scalia's death from a reporter. He quickly followed McConnell's lead, sending out his own statement declaring he would not act on any nomination before the November election.

"The fact of the matter is that it's been standard practice over the last nearly 80 years that Supreme Court nominees are not nominated and confirmed during a presidential election year," Grassley said, aping McConnell. "Given the huge divide in the country, and the fact that this President, above all others, has made no bones about his goal to use the courts to circumvent Congress and push through his own agenda, it only makes sense that we defer to the American people who will elect a new president to select the next Supreme Court Justice."

Grassley's statement touched on a sore point with Republicans when it came to Obama. Stymied legislatively by the Republicans in the House and Senate since 2011, the president had increasingly relied on his own executive authority to enact policy over the objections of Republicans.

The Deferred Action for Childhood Arrivals program, or DACA, was a prime example. Created in 2012 through a presidential memorandum, it protected people brought into the country unlawfully as children from being deported. Obama had also angered Republicans with his declaration in 2014 that "I've got a pen to take executive actions where Congress won't and I've got a telephone to rally folks around the country on this mission." It became known as Obama's "pen and phone" promise to sign executive orders and work around Republican resistance. The Scalia vacancy would give the president a Supreme Court likely to uphold those executive policies, and McConnell, Grassley, and their colleagues wanted none of it.

Democrats immediately howled at the declarations by the top Republicans.

McConnell, their archnemesis for the past seven years, had not even waited for Obama to choose a nominee before declaring the Senate would not fulfill its iconic role of "advice and consent"—the constitutional responsibility that is probably the best-known feature of the Senate after the filibuster. To them, the idea that the "American people" would need to have a role as demanded in the McConnell statement was ridiculous—the American people had played a role in 2012 when they reelected Barack Obama over Republican Mitt Romney, they argued. This was clearly Obama's vacancy to fill, and McConnell's statement was a laughable attempt to find a rationale to deny the president his indisputable right to carry out his constitutional duty.

Appearing at a fundraising dinner in Denver the night of Scalia's death, Hillary Clinton, the Democratic front-runner to succeed Obama, lashed out at McConnell as well as Republican presidential contenders who were already backing the idea of holding the seat open.

"For any of us who needed a reminder of just how important it is to take back the US Senate and hold on to the White House, just look at the Supreme Court," she said. "I know that our thoughts and prayers are with the Scalia family tonight, and I am also thinking and praying for the future of our country. It is outrageous that Republicans in the

Senate and on the campaign trail have already pledged to block any replacement that President Obama nominates.

"Now, I'm sure we'll all have a lot more to say about this in the coming days, but let me just make one point: Barack Obama is president of the United States until January 20, 2017. That is a fact, my friends, whether the Republicans like it or not. Elections have consequences. The president has a responsibility to nominate a new justice, and the Senate has a responsibility to vote, and all of us Democrats, we have a responsibility to make sure a Republican doesn't win in November and rip away all the progress we've made together."

Clinton had served in the Senate with McConnell and was well acquainted with his intense partisanship. Many elected Democrats and their activist allies had nothing but contempt for the majority leader. This was the taciturn man who had set out from the start of the Obama presidency to thwart the president, the man who had famously said that his top priority was to make Obama a one-term president. To them, McConnell was a poisonous presence on Capitol Hill and in American politics—the obstructionist in chief.

All of that was fine with Mitch McConnell, who didn't mind what the opposition thought of him if he was winning. He happily embraced his image as the dark lord of the Senate. One wall of his personal office in the Russell Senate Office Building was covered with framed prints of editorial cartoons saying all sorts of nasty things about him. McConnell, often caricatured by his foes as physically resembling a turtle, would even wear turtle-shaped cuff links on occasion.

Privately, Democrats had grudging respect for McConnell's ruthlessness and his win-at-any-cost mentality. "What he did was just incredibly shrewd," said one Obama White House insider, marveling at McConnell's willingness to act so quickly after Scalia's death. But no one was about to say that publicly, particularly when it came to the federal courts.

McConnell was more than slightly obsessive about the Supreme Court and the Senate due to his early exposure to the high drama of court confirmation fights. He was on the staff of the freshman senator

Marlow Cook, his mentor, when Richard Nixon nominated Clement Haynsworth in 1969, followed by G. Harrold Carswell in 1970, resulting in the storied case of two ugly back-to-back rejections by the Senate. (Carswell's rejection came after an iconic Senate moment when Senator Roman Hruska, the Nebraska Republican, defended the nominee against complaints he was mediocre. "Even if he were mediocre, there are a lot of mediocre judges and people and lawyers. They are entitled to a little representation, aren't they, and a little chance?" Hruska asked. "We can't have all Brandeises, Frankfurters, and Cardozos.")

McConnell's front-row seat as an aide to Cook, a junior member of the Judiciary Committee, resulted in McConnell writing a 1970 article on the failed confirmations for the *Kentucky Law Journal*. In it, he noted that he had been a witness to "possibly the most interesting period in Supreme Court history."

He was wrong about that. Now he was about to create his own interesting period of Supreme Court history through his handling of the nomination to replace Scalia and what would become its transformative aftermath. He could deal with the outrage from the Democrats. What he didn't want was his fellow Republicans breaking from their colleagues, to weaken or wilt in the face of the coming critical onslaught. He was quickly in contact with those who would be crucial to helping him secure his position—as well as those who might be shaky. A few required reassurance that this was the right move, that Republican voters would much more strongly reward the obstruction of Obama than Democrats and independents would revolt against it. But the internal concern was actually less than McConnell anticipated, and he said the "hand-holding" was kept to a minimum.

"A couple of people were a little nervous Nellies," McConnell said. "But I only had to make two or three calls. We were monitoring what anybody might be saying in case I needed to make further calls. It was actually fairly smooth."

McConnell didn't intend to lose now that he had made his own play.

4

"Of Course the President Is Going to Nominate Someone"

Denis McDonough, the White House chief of staff, was at his son's soccer game when he was alerted about Scalia. One of the first calls he received was from Senator Chuck Schumer, the New York Democrat who was also a veteran of decades of judicial nomination fights. Anticipating McConnell's reaction, he warned McDonough that Republicans were going to urge President Obama not to nominate a replacement for Scalia and to leave the seat open—a notion the White House chief of staff considered preposterous.

"I said, 'Of course the president is going to nominate someone,'" recalled McDonough, a known stickler for going by the book when it came to running the White House. "It is the president's constitutional responsibility."

Out in Rancho Mirage, California, where the president was playing golf on what was expected to be a quiet holiday weekend, aides who had been lounging at the pool sprang into action. They quickly learned of McConnell's view and debated whether the president's statement should be delivered personally or as a White House release. They also discussed whether it should focus, as would be traditional, on the deceased and his life of service or be more political given the rapid pace of developments. They were leery of ceding the political terrain—and the news cycle—to McConnell's declaration. They too were cognizant that the Republican presidential candidates were gathering for the primary debate in South Carolina.

To start, they needed to round up a suit for the vacationing chief executive.

In the end, the team on the ground thought they hit the sweet spot—a video and a written statement that allowed the now suitably attired president and former constitutional law professor both to recognize Scalia and to make clear his intentions to select a nominee no matter what Mitch McConnell might think.

"Justice Scalia dedicated his life to the cornerstone of our democracy: the rule of law," Obama said in the statement. "Tonight, we honor his extraordinary service to our nation and remember one of the towering legal figures of our time."

While Obama said that it was the moment to remember Scalia, he also made clear he had his own ideas about what to do with the seat. "I plan to fulfill my constitutional responsibilities to nominate a successor in due time," he said. "There will be plenty of time for me to do so, and for the Senate to fulfill its responsibility to give that person a fair hearing and a timely vote. These are responsibilities that I take seriously, as should everyone. They're bigger than any one party. They are about our democracy. They're about the institution to which Justice Scalia dedicated his professional life and making sure it continues to function as the beacon of justice that our founders envisioned."

Don McGahn, Trump's campaign lawyer, was driving along Route 50 to Ocean City, Maryland, his car packed with band gear for a weekend gig as a guitarist with a group called Scott's New Band. He glanced at an incoming text from his wife, Shannon. "Scalia died," she wrote. McGahn pulled off the highway into the parking lot of a Wawa gas station and convenience store, shocked, shaken, and saddened by the news. Then, like McConnell, he immediately turned to the political implications.

McGahn knew that his candidate might be at a disadvantage at that night's debate against senators who had more experience with judicial politics. He was particularly worried about Cruz, the obstreperous Texan who served on the Judiciary Committee and had also clerked on the court for Chief Justice William Rehnquist. Cruz was still hanging on as a rival and potential conservative alternative to Trump, and he would inevitably try to capitalize on the political implications of Scalia's death.

McGahn called Trump to warn him not to be the first to politicize Scalia's passing.

"What about putting out some names?" Trump asked, instinctively recognizing that specific prospective nominees might go over well with the conservative audience he was courting.

McGahn agreed that was a good idea and quickly ran through some possibilities. "Brett Kavanaugh," McGahn offered as the first name that came to mind, promoting the judge recognized in Washington as a rising conservative star of the federal bench. He and Trump kicked around a few others, including the appeals court judges William Pryor Jr. of Alabama and Diane Sykes of Wisconsin—two favorites of hardline conservatives. As they weighed the pros and cons, the candidate and his lawyer concluded that perhaps it wasn't the best time for Trump to embrace Kavanaugh, a Washington insider and a George W. Bush appointee to the court that had also produced Chief Justice John G. Roberts Jr., another W. appointee currently in Republican disfavor for upholding the new health care law.

The moderator, John Dickerson of CBS News, opened the debate with a moment of silence for Scalia, but the silence didn't last long. Dickerson asked Trump if, with eleven months to go in his hypothetical presidential term, he would bow to Democratic demands that he not put forward a nominee for the vacancy.

"If I were president now I would certainly want to try and nominate a justice," he acknowledged. "I'm sure that, frankly, I'm absolutely sure that President Obama will try and do it. I hope that our Senate is going to be able—Mitch, and the entire group, is going to be able—to do something about it."

And by doing something about it, Trump meant doing nothing about it. Then, the phone conversation with McGahn fresh in his mind, Trump tossed out some names. "In times of delay, we could have a Diane Sykes, or you could have a Bill Pryor, we have some fantastic people," he said. "But this is a tremendous blow to conservatism. It's a tremendous blow, frankly, to our country."

"I think it's up to Mitch McConnell, and everybody else to stop it," he said in answer to a follow-up question. "It's called delay, delay, delay."

Those words were music to the ears of McConnell, the master of delay.

McGahn's instincts about Cruz proved correct. During the debate, Cruz emphasized his own twenty-year history with Scalia and how he would handle the job of filling court vacancies. "One of the most important judgments for the men and women of South Carolina to make is who on this stage has the background, the principle, the character, the judgment, and the strength of resolve to nominate and confirm principled constitutionalists to the court," he said, trying to draw a contrast with Trump. "That will be what I will do if I'm elected president."

Traveling around South Carolina after the debate, Cruz was even more direct, noting that Trump had said that his sister Maryanne Trump Barry, a federal judge in Pennsylvania, would make a phenomenal judge. "Now, it's good to stand with your sister, but Donald's sister was a Bill Clinton–appointed federal appellate judge who is a radical pro-abortion extremist," Cruz said at a news conference. He also warned that Trump would appoint judges who would roll back gun rights.

Cruz's comments persuaded the Trump campaign that, with a court vacancy potentially at stake in the election, he could benefit from doing more to be specific about the judges he would appoint.

At home in Maine, Senator Susan Collins was already preparing in her mind for contentious Supreme Court hearings. One of just two remaining Republican centrists in the Senate, Collins was the perennial swing vote in that chamber, a role that had grown more significant as Senate Republicans had become more conservative.

Meticulous and thoughtful, Collins sometimes seemed more like the studious Senate staffer she had been before her successful political career. She had a welcoming, friendly manner and a deliberate speaking style that led some to mistakenly believe she was a pushover. Far from it. She was not afraid to take on her colleagues, including McConnell. The former high school student body president was always well prepared and not one to be intimidated.

She also drove some Democrats crazy. They saw her as a Republican who was masquerading as a moderate but would almost always vote with her party in the end. As much as Democrats wanted Collins to be a Democrat, she was still a Maine Republican, one in the establishment, government-service mold of the Bush family, which had deep ties to Maine from their summer residence in Kennebunkport. Collins would invariably grab the spotlight in any confirmation fight as a gettable Republican vote for the nominee of a Democratic president. In the case of a Republican president, Collins, as a supporter of abortion rights, would be pressed by activists not to support any nominee considered a threat to the landmark *Roe v. Wade* ruling.

When it came to the Scalia seat, Collins was thinking like a Bush, not McConnell. "I just assumed the president would nominate someone and we would have a big battle," Collins said. "It never occurred to me that we would not go through the normal process of considering the nomination."

Top Democrats were confident that was what eventually would happen. They believed that McConnell's strategy could never hold under the political and public pressure they intended to bring, particularly with an election that would decide control of the Senate just nine months away. The public wouldn't stand for it. "I think there is at least a fifty-fifty chance that pressure from the Republican Senate caucus will force McConnell to reverse himself and at least hold hearings and a vote," Schumer predicted the day after Scalia's death.

Privately, some Democratic strategists were jubilant, believing that the cagey McConnell had made a gigantic blunder and handed them potent ammunition that would not only allow them to take back the Senate but would help elect Hillary Clinton to the White House.

David Krone, a former chief of staff to Harry Reid, the Senate Democratic leader, had regularly clashed with the White House and had little regard for the administration's strategic ability or political skills. But he saw this as a major misstep by McConnell. "I am the very last person in the world to defend Obama or Dems, but this is a gift from heaven," wrote Krone, the frequent Obama critic, in an email at the time. If Republicans held firm, it would give Hillary an issue on which to pound them for months. And with a Supreme Court seat at stake in November, she could stress her electability over her primary foe, Senator Bernie Sanders. Krone calculated that it might also help her rally the younger women who had so far been cool to her campaign.

"Those young women who might not have voted in November now do have a real reason to vote—their future. It's no longer about theory but reality.

"Of course," he added, "that would mean the Clinton campaign would have to get their heads out of their asses, but that's another issue altogether."

Publicly, Krone's former boss Reid of Nevada was supremely assured about the outcome as he met with reporters on February 17 in Reno. "I think my Republican counterpart McConnell has made a terrible mistake by saying that he is going to ignore the president," said Reid, who had gone toe-to-toe with McConnell for years. "Presidents are elected for four-year terms. The president was reelected for a four-year term, not a three-year term.

"So I would think that McConnell's going to have to come around. He can't keep this position. It would historically change our country."

Democrats saw the judicial maneuver as an attempt by McConnell to protect himself as much as the conservative majority on the court. He had been under fire from the Right for years for being too accommodating—a view that left Democrats incredulous, since they saw him as just the opposite. But McConnell had been determined to beat back Tea Party challenges to Senate Republicans and in 2014 had to fight off a primary challenge of his own. To Democrats, the decision to resist an Obama nominee was another example of McConnell's well-honed instinct for self-preservation. By vowing to block any nominee, McConnell could ingratiate himself to the Right and say he had done all he could. Democrats didn't think he could prevail.

"He did it for himself," Reid would say later.

Of course, Reid's hands were not exactly clean on the subject. He had led the blockade of appeals court nominations by President George W. Bush beginning in 2003. More important, he had engineered a change in Senate practices in 2013 that had gutted the ability to filibuster judicial and executive branch nominees—except for Supreme Court picks. After years of threats, it was the first time the so-called nuclear option weakening the filibuster had been detonated. Republicans were still steaming over that maneuver, which had allowed Obama to fill multiple judicial vacancies, most notably three on the important US Court of Appeals for the District of Columbia Circuit, a court that has historically served as an incubator for future Supreme Court justices and reviews conflicts over federal policy.

Reid declared that "the president's going to give us a nominee that's a good one, and I think they're going to have to hold hearings and have a vote. And I think it's going to be a very, very tough deal for them because we have held hearings continually, we have voted on some of these characters they've put up."

Reid cited Justice Clarence Thomas, whom he called "a disaster for the country. Sits up there mute, doesn't say anything. Joins in opinions, usually with Scalia. And we approved him. He got fifty-three votes. Now think about that. We didn't filibuster anybody, we could have stopped that so easy, but we didn't do that. It's not the right thing to do. But that's what they've done. Time and time again, they've filibustered everything. We haven't. [Anthony] Kennedy, [John] Roberts, [Samuel] Alito, there were no filibusters there," said Reid, overlooking a failed attempt to block Alito. "I think they should just have a vote."

"The American people are going to make them pay if they jerk the president around on this," Reid declared in his usual blunt style.

Despite the threat of political consequences, Republicans quickly fell in line behind McConnell. On the Sunday following McConnell's dramatic decision, Republicans were generally in sync. "I don't see anyone getting confirmed," Senator Mike Lee, a conservative Utah Republican who sat on the Judiciary Committee, said that Sunday afternoon. "I suspect that probably means no hearings."

Even more telling was a statement released on Twitter by Senator Kelly Ayotte of New Hampshire, one of the most endangered Republican incumbents up for reelection. She was certain to anger crucial independent voters in her home state if she helped stall the eventual nomination. But she quickly backed McConnell's position. "We are in the midst of a consequential presidential election year and Americans deserve an opportunity to weigh in given the significant implications this nomination could have for the Supreme Court and our country for decades to come," she wrote.

McConnell's aides said that Ayotte, despite her public posture, was nervous and needed assurances, as did Senator Rob Portman, the Ohio Republican, who was not one to embrace big political risks.

Trump sounded the alarm for conservatives in one of what were becoming his ubiquitous tweets. "The totally unexpected loss of Supreme Court Justice Antonin Scalia is a massive setback for the Conservative movement and our COUNTRY!" Trump tweeted with his characteristic capital letters.

Trump went on in a statement extolling Scalia's ideology. "His career was defined by his reverence for the Constitution and his legacy of protecting Americans' most cherished freedoms. He was a Justice who did not believe in legislating from the bench and he is a person whom I held in the highest regard and will always greatly respect his intelligence and conviction to uphold the Constitution of our country."

Trump instinctively recognized the tremendous importance of the Supreme Court—and now this potentially court-shifting vacancy—to the voters he was trying to sway.

Playing It Straight

A FEW DAYS after Scalia's death, Chief of Staff McDonough convened a meeting in his West Wing office to map out how to approach the vacancy and McConnell's shot across the bow. Despite all their clashes with the Senate leader, White House officials were stunned by both the content and the timing of the statement. "I was pretty surprised that he turned it into a political thing before he expressed any condolences," recalled McDonough. "Maybe I shouldn't have been, but I was."

Among those attending either in person or by phone were Bob Bauer, a former White House counsel and election law expert; Kathryn Ruemmler, a former White House counsel who had been Obama's point person on judges earlier in his administration; and Ron Klain, a former chief of staff to Vice President Biden and a veteran of multiple Supreme Court fights.

It was an impressive assemblage of talent, experience, and political acumen. McDonough was a devout Catholic whose brother was a priest. Like many in Obama's inner circle, he was an alumnus of the staff of Tom Daschle, the former Democratic Senate leader whose experienced personnel had moved over from the leader's office when Daschle was defeated in 2004 and Obama joined the Senate. A fierce defender of Obama, McDonough was a straight arrow who lacked the pretentiousness typical of those at the top of the Washington power pyramid. He had continued to bike to the White House from his

Takoma Park home until an accident and his appointment as chief of staff got in the way.

Klain, who had clerked for the Supreme Court justice Byron White, had been chief counsel for the Judiciary Committee in the early 1990s, including during the tumultuous Clarence Thomas confirmation hearings. He had led judicial selection efforts for President Bill Clinton and had overseen the confirmation of Ruth Bader Ginsburg. He later became the chief of staff to Vice President Al Gore and was in and out of the Gore presidential effort, ultimately heading up the vice president's unsuccessful recount fight. He went on to be a central player for Obama in the confirmations of both Sonia Sotomayor and Elena Kagan.

Despite McConnell's declaration of war, the White House team was determined to play it straight. They considered Obama's brand to be "institutional"—that of a president determined to follow the rules and observe the norms even if his opponents did not.

Obama, as a former constitutional law professor, brought his own academic credentials to the fight. Plus, the White House was hardly starting from scratch. The president had already named two justices, and the White House was keenly aware that Justice Ginsburg, a cancer survivor, might have to leave the court.

Obama had a weak spot of his own, though, when it came to Supreme Court nominations. As a junior senator in 2006, he had joined an unsuccessful Democratic effort to filibuster the confirmation of Samuel A. Alito, a very rare move at the time. The White House said the president had come to regret his decision, and that the Senate Republicans were well over that line in their determination to prevent even hearings for any Obama nominee. Republicans would repeatedly raise Obama's participation in the failed filibuster as evidence of presidential hypocrisy.

While Obama had addressed Scalia's legacy in his statement the night of the death, he had also made it clear he had no intention of passing on the vacancy to his successor—even if that successor was going to be Hillary Clinton. The chance to appoint three justices was a rare opportunity for a president, allowing him to leave a lasting imprint on the court. Obama intended to move ahead. Still, after seven years of conflict and butting heads with Mitch McConnell and congressional Republicans, Obama was clear eyed about the prospects for overcoming the opposition.

"I think the president was the most realistic about it and the staff was more bullish," said one close Obama adviser who was deeply involved with the fight over the vacancy. "He was the most realistic of how uphill this was. I think he was the most socialized to their shamelessness over the past eight years."

McDonough began assembling a team that he thought was perfect for a difficult job, one to be headed by Brian Deese, a high-level Obama administration projects director who had worked on the auto industry bailout and the Paris climate deal.

"He could pull together the team," McDonough said. "Everybody respects him. Nobody thinks he is going to run a shoddy process." McDonough also called in Mark Childress, another former Daschle staffer with experience in judicial fights.

In the gathering, the White House aides and advisers agreed to start putting the paperwork together and begin vetting candidates from the lists they had ready. They would start sounding out the interest groups, consulting with senators, putting together bios for the prospective candidates, gauging their relative weaknesses and strengths, and planning a rollout and extended public relations drive. Supreme Court confirmation fights were somewhat like political campaigns but greatly compressed. Still, the Obama approach was going to take some time.

Klain, the veteran of so many court fights, had a different idea. He didn't want to wait at all and pulled McDonough aside as the meeting broke up.

"I said, 'Look, I think you guys are doing this all wrong,'" Klain recalled. "The president ought to go to the Rose Garden tomorrow and name Merrick Garland. Tomorrow. Not a month from now. Tomorrow. Every day that ticks by is a day you are letting McConnell consolidate his position."

Klain was certain that Obama would end up picking Garland, a highly respected legal mind who was the chief judge of the US Court of Appeals for the District of Columbia Circuit—often referred to as the second-highest court in the land, because it considers so many government cases. The sixty-three-year-old Garland was a centrist, highly popular in Washington's rarified legal circles, and considered a judge's judge.

As Klain talked to McDonough, he grew "one hundred percent certain that Obama [was] going to pick Merrick Garland and he [was] going to do it a month from now, and a month from now it [would] be dead."

Obama himself had made no secret that he had held Garland in reserve for this very situation—a time in his presidency when he needed to make a pick acceptable to Senate Republicans. That view grew out of the fact that Orrin Hatch of Utah, the most senior Republican and a former chairman of the Judiciary Committee, had in 2010 urged Obama to pick Garland for the vacancy that year, saying he was a consensus candidate who could be easily confirmed.

Garland had been in the mix for both of Obama's previous two appointments but was narrowly passed over for Justice Kagan.

"It was a close call," recalled Klain about the decision to choose Kagan. "[Obama] knew her better than Merrick Garland. He liked her very much. At the end, one thing he said to those of us involved in that process was, 'Look, I am going to do Kagan now because if I have to do this later in my presidency with a Republican Senate, Merrick Garland is the kind of guy I think that could be confirmed by a Republican Senate.'"

Not only did Klain think it folly to wait and give McConnell time to strengthen his position; a delay would also give liberals more time to contemplate the possible choice of Garland and conclude they would much prefer a younger, more liberal nominee who could spur enthusiasm among the party's growing progressive left.

Klain knew that moving so quickly would be uncharacteristic for a cautious Obama team. But he believed it the best chance for success. "Extreme times require extreme measures," he said. "It was incumbent on the White House to do something different. Again, it was not reckless. He had interviewed Merrick twice already. It was a mistake in many ways. They failed to appreciate they were facing different circumstances. The game has changed and you've got to change."

McDonough listened attentively but, in the end, chose to go in the traditional direction.

"He nodded," Klain recalled, "he said thanks for the advice, and a month was gone."

The Obama White House was doing this one by the book, even though McConnell had thrown his book out the window.

Swift timing had been crucial to McConnell's strategy. He calculated that the Republican stand would have to be against filling the vacancy, not against any individual who might be picked by President Obama. Thus Republicans could not afford to wait and see if the president made an objectionable choice. In fact, McConnell was certain the president would nominate a candidate who would be hard for Republicans to refuse, someone with impeccable qualifications and a record of bipartisan confirmation by the Senate for previous judicial positions.

"Believe me, we are going to get a qualified nominee," he told his colleagues. "You make him the issue and you've got a problem.

"We decided no hearings, no votes, no nothing if we were going to be able to credibly say this. The nominee needs to be irrelevant if you are serious," he said.

It was a prescient move. When Obama finally spoke out on the developing fight during a joint appearance with King Abdullah of Jordan on February 24, he said he hoped the imminent selection of the nominee would shift the trajectory of the court showdown.

"My hope and expectation is that once there is an actual nominee and once this is no longer an abstraction, that those on the Judiciary Committee recognize that their job is to give this person a hearing, to show the courtesy of meeting with them. Then they are free to vote whatever their conscience dictates as to whether this person is qualified or not. In the meantime, the American people are going to have to gauge whether the person I've nominated is well within the mainstream, is a good jurist, is somebody who is worthy to sit on the Supreme Court."

In his typically understated, professorial, and droll manner, Obama predicted the public would back him once his choice was announced. He said it "will be very difficult for Mr. McConnell to explain how, if the public concludes this person is very well qualified, that the Senate should stand in the way simply for political reasons."

The president also jabbed at Republicans for their argument that there was some deeply embedded tradition that presidents, in their last year of office, couldn't fill a court seat. To him it was a shameless clash with the party's—not to mention Justice Scalia's—preferred strict interpretation of the Constitution.

"Ironically, these are Republicans, who say they believe in reading the text of the Constitution and focusing on the intent of the Constitution. But none of the Founding Fathers thought that when it comes to the president carrying out his duties, he should do it for three years and then on the last year stop doing it."

The battle lines were hardening; both sides were committed. When lawmakers returned to Washington for the first time since Scalia's death, hostilities quickly broke out in what would become the most consequential conflict yet in the judicial wars that had consumed the capital for decades.

Pulling a Biden

It was nearly ten days after Scalia's death before members of the Senate returned to Washington on February 22. In the intervening week, the two parties had been jousting at a distance and via television news interviews. But partisan disputes often took on a different aspect when lawmakers were captive in the Capitol and could be buttonholed by reporters in the Senate hallways. Statements and long-distance interviews were one thing; being put directly on the spot was another.

Throughout the corridors of the Senate office buildings and in the austere Capitol basement, where the subways for members and staff come and go, journalists pressed Republicans for an explanation of how they could so easily dismiss a presidential Supreme Court nomination. Democrats seized the opportunity to tear into Republicans for basically thumbing their noses at a still-popular president.

Some Republicans were clearly nervous about the path they were on, but most seemed comfortably behind McConnell's strategy.

All the Republican members of the Senate Judiciary Committee signed a letter to McConnell resoundingly supporting his decision and vowing to hold no hearing on any nominee until after January 20, 2017, when the next president would be inaugurated. In the letter, they sought to turn the debate on its head, arguing that they would use their constitutional role *not* to act on the vacancy.

"We intend to exercise the constitutional power granted the Senate under Article II, Section 2 to ensure the American people are not deprived of the opportunity to engage in a full and robust debate over the type of jurist they wish to decide some of the most critical issues of our time," the letter said. "Not since 1932 has the Senate confirmed in a presidential election year a Supreme Court nominee to a vacancy arising in that year. And it is necessary to go even further back—to 1888—in order to find an election-year nominee who was nominated and confirmed under divided government, as we have now. Accordingly, given the particular circumstances under which this vacancy arises, we wish to inform you of our intention to exercise our constitutional authority to withhold consent on any nominee to the Supreme Court submitted by this President to fill Justice Scalia's vacancy."

The letter, trying to bolster the Republican case, noted that a few presidential primaries had already been held. "The presidential election is well underway," it read. "Americans have already begun to cast their votes.

"The American people are presented with an exceedingly rare opportunity to decide, in a very real and concrete way, the direction the Court will take over the next generation. We believe The People should have this opportunity," the letter stated, capitalizing "The People" for an added flourish. Republicans were showing no signs of weakening—in fact, they were showing surprising unity.

The fight was now beginning to unfold in the Senate chamber, which was quiet and nearly empty as the Senate returned to work.

Reid started things off, beginning his remarks with a brief tribute to Scalia and the recent funeral observance, which had been highlighted by a eulogy from the justice's son Paul, a Catholic priest. "Justice Scalia and I had our differences," Reid said. "However, there was no doubting his intelligence or dedication to the country."

Reid quickly got to why he was truly there—the beginning of a concerted effort to undermine blanket Republican opposition to so much as holding a hearing for an Obama nominee. He reminded anyone watching on C-SPAN that McConnell was "the guardian of gridlock" when it came to Obama, beginning the minute the Democrat had taken office.

But it wasn't McConnell whom Reid was really aiming at—his target was Chuck Grassley, the Iowa Republican who chaired the Judiciary Committee and was a central player. As chairman, he could theoretically hold a hearing on any nominee no matter what McConnell said. McConnell might control the floor, but Grassley had unquestioned authority over his committee's agenda. Grassley, then eighty-two, was in his sixth term in the Senate and would face the voters for reelection in just a few months.

Grassley considered himself a highly principled member of the Senate with a wealth of experience who, incredibly, had served in public office since 1959, beginning with the state House in his beloved Iowa. He could be an ornery Midwestern crank, a characteristic that seemed to become more pronounced as he got older. But Grassley valued his image and reputation and saw himself as a fair man, a senator who until recent years had worked his own farm and was viewed by constituents as the salt of the earth. His quirky Twitter feed got him a lot of good-natured attention, particularly his running criticism of the History channel for showing little real history. Grassley was among the first senators to write his own tweets, and their eccentric, grandfatherly nature had brought him quite a following.

Reid doubted that McConnell would crack under public pressure but calculated that Grassley was a weak link and could be badgered into relenting if his reputation was at risk. Grassley might agree to convene a hearing or at least meet with the eventual nominee. And from there, events might take their course.

Grassley had joined McConnell in objecting to any nomination by Obama on the night of Scalia's death. And his statement added that he felt it important to do so because Obama was intent on circumventing the Republican Congress through executive orders that would eventually be challenged in court.

But Reid was not about to give up so quickly on Grassley. He pounced on past remarks and noted that Grassley was among his own colleagues in 1988 who voted to confirm Justice Kennedy during the last year of President Reagan's tenure. The idea was to undermine the Republican argument that it had been eight decades since a Supreme Court justice had been confirmed in a president's final year. The fact that the vacancy occurred the year before was incidental to Reid and his fellow Democrats.

"Senator Grassley had no trouble supporting Justice Kennedy then, notwithstanding the fact that it occurred during President Reagan's last year in office," Reid noted archly. "Since that time, the senior senator from Iowa has been on record defending the president's right to put forward nominees during a presidential election year. In 2008, in fact, Senator Grassley said: 'The reality is that the Senate has never stopped confirming judicial nominees during the last few months of a president's term.'"

Reid was pulling the veil back on another of the Senate's most defining characteristics after the filibuster—blatant hypocrisy. With control of the Senate frequently shifting between the parties, senators had to master the art of the 180-degree turn, instantly adopting the language and tactics of the opposition party as soon as they exchanged places. It was a role reversal that would play out repeatedly during the struggle over the Scalia vacancy, and Grassley, frequently under attack, would often counter by firing back old words from his Democratic colleagues.

Reid, indeed, had his share of problematic past positions, and he was far from the only Democrat with old statements to live down.

As George W. Bush's second term wound down in 2007, Chuck Schumer told a meeting of the American Constitution Society that the majority Democrats would be within their rights to refuse a nominee by the president based on the misleading testimony the most recent Republican nominees had provided. "Given the track record of this president and the experience of obfuscation at the hearings," Schumer said, "with respect to the Supreme Court at least, I will recommend to my colleagues that we should not confirm a Supreme Court nominee unless in extraordinary circumstances."

Reid, during a judicial clash in 2005, claimed that the Senate had no constitutional duty to vote on judicial nominees. "The duties of the Senate are set forth in the US Constitution," he said in a floor speech. "Nowhere in that document does it say the Senate has a duty to give presidential appointees a vote. It says appointments shall be made with the advice and consent of the Senate. That is very different than saying every nominee receives a vote."

But that was then.

As he continued his assaults on both Grassley and McConnell, Reid seemed to be thoroughly enjoying himself. The onetime boxer from tiny and rugged Searchlight, Nevada, still relished nothing as much as a good scrap. He concluded his opening argument by again quoting Grassley:

"I hope my Republican colleagues will heed the counsel offered by the senior senator from Iowa and chairman of the Judiciary Committee, Charles Grassley, just a few short years ago when he said: 'A Supreme Court nomination isn't the forum to fight any election. It is the time to perform one of our most important constitutional duties and decide if a nominee is qualified to serve on the nation's highest court.'"

Reid cautioned his Republican colleagues not to "manipulate our nearly perfect form of government in an effort to appease a radical minority."

Reid sat down, pleased with himself. But unbeknownst to him, Grassley had quietly come onto the floor while he was speaking. When Reid glanced around the chamber, he seemed noticeably startled by Grassley's sudden presence. Grassley was about to prove that Reid and the White House were indeed caught off guard. He was recognized to speak and immediately sought to frame the situation to his advantage. Obama shouldn't be able to fill the seat, Grassley argued, because the election was well under way.

"The campaign for our next commander in chief is in full swing. Voting has begun." In addition, he said, a "term-limited Democrat in the twilight of his presidency occupies the White House." One would have thought that Obama had one foot out the door and the moving vans were lined up in the White House drive rather than there being nearly eleven months before the next president—whose identity was quite unknown on February 22, 2016—would take the oath of office.

The best was yet to come. Senators utter a lot of words over the years, and Grassley and his staff had uncovered particularly compelling ones delivered by none other than the vice president of the United States, Joe Biden, back in June 1992, another combative presidential election year. With a week to pull together talking points and do research to bolster their position, aides to Grassley and McConnell had uncovered a doozy of a justification.

It was a speech by then-senator Biden seeming to side with McConnell's argument by declaring that President George H. W. Bush should withhold making a nomination if a vacancy cropped up during a presidential election year.

"It is my view that if a Supreme Court justice resigns tomorrow or within the next several weeks, or resigns at the end of the summer, President Bush should consider following the practice of a majority of his predecessors and not—and not—name a nominee until after the November election is completed," Mr. Biden, the chairman of the Senate Judiciary Committee, had argued on June 25, 1992.

It was a typical long-winded Biden speech and provided plenty of material for Republicans to mine, in addition to offering another vivid reminder of how deep hypocrisy runs in the Senate. The fight for the Scalia seat graphically and embarrassingly exposed the shape-shifting ability of senators.

Never mind that there was no vacancy in 1992. Republicans branded Biden's old speech as proof that Democrats, if put in the same position as McConnell and the Republicans, would not confirm a nominee.

Grassley even gave it a catchy name—"The Biden rules." The name would evolve over the coming months, but the remarks themselves would prove problematic.

"The Biden rules recognize the wisdom of those presidents—including another lawyer and state lawmaker from Illinois—who exercised restraint by not submitting a Supreme Court nomination before the people had spoken," said Mr. Grassley, drawing a rare Republican comparison between Lincoln and Obama when it came to the court.

Republicans were bolstered by the discovery of the Biden speech, though there were some small cracks in the unity as well—cracks that McConnell moved swiftly to seal. A few Republicans, including Orrin Hatch, opened the door to considering a nominee in a lame-duck session. So did Senator Jeff Flake of Arizona. But those comments were carefully walked back under pressure from the leadership.

The Biden statement rocked both Senate Democrats and the White House, where they seemed to come as a total surprise, though Biden's views had received news coverage when the speech was given nearly a quarter-century earlier. One top staffer recalled that it seemed the vice president did not remember the speech—one of many he had given. The White House official said that Biden, still mourning the death of his son, Beau, was also resentful at essentially being pushed out of the presidential race the year before and had withdrawn from the White House day-to-day. And he remembered the speech differently. In any event, it took the administration days to come up with a rebuttal.

Schumer and top Democrats played it down, arguing that if it had not been the Biden speech, Republicans would have simply found another way to undergird their argument. But the pushback wasn't very convincing. The damage was done, and Republicans won an early debating point on the very first day the Senate convened following Scalia's death. It stung.

7

The Oval

It is traditional for top lawmakers to confer with the president when a Supreme Court vacancy occurs, to give visibility to the "advice" part of the advice and consent clause of the Constitution. No matter if it is all a charade, the parties get together and the senators pretend that the president is consulting with them and the president pretends to weigh their advice.

But no previous Supreme Court discussion was like the one that took place on March 1, 2016, in the Oval Office after days of nasty political back-and-forth.

The two Senate leaders, Republican McConnell and Democrat Reid, traveled down Pennsylvania Avenue accompanied by the top two members of the Judiciary Committee—Chairman Grassley and Patrick J. Leahy of Vermont, the senior Democrat. Vice President Biden, also a former chairman of the Judiciary Committee, was on hand as well.

It was a tense standoff. The Oval is often described as one of the most powerful negotiating tools in existence, and people called in to meet with the president often find it hard to hold their ground in such a powerful and persuasive setting. It has been called the ultimate home field advantage. Hoping to break the impasse over choosing a successor to Scalia, Obama asked the Republicans if they had names of judicial candidates they wanted him to consider.

McConnell had been in the Oval Office plenty of times with presidents of both parties. He was not about to succumb to pressure from a president for whom he had little respect and a man he did not fear.

As for advice, McConnell essentially told the president not to waste time with a nomination, because the Senate would not take it up no matter who he put forward.

"McConnell was emphatic that he would not have a hearing," said Leahy, remembering the heated atmosphere in the room.

It was a triumph for McConnell, so much so that just six months later he reveled in the memory before a cheering crowd back home in Kentucky. "One of my proudest moments was when I looked at Barack Obama in the eye and I said, 'Mr. President, you will not fill this Supreme Court vacancy,'" McConnell declared.

During the meeting, Obama was not about to give up despite McConnell's intransigence, insisting that he intended to follow through on his constitutional duty and make a nomination. McConnell stuck with his argument that it had been eighty years—1932—since a vacancy occurred and was filled in a presidential election year.

"We went back and forth on this," recalled Leahy, "and pointed out that it is unusual to have a vacancy in a presidential election year but we have had it." Leahy reminded McConnell that every Senate Democrat voted for Justice Kennedy in 1988—the last time a justice was confirmed unanimously.

"He didn't want to talk about it," said Leahy. "Things got a little bit heated, but it was obvious that McConnell could care less about the facts."

Leahy and Reid exited the Oval and headed out to the White House driveway to lambaste the Republicans before the White House press corps. Reid, in his signature sarcastic style, took what he thought was a shot at the outlandish position of McConnell and Grassley. "They think they are going to wait and see what President Trump will do,

I guess, as far as the nomination is concerned," Reid said, raising the then-unimaginable prospect of a Trump presidency.

The two Republicans held their fire until they got on friendlier ground back at the Capitol. They were emphatic in what they had told the president. "Mr. Grassley and I made it clear that we don't intend to take up a nominee or to have hearings," McConnell told reporters. "We will look forward to the American people deciding who they want to make this appointment through their own vote."

Clearly, McConnell was not budging. Neither was Obama. A nominee was coming, and who it would be would determine the Democratic strategy going forward.

Despite Klain's belief that Merrick Garland was a shoo-in, the White House team responsible for managing the selection and the nomination fight went in with a more open mind. They wanted to show that while Republicans might be violating governing norms, they would follow their game plan.

The main tension was always what kind of nominee to go with—a more mainstream person or a more liberal figure whom the Left could rally behind. While Garland was always a leading candidate, the president and his inner circle wanted to consider other candidates, including Sri Srinivasan, who sat with Garland on the federal appeals court for the District of Columbia and if picked would be the first South Asian named to the court.

Obama recognized the historic opportunity to shape the court in his image and ideology. Elevating another minority candidate or a woman would be a coup. Srinivasan was tempting even though his centrism would anger the Left, particularly given some of his past decisions and clients as well as a stint in the solicitor general's office during the administration of George W. Bush. But he had been confirmed for his appeals court seat on a vote of 97–0, and the White House's thinking was that it would be much harder for Republicans to block someone with a history of such strong bipartisan support.

At worst, the White House believed the nominee could be approved in a lame-duck session after the election, when Republicans would capitulate in fear of Hillary Clinton making a new, more liberal choice as one of her first acts as president.

A centrist might make more sense but presented multiple problems for the White House: It would be harder to predict how a more centrist choice might act on the court. A centrist could also sap enthusiasm from Democratic voters and potentially harm the Clinton campaign. Many wondered about the wisdom of nominating a candidate who appealed to Republicans at such a crucial moment in deciding the balance of the court.

White House officials were leery of nominating some of the younger candidates out of fear that they would be put through the political grinder and have their records distorted, ruining their future chances for a high court appointment. "There were these fantastic people who had big legal minds that would have just been shredded," said Shailagh Murray, a former reporter for the *Wall Street Journal* and the *Washington Post* who had become a top adviser to Obama in his second term. "It could destroy the person you put forward."

Part of the rationale also revolved around the seat being filled. To Republicans, the Scalia seat was special, given his position as a conservative thought leader, and Democrats would have a hard time justifying filling it with a liberal flamethrower. No rule said they couldn't, but it would no doubt set off Republicans.

The escalating court fight was spilling into the presidential race, which was clarifying as February came to a close. By the end of the month, the Republican field lost six candidates, including Jeb Bush and Rand Paul, as Donald Trump emerged as the front-runner by winning the New Hampshire and South Carolina primaries and the Nevada caucuses. Despite the Washington establishment view within both parties that Trump was a ludicrous figure, a fast-talking real estate developer with a long history of hyperbole and deceit, he was shaping up as the likely nominee.

Trump along with McGahn wanted to realize the potential advantages of the court fight for his unusual candidacy. They quickly went to work behind the scenes to make the court opening a main argument for Trump's election and a means to rally conservative support behind a man whose ideological impulses and personal behavior were unsettling and reprehensible to many on the right.

The List: Part I

IT WAS A Washington coming-out party for Donald Trump on March 21, 2016, at the offices of a well-connected law firm just a few blocks from the Capitol on the Senate side of the hill.

Trump was showing real strength as a candidate in the Republican primaries, though he remained suspect in the eyes of many top Republicans in Washington. The idea was to gather together a couple dozen Republican lawmakers and other party heavyweights willing to entertain the idea of backing him at a get-to-know-him session at the headquarters of Jones Day, a prestigious law firm where McGahn worked.

The New York–centric presidential candidate hadn't been in Washington much during the campaign—he was not particularly popular with the establishment Republicans who dominated the capital. But he was speaking later in the day to the American-Israeli Public Affairs Committee, a must-stop for any serious presidential contender who wanted to demonstrate his devotion to Israel, and Trump certainly wanted to do that. It was an opportunity to court some new allies—and to promote his new luxury hotel taking shape in the Old Post Office building, a prominent architectural sentinel on Pennsylvania Avenue that was a sadly underutilized food court and tourist center. The landmark building and its twelve-story tower were about to become a local version of Trump Tower, just a few blocks from the White House.

In addition to McGahn, Jeff Sessions, the conservative Alabama lawmaker who was the first senator to publicly embrace Trump, would also be on hand. A scattering of other conservative lawmakers such as Senator Tom Cotton of Arkansas joined onetime House Speaker Newt Gingrich and the former congressman Bob Livingston, now a superlobbyist in Washington who had once almost replaced Gingrich, before his dramatic admission of marital infidelity on a memorable Saturday morning in the House in 1998. No Republican congressional leaders attended.

One person invited with a specific purpose in mind was Leonard Leo, the Federalist Society official. Like many in Washington's rarified Republican circles, Leo did not know Mr. Trump well.

Leo's first contact with the campaign came on the day of Scalia's death, from Stephen Miller, a far-right anti-immigration staffer who had been an aide to Sessions before becoming an influential adviser to the Trump campaign. Miller sought advice from a colleague of Leo's as to how they should respond to the passing of Scalia and what to say if they were asked about who they would appoint.

"It was at that time I had some inkling they were very seriously thinking about these issues or that the justice's passing had prompted them to do so," Leo recalled. "And secondly, that they were prepared to go a little bit further than presidential candidates had in the past."

Leo was soon to learn just how much further.

Before the scheduled session at Jones Day, Leo got a call from McGahn, asking if he would remain a few minutes after the main session broke up to have a private word with Trump so the candidate could run an idea by him. Intrigued, Leo said he would be happy to but wanted to know a little more so he could prepare.

McGahn let him in on a secret—the campaign wanted to put together a list of potential Supreme Court nominees to assure conservatives still nervous about Trump's occasionally liberal past that his administration would put solid conservatives on the court. With the Scalia seat looking to remain open until the next president took office,

Trump saw it as a prime chance to build credibility with conservatives, who always put more weight on the court when casting their vote than Democrats did.

Republican voters had reason for skepticism. Trump, after all, had been publicly pro-choice at some points in his life. And his sister Maryanne Trump Barry, a federal appeals court judge in Pennsylvania who had been nominated by Bill Clinton, had ruled against a tough anti-abortion law. That was the decision Cruz had cited in taking a swipe at Trump and his sister after the Republican presidential primary debate the night of Scalia's death, hoping to instill nervousness among the party about Trump's potential court picks. Trump wanted to quiet those trying to sow distrust about his judicial intentions. The vacancy had created an entirely new political imperative.

In McGahn's mind, the list would mainly be a resource for Trump to draw on when speaking at rallies. If he suddenly decided to throw out the name of a potential judicial nominee, it would at least be a name of someone who had been vetted, a person whose opinions had been researched for possible landmines. It was insurance for an unscripted and unpredictable candidate.

During the meeting with Leo, Trump began expounding on the list and his plans. As he continued, it became clear that the list was not going to be made known just to conservative insiders or serve as a cheat sheet for the president when discussing his intentions about the Supreme Court. He wanted to release it to the general public.

McGahn almost fell out of his chair. This had never been done, and it could box in Trump on his nominees. Trump, as his business career demonstrated, was not someone who wanted to be boxed in when it came to big decisions.

A list would also be a huge shift from how presidential candidates of both parties typically handled the issue. Candidates usually assured their voters that they would appoint someone "in the mold" of a Scalia or Clarence Thomas for Republican voters or a Ginsburg for Democrats—soothing voters with a name that would provide some comfort and familiarity. The idea was to placate voters without going out too far on a limb or providing too much fodder for political opponents.

Leo then had his first extended conversation with Trump while McGahn and Sessions—two men personally familiar with the Senate confirmation process—outlined a plan for a definitive list of conservative judges and lawyers around the country who could be in line for a high court seat should Trump prevail in November. Eager to cultivate Leo as an ally, Trump treated him with unusual respect and deference, really "making him feel like a player," according to those familiar with the meeting.

Leo recalled: "I started out by saying to then-candidate Trump, 'Well, it has never been done before.' He said, 'Then should we not do it?' I said no, but 'I'd like to know why you want to do it' was my first question. He said, 'Well, I want to do it because nobody really knows who I am, and I want to make it clear what I would do on the Supreme Court and with the Scalia vacancy.'"

Leo warned Trump and McGahn that there were risks involved, that putting out the names of prospective judges would provide opponents added opportunity to dig into their backgrounds and potentially uncover disqualifying material. But Leo recognized that the benefits could outweigh the risks. With the Internet and modern research capabilities, anything major would likely be found quickly, even if the judicial prospects hadn't been publicly identified previously.

"I said, look, in the modern information age, most of these people even after they were nominated would be digested very quickly," said Leo, who told Trump and his team that the proposal made sense and they should move forward.

"No one has ever wanted to go so far as to say, 'I might appoint A, B, or C, among others.' That is what really broke new ground," said Leo. "They were in the game and they were serious."

In a press conference later that day at his hotel—"Close to three hundred rooms, super luxury, going to be amazing"—Trump was upbeat about his meeting with the Republicans. He took the chance to crow about his own prospects and that of the high-end hotel that would be opening in a few months.

"We had a good meeting and can't believe how far we've come," Trump said at the news conference, held in the future lobby still under construction, as workers in hard hats stood alongside. "I think maybe a lot of people wouldn't have predicted that."

He wanted to drive home the point that influential members of the party were finally beginning to take him more seriously and accept the possibility that he could be the Republican nominee. "It is a beginning meeting, but it was a very good one with a lot of the most respected people in Washington," he said.

Then, with the meeting with Leo fresh in his mind, he began outlining his unique Supreme Court plans, saying he would be distributing a list in coming days of specific people he would name to the high court. "I've already shown it to a lot of people and, you know, a lot of people are worried about which judges," Trump acknowledged, though in reality his campaign had very few names on the list at the time. "We're going to have a conservative, very good group of judges. I'm going to submit a list of justices, potential justices of the United States Supreme Court, that I will appoint from that list. I won't go beyond that list. I'm going to let people know because some people say, maybe I'll appoint a liberal judge. I'm not going to appoint a liberal judge. Heritage Foundation and others are working on it already and with some thoughts of mine."

Trump was still learning. He often confused the Federalist Society with the Heritage Foundation, the limited-government conservative advocacy group on Capitol Hill. Both would be engaged in putting together the list.

But Trump had clearly intuited the court as something he could use to entice wary Republican voters by raising the prospect of the court being filled with judges selected by Hillary Clinton. The fact that his sister had a career on the federal bench—a liberal one, by Cruz's measure—gave him at least a passing familiarity with the judicial branch, the confirmation process, and judicial qualifications. He was ahead of the game when it came to judges, compared with his very loose grasp on a multitude of other federal issues and responsibilities.

That is not to say he understood the courts perfectly. In defending himself against Cruz's continuing insinuation that he would appoint liberal judges and that his sister had joined in an antiabortion decision, Trump noted at a debate in Texas that she was not the only judge who had done so. "He's been criticizing my sister for signing a certain bill," Trump snapped back. "You know who else signed that bill? Justice Samuel Alito, a very conservative member of the Supreme Court, with my sister, signed that bill. So I think that maybe we should get a little bit of an apology from Ted. What do you think?"

Federal judges don't sign bills.

At his hotel press conference, Trump promised that his candidates would meet the "highest standards" and that "we'll look at pro-life.

"We'll look at intellect, very important. Like, we want very, very smart people.

"I make that pledge because I want people to understand, that is the single biggest problem. It will be terrible losing the election because the country's going in the wrong direction. If the new president is a Democrat and picks very liberal people, this country is in big, big trouble."

His visit to the nation's capital wasn't a complete success. He gave head-scratching answers in a meeting with the editorial board of the *Washington Post* and went public with a run-down of foreign policy advisers who, to put it mildly, were not well known among the foreign policy intelligentsia in Washington. His address later to the pro-Israeli lobbying group was, in a precursor of future events, a complete fiasco. Trump unleashed an inappropriate ad hominem attack on President Obama, and leaders of the group were forced to apologize the next day, one of them in tears.

Still, it was a productive visit to DC for Trump when it came to judges. Though its import was not yet fully understood, he had set in motion a judicial confirmation strategy that brought him support from conservative advocacy groups and conservative voters. Both would turn out to be extremely beneficial to his candidacy and later to his presidency.

9

Lack of Judicial Temperament

THE IMPASSE WAS almost unthinkable. McConnell's position seemed so outrageous and beyond reasonable norms to many Democrats in Congress and the White House that they just assumed Republicans would eventually relent. Even some Republicans were stunned by the nerve of the decision.

But the determination to blockade Obama's nominee was just the next progression in a steadily escalating partisan war over the courts that had ebbed and flowed for three decades, most visibly at the Supreme Court level, but equally furiously at lower branches of the federal judiciary. The conflict did not erupt overnight; it had evolved and intensified, fueled by the fierce partisanship that had enveloped Washington and simultaneously elevated the role of the courts in serving as referee over policies crafted in the heat of that partisan atmosphere.

The thunderous 1987 confirmation hearings for Judge Robert Bork are typically marked as the birthplace of the modern era of judicial warfare, as well as of the broader politics of personal destruction. Senator Edward M. Kennedy's denunciation of "Robert Bork's America"—a dark place where women and minorities would be second-class citizens—still rings in the ears of conservatives who consider that a blasphemous attack on one of their leading lights nominated by President Reagan and the intellectual godfather of constitutional originalism.

It is illuminating now to watch Kennedy's remarks courtesy of

C-SPAN, since the three-and-a-half-minute speech is delivered not in the thunderous, over-the-top style that Kennedy sometimes employed to drive home his partisan points on the Senate floor. Instead, it is a matter-of-fact denunciation of Bork's conservative philosophy. Staff sit somewhat indifferently in the background and others walk behind Kennedy, unaware that the words he is saying will be burned for decades into the souls of conservatives who revered Bork.

In his now-famous speech, Kennedy, noting that Bork had fired the Watergate special prosecutor at President Nixon's behest and that the nomination was coming during the Iran-Contra scandal, gave grudging acknowledgment that while President Reagan's years in office were coming to an end, he still had the authority to fill a Supreme Court vacancy.

"President Reagan is still our president," Kennedy said in his July 1, 1987, remarks. "But he should not be able to reach out from the muck of Irangate, reach into the muck of Watergate, and impose his reactionary vision of the Constitution on the Supreme Court and on the next generation of Americans. No justice would be better than this injustice."

Allies of Kennedy at the time believe he toned down his approach on Bork that day because he was aware he was taking a risk by jumping out immediately on the day of the nomination. But it wasn't Republicans he was worried about upsetting; it was Democrats, who were not accustomed to waging partisan warfare over high court judges and might be pushed to the Republican side by such a frontal attack.

That speech is still seen as the starting point for judicial clashes, as Bork was ultimately defeated. Republicans believe that the Reagan White House was caught flat-footed and didn't understand the threat posed by Kennedy's speech, which set the narrative for months heading into the hearings and vote while the White House was slow to respond.

After a bitter back-and-forth at his confirmation hearing, Bork was rejected by the Judiciary Committee, and the assumption was that he would withdraw his nomination to avoid the humiliation of a defeat on the Senate floor. But Bork was a proud man and he insisted on getting the Senate's final verdict.

His goal, he said, was to protect the process of filling the courts.

"The tactics and techniques of national political campaigns have been unleashed on the process of confirming judges," he said in a statement delivered at the White House. "That is not simply disturbing, it is dangerous."

Bork insisted that "in deciding on this course, I harbor no illusions.

"But a crucial principle is at stake. That principle is the way we select the men and women who guard the liberties of all the American people. That should not be done through public campaigns of distortion. If I withdraw now, that campaign would be seen as a success, and it would be mounted against future nominees. For the sake of the federal judiciary and the American people, that must not happen. The deliberative process must be restored."

On October 23, 1987, Bork was defeated by the Senate on a 58–42 vote, with 2 Democrats joining 40 Republicans in backing him and 6 Republicans joining 52 Democrats in opposition. Adding insult to injury for conservatives, the seat of Lewis Powell then went to Anthony M. Kennedy, the last justice to be confirmed with a unanimous vote and a member of the court scorned by many on the right for swinging it to the left on major cultural issues such as same-sex marriage.

Denying Obama a chance to fill the Scalia seat would no doubt be a salve for those conservatives still fuming decades after Bork's defeat. But others who had lengthy service in the judicial trenches felt that the fight over the federal judiciary entered a new phase a few years before Bork was nominated to the high court.

Federal judgeships had long been one of the patronage plums available to senators, and they took advantage where they could, recommending friends and political allies for the lifetime appointments and using their influence to make sure the White House mainly put forward their recommendations. Jimmy Carter instituted significant reforms in federal judicial appointments, establishing nominating commissions, setting basic qualifications, and opening the process to more women.

As a candidate in 1980, Ronald Reagan pledged to shift what he and close advisers like Edwin Meese, the future US attorney general and a close Reagan ally from California, saw as the liberal tilt of the federal courts, with a strong emphasis on selecting judges opposed to abortion. In a dramatic appeal, the future president on October 14, 1980, also declared that he would name a woman to one of the first Supreme Court openings that occurred if he was elected.

After his election, he was successful in pushing notable conservative jurists onto the court with little resistance from Democrats and their liberal allies. Initially, he had only one chance at the Supreme Court, and he fulfilled his pledge by nominating Sandra Day O'Connor, the first woman ever to sit on the high court. He also named about 375 people to district and appellate courts during his tenure.

At the same time, conservatives gained a powerful new ally in the court fights. In April 1982, midway through Reagan's first term, about two hundred students from Yale University and other campuses met at Yale for a weekend symposium on federalism that would blossom into the Federalist Society, a group that would prove crucial in feeding conservatives to the federal bench. One of that weekend's keynote speakers, Robert Bork, warned attendees that the Supreme Court was trying to "nationalize morality."

Reagan encountered a first challenge in 1983 when Democrats sought to derail the nomination of J. Harvie Wilkinson III, a thirty-nine-year-old law professor with little courtroom experience, who was nominated for an appeals court post. Liberal groups and Democratic senators accused Wilkinson, also a Justice Department official, of lobbying for the job. Ted Kennedy called him the "least experienced" person ever nominated for a federal circuit court, since he had bypassed the district court level. Democrats tried to filibuster Wilkinson—a very rare effort at the time—but it was easily overcome in a bipartisan vote and Wilkinson went on to a long and highly regarded career on the bench.

The success that Reagan and his allies had in populating the courts did not go unnoticed among liberals or Democratic senators, and they began to push back, beginning with one notable case in 1985—two years before the Bork showdown.

The nominee in question was Alex Kozinski, a thirty-four-year-old who at the time was the chief judge of the US Claims Court and was selected to join the US Court of Appeals for the Ninth Circuit. An immigrant from Romania, he had been a campaign aide to Reagan and a law clerk both to Anthony Kennedy before his elevation to the Supreme Court and to Warren Burger on the Supreme Court. Kozinski was an ambitious up-and-comer.

Democrats had reservations about Kozinski and his tenure on a civil service board, the Merit Systems Protection Board, that suggested a "lack of judicial temperament." But he survived the Judiciary Committee hearing, and his confirmation headed for a vote on the Senate floor. Then Democrats obtained sworn statements from some former colleagues of Kozinski who said he had misled the committee the first time and that he had been imperious while badly mistreating those who worked for him. Democrats called for new hearings, a highly unusual move, and Republicans were forced to convene one. In a daylong hearing in November 1985, Democrats grilled Kozinski much to the displeasure of majority Republicans.

Senator Orrin Hatch, a member of the panel, called Kozinski outstanding. During a recess that day, he sent a young intern out for a tuna sandwich. Mulling over the situation in a committee conference room as he ate, an angry Hatch told the intern, Leonard Leo, that the Democrats would come to regret their mistreatment of Kozinski.

Strom Thurmond, the South Carolina Republican who chaired the committee, accused Democrats of making the "puniest, most nitpicking charges" against the nominee. Republicans on the panel again sent the nomination to the floor, and Kozinski was approved 53–43—an unusually close vote for the lower courts, whose nominees typically breezed through. Though they lost, Democrats were energized by their success at putting new scrutiny on a judicial nominee and subjecting his record to greater exposure. More than thirty years later, Kozinski would be forced off the federal bench after an illustrious career, fleeing accusations of sexual harassment; improper physical contact with staff, clerks, and others; as well as abusive treatment of employees. He may have survived his 1985 accusations of a lack of judicial temperament, but the issue eventually caught up with him as the culture shifted and spurred a new willingness to challenge those holding power, including lifetime federal judges.

Despite their inability to block Kozinski, Democrats stepped up their efforts and scored a major victory the next year at the expense of Jeff Sessions, the future senator and US attorney general.

Nominated by Reagan to a federal district court seat in Alabama, Sessions, then a US attorney, came under fire for racially charged comments and prosecutions. He ultimately lost a vote in the committee and his nomination died, a bitter defeat that haunted him for decades and motivated him to seek a seat in the political body that he believed had unjustly wronged him.

During the administrations of both George H. W. Bush and Bill Clinton, the parties continued to maneuver over federal judges with mixed success.

The most explosive moment of the Bush administration came in 1991 following the nomination of Clarence Thomas to the Supreme Court and the subsequent uproar after he was accused by a former colleague, Anita Hill, of sexual harassment and misconduct. He was ultimately placed on the court after an incredibly contentious fight that continues to shape confirmation politics to this day.

In an illustration of how reluctant both parties were at that time to deploy the filibuster in a Supreme Court confirmation, Democrats refrained from doing so and allowed Thomas to be seated despite fervent opposition. Part of their rationale was political, of course. As the potential successor to Thurgood Marshall, Thomas had some support in the African American community, and Democrats were leery of alienating that voting bloc. But the caution proved ill advised. The backlash claimed at least two Democrats, Senators Alan Dixon of Illinois and Wyche Fowler of Georgia, the next year, and others never escaped the shadow of their performances during the public hearings, including Joe Biden, who chaired the panel.

The eight years of the Clinton administration were marked by more disputes with Republicans over perceived liberal nominees as well as complaints from Democrats that the president was insufficiently devoted to the cause of taking on Republicans over their objections. In one notable instance, Republicans in 1999 rejected the confirmation of Ronnie White, an African American judge serving on the Missouri Supreme Court, partially due to White's reservations toward the death penalty. The outcome—the first defeat of a judicial pick on the floor since the Bork nomination—provoked Clinton to suggest that "the Republican-controlled Senate is adding credence to the perceptions that they treat minority and women judicial nominees unfairly and unequally."

In another case, Judge Richard A. Paez, a district court judge in Los Angeles, was confirmed to the US Court of Appeals for the Ninth Circuit after a wait of four years due to Republican objections that he would amplify the liberal bias of that court. The stalled nominations of Paez and another long-delayed Clinton nominee to the Ninth Circuit, Marsha Berzon, were able to move only in March 2000, after Democrats made an agreement with Senator Trent Lott, the Republican leader and a politician always looking to cut a favorable deal, to confirm a stalled nominee to the Tennessee Valley Authority. As unseemly as it sounds, such agreements were often the way nominations got done—when both parties had something to gain.

Despite the toxic legacy of the Bork and Thomas nominations and the deal-cutting during the Bush and Clinton years, the history-changing fight over the Scalia vacancy was more rooted in recent events that began during the presidency of George W. Bush, an era when the clashes over judges reached a new level.

The personification of this fight was Miguel Estrada, a Honduran-born constitutional lawyer who became the victim of the first-ever successful filibuster against an appeals court nominee and the subject of an ugly and protracted fight in the Senate that led in a straight line to the showdown over the Scalia seat.

10

Should Ideology Matter?

WHEN GEORGE W. BUSH took office as president in January 2001, his party ruled the 50–50 Senate by virtue of controlling the White House, making the vice president, Dick Cheney, the deciding vote in all ties. It was the thinnest of margins, and Democrats had no intention of being pushed around when it came to judicial confirmations.

In the spring, most of the fifty Democrats gathered at a retreat in Farmington, Pennsylvania, to discuss how to be more aggressive in challenging the new administration's judicial nominees—a group that they fully expected to be composed of scores of the nation's most conservative judicial prospects as assembled by the president and his inner circle. Democrats wanted to be ready.

"What we're trying to do is set the stage and make sure that both the White House and Senate Republicans know that we expect to have significant input in the process," Senator Chuck Schumer, then a Democratic force on the Judiciary Committee, told the *New York Times*. "We're simply not going to roll over."

Schumer and his allies were trying to persuade some reluctant colleagues that it was well within bounds to weigh judicial nominees not just on experience, stature, and knowledge of the law, but on ideology as well. That would represent a shift to many, mainly the moderate Democrats from the South and Midwest who were more used to viewing judicial nominations through the prism of years in the law, lack of a criminal record, rating by the American Bar Association (ABA), and whether lawyer friends back home spoke well of them or not. But Schumer's groundwork, as it turned out, was being laid just a bit early.

Unbeknownst to most of them, Democrats were about to get a remarkable turn of good fortune that would, for the moment at least, give them the upper hand when it came to judges. Senator James Jeffords, the liberal Vermont Republican, was unhappy with the initial course of the new Bush administration and began making his concerns known. On May 24, he announced he would become an independent but caucus with the Democrats, suddenly handing them the majority just as the second Bush in the White House was trying to get his feet under him.

Senator Harry Reid from Nevada, the number two Democrat, had wooed Jeffords feverishly. The linchpin of the deal was Reid's willingness to give his chairmanship of the Environment and Public Works Committee to Jeffords, handing him a prime spot to pursue his liberal environmental agenda. Years later Reid still chortled at the thought of it. Not many senators would sacrifice a committee chairmanship, but the reward was worth it from Reid's perspective.

"It is hard for me to accept what I did," said Reid, who was willing to sacrifice the very thing most senators yearned for—committee power. "I knew my way around. I had a big staff, I gave it all up. That was the clincher."

Reid said his only demand was that Jeffords keep on the Democratic staff a friend of one of his sons. That man was still working for the committee when Reid retired in 2016.

The Jeffords flip was an astonishing development that rattled the Republican Party, though to soften the blow Jeffords agreed to delay the switch until after the new president's tax cut, Bush's top priority, was passed. Jeffords's relationships with some Republican colleagues were never the same. He had been a member of a corny barbershop quartet with the Republican senators John Ashcroft, Larry Craig, and Trent Lott. Lott lost his slot as majority leader due to Jeffords.

Republicans might have been singing the blues, but the Singing Senators were no more.

The switch had a direct bearing on the Bush administration's judicial plans. The president had made his first picks public just days earlier, and Democrats were not happy with the names they saw. Now Democrats were no longer just standing in the way. They controlled the floor and the committees and could pick and choose which nominees they intended to bring to a vote.

All this was happening against the backdrop of the recent election, when the high court itself had intervened to halt a presidential vote recount in Florida, making Bush the winner over Al Gore in a decision that was widely condemned as nakedly partisan. "Although we may never know with complete certainty the identity of the winner of this year's Presidential election, the identity of the loser is perfectly clear," Justice John Paul Stevens famously wrote. "It is the Nation's confidence in the judge as an impartial guardian of the rule of law." To elected Democrats, that high court decision was proof of what could happen to their priorities if a president many considered illegitimate had his way in filling court seats.

To the Democrats' way of thinking, President Bush should not have been able to forward any nominees. They should have been coming from President Gore, and Democrats were willing to do whatever it took to impede the new president. "We will not have nominations of right-wing after right-wing after right-wing judges," Schumer said at the time. "Judges will have to be moderate. The president will get some he wants, we will get some we want, and there will be a compromise that, overall, the bench will be a moderate bench."

Handed control of a judiciary subcommittee on the courts, Schumer, a former House member known then for a thirst for media attention, wasted no time in trying to make his case that judges could be opposed on their basis of their political philosophy. The hearing was entitled "Should Ideology Matter?"

"Politically, the American people were divided in our recent national elections, sending a message of moderation and bipartisanship," Schumer said in opening the hearing. "This era, perhaps more than any other before, calls out for collaboration between the president and the Senate in judicial appointments. The 'advice' in 'advice and consent' should play a new and more prominent role. It also certainly justifies Senate opposition to judicial nominees whose views fall outside the mainstream and have been selected in an attempt to further tilt the courts in an ideological direction."

To support his position, Schumer called as a witness Cass Sunstein, a University of Chicago law professor who had spoken just weeks earlier at the Democratic retreat. Sunstein said that applying an ideological test was fully within the rights of senators when considering judges.

"In an era, like our own, in which the federal judiciary is showing too little respect for the prerogatives of Congress, an excessive willingness to intrude into democratic processes, and a tendency toward conservative judicial activism, it is fully appropriate for the Senate to try to assure more balance, and more moderation, within the federal courts," Sunstein said.

Schumer believed being up front about weighing the ideology of a nominee would in fact make the process more transparent. Senators already had been considering judges' ideology regularly but then had to find other reasons for opposing judges since political philosophy wasn't supposed to be an issue.

"This unwillingness to openly examine ideology has sometimes led senators who oppose a nominee to seek out nonideological disqualifying factors, like small financial improprieties from long ago, to justify their position. This, in turn, has led to an escalating war of 'gotcha' politics that, in my judgment, has warped the Senate's confirmation process and harmed the Senate's reputation."

Republicans were having none of it, with Mitch McConnell, then a member of the committee, taking the lead in lambasting the idea. "What I fear is going on here is an effort to establish a new standard under which nominees are judged and a litmus test is established that substantially is at variance with the majority of the American people," he shot back. "What appears to be happening—and I hope this will not prove to be the case—is that some on the left are increasingly dedicated to shutting down the vibrant marketplace of ideas and replacing it with a monopoly of thought where the only commodity to be bought is a kind of liberal orthodoxy."

McConnell went on to suggest that what Schumer and other Democrats might consider mainstream was far from what much of the country might rate as middle-of-the-road acceptable.

"Where is the mainstream?" he asked. "All across most of America, in most of the states, I think the mainstream would be quite different from what may be under way here today to establish as sort of acceptable views things that are far different from what most Americans hold.

"That is why the safest place to be and the sound place to be, and the place where the Senate has been most of the history of our country is largely deferring to the president on the question of ideology and judging the competence and the integrity of the nominee.

"The president was elected, not the editorial board of the *New York Times*. And as astonishing as it may sound to some here," he said with a gibe at the New Yorker chairing the panel as well as the newspaper McConnell frequently used as a foil, "the editorial views of the *New York Times* are not mainstream values. Those are not the values of the vast majority of Americans."

Despite the effort by Schumer, the parties remained split on the question he posed as the Senate moved slowly on Bush's judicial nominations while Democrats held control.

Miguel Estrada, nominated in early May 2001, finally got a hearing on September 26, 2002, and Democrats were clearly skeptical. Their main concern was that because he had never served as a judge, Estrada had too slight a paper trail to make an assessment, given that the Bush administration was refusing to release memos he had written while in the solicitor general's office.

"There is a lot we do not know about Miguel Estrada," Schumer said before beginning the questioning at the nomination hearing. Estrada had also come under criticism from a former supervisor in the Clinton administration for being too much of a conservative ideologue and temperamentally unfit for the office.

But, as would be confirmed later, there was also a much larger issue at work.

Democrats were concerned that Estrada, with his Hispanic background and inspiring life story, was being groomed by the White House for a seat on the Supreme Court. It would be a real coup for Bush, the former Texas governor who was popular with Hispanics (for a Republican), to name the first Hispanic to the court. And it would be a huge bonus for his party in its struggle to attract more Latino voters. Estrada's nomination to the US Court of Appeals for the District of Columbia Circuit—always a jumping-off point for the high court— was strongly supported by some of the more conservative Hispanic-advocacy and business groups, though some of the liberal organizations were strongly opposed or remained neutral. At the same time, there were some—much to the offense of Estrada and Senate Republicans— who suggested his success and conservative leanings meant he could not truly understand the Hispanic experience in the United States, a whisper campaign that persisted during his nomination.

Estrada was born in Tegucigalpa, Honduras, and had moved to the United States at age seventeen to live with his mother after his parents divorced. He went to Columbia University and Harvard Law School, where he edited the law review, and had distinguished clerkships, including with Justice Kennedy. At the time of his nomination, he had already argued fifteen cases before the Supreme Court. It was an impressive run for a man who grew up not speaking English. Of primary interest to the Democrats was his work in the Department of Justice in the administrations of Presidents George H. W. Bush and Bill Clinton. The Justice Department, in a wrestling match over documents that would become a fixed element of the judicial wars, was not willing to part with those papers, though previous administrations had in similar circumstances, including the Bork confirmation battle.

"It is highly unusual, even though there may be some precedent in the past, but highly unusual, to ask attorneys for opinions that they gave and writings that they made while in the solicitor's office," Orrin Hatch argued in mounting a defense of Estrada. "That would put a chill across honest thinking, it seems to me, like never before. And keep in mind, he served the administrations he served, and I presume that many of the briefs that were written, the opinions that were given, were consistent with the administration that he served."

Hatch also said the former Clinton official who had criticized Estrada had been widely discredited over the years, and that even in the time the men worked together, the supervisor had provided glowing performance reviews.

Then it was Estrada's moment to speak for himself. He said he too would like his previous work made public. "I have been a lawyer in practice for many years now, and I would like the world to know that I am exceptionally proud of every piece of legal work I have done in my life," he told the panel. "If it were up to me as a private citizen, I would be more than proud to have you look at everything that I have done for the government or for a private client. I do recognize that there are certain interests that have been asserted in this case that go beyond my own personal interest, and those are the institutional interests of the Justice Department, and that those interests have been seconded, as it were, by men—and, unfortunately, only men—who have held the job of solicitor general in both administrations going back to Mr. Kennedy."

It was an easy position for Estrada to take, since it was not up to him and he could be certain that the stubborn Justice Department would not comply. The refusal, repeated in the years ahead in other confirmations, allowed opponents to accuse the executive branch of covering up objectionable writings.

Pressed again by Schumer to push harder for the documents, Estrada bristled a bit. "Let me say that I would like to think that my life in the law is an open book and that there are tons and tons and reams of stuff out there that can speak to the committee about the sort of thinker that I am and the sort of lawyer that I have been," he said. "Obviously, as I said, I have been in practice or have been a lawyer since 1986."

He and Schumer then clashed over reports that Estrada had prevented applicants he considered too liberal from getting to serve as clerks to Justice Kennedy—a charge he sharply rejected. "Senator Schumer, I have taken a cab up to Capitol Hill and sat in Justice Kennedy's office to make sure he hired people that I knew to be liberal," Estrada said.

The rest of the hearing was more of the same, as Democrats challenged him and Republicans defended him strenuously, asking few questions. It didn't matter. With the midterm election so close, Democrats were not going to give Estrada a committee vote, let alone bring his nomination to the floor. He was stuck, and the bigger showdown was ahead.

11

Filibusted

THE NOVEMBER 2002 midterms were unique. Traditionally, the president's party loses seats in the first national vote after being inaugurated. But this was the first election after the September 11, 2001, attacks and America was still fearful and in crisis. Republicans, who issued immediate calls for national unity in the aftermath of the attacks that occurred on their watch, changed their tune during the run-up to the midterms and sought to portray Democrats as weak on terror. It worked. Republicans netted two Senate seats and took back the control that was abruptly snatched from them with the party switch by Senator Jeffords. There was one significant postelection hiccup, however. While celebrating Senator Strom Thurmond's one hundredth birthday in a Senate hearing room on December 5, Senator Lott, thrilled to be returning as majority leader in the wake of the election, got carried away at the ceremony.

In lionizing Thurmond, the South Carolina legend, Lott referred to Thurmond's 1948 run for president on a segregationist platform. "I want to say this about my state," Lott said. "When Strom Thurmond ran for president, we voted for him. We're proud of it. And if the rest of the country had followed our lead, we wouldn't have had all these problems over all these years either."

The comments didn't attract much attention at the birthday party. But as they sunk in over the weekend, an angry backlash built. To many, Lott, a slick congressional operator and onetime University of Mississippi cheerleader with a deep love for the South, was implying that if America had put a segregationist in the executive mansion, it would have been better off. Lott insisted he hadn't meant it that way, that he was just paying lighthearted reverence to a man who'd had a remarkable career as well as a later-in-life change of heart about race relations.

As he fought to hang on to his job, it didn't help that Lott was found to have made a similar comment when speaking after Thurmond at a Reagan political rally in Jackson, Mississippi, just days before the 1980 presidential election. "You know, if we had elected this man thirty years ago, we wouldn't be in the mess we are today," Lott had said.

Lott's problems were not confined to Democrats and civil rights groups. In the aftermath of a big election victory, President Bush and Karl Rove, his political guru, did not want the Senate face of their party to be a man under attack for racially charged remarks. There was no administration love lost for Lott, a man who considered himself an equal partner with the White House and a much more astute Washington insider. Bush, Rove, and a few ambitious Republican senators were in the market for a leader they felt more comfortable with, one over whom they could exert more influence.

After days of backroom maneuvering, the White House helped usher Lott out of the leadership and installed Senator Bill Frist, the Tennessee Republican and a renowned heart-lung transplant surgeon who had led the successful midterm political operation for Senate Republicans. It was a mortifying outcome for Lott, who was about to resume the majority leader's job that he had lost in 2001 to Jeffords's party switch. Lott never again seemed the same in the Senate. He abruptly resigned in November 2007, less than a year after being elected to a new six-year term, to open a lucrative lobbying practice with John Breaux, a former Democratic senator from Louisiana.

Frist, first elected in 1994, was barely into his second term in the Senate, and now he was going to lead it in a very difficult political environment. Democrats were only too willing to test him when it came to judicial nominations.

After watching Estrada's nomination languish under Democratic control of the Senate, Republicans were eager to move it forward, figuring their new majority could push it through. He finally received a vote in the Judiciary Committee in January 2003 and was approved 10–9 on a party-line vote. Schumer referred to him as a "sphinx-like" nominee who would tilt the important appeals court out of the American mainstream.

A few days following the committee vote, Democratic members of the Senate Judiciary Committee gathered privately in the Capitol leadership suite of Senator Tom Daschle, the Democratic leader from South Dakota. In that meeting, later disclosed by the columnist Bob Novak, the Democrats agreed to block Estrada through a filibuster in what would be an extraordinary move.

Senator Kennedy was adamant in the session that Democrats needed a coherent strategy for preventing the confirmation of multiple judges they found objectionable. Democrats feared that allowing Estrada to escape without providing his solicitor general memos would set a bad precedent and make it harder to force other nominees to comply, as well as make it hard to block Estrada should he, as anticipated, be put up for a Supreme Court seat. Daschle then took the proposal to the full Democratic caucus at one of its weekly luncheons and most came on board, itching for a fight with Bush.

Unaware of the depth of Democratic resistance and confident that Democrats would break, Republicans quickly moved the Estrada nomination to the floor for a vote. In keeping with their leadership decision, Democrats dug in against Estrada, telling Republicans they had the votes to prevent the nomination from coming to a final vote, infuriating Republicans and the White House.

As the debate wore on for nearly two weeks, Republicans sought to put the pressure on Democrats and make them squirm. They recorded a bit of success when Senator Bill Nelson, the Florida Democrat, told

Daschle that he would join Senators John Breaux of Louisiana, Zell Miller of Georgia, and Ben Nelson of Nebraska in backing Estrada's nomination. It was lost on no one that Hispanic voters were a force in Florida, particularly the Republican-leaning Cuban Americans in the Miami area.

"I am troubled by those who have suggested that some senators are anti-Hispanic because they seek additional information about this nominee," Nelson said in a statement. "Poisoning the debate with baseless accusations demeans the nomination process." Still, Nelson said that "after reviewing Mr. Estrada's personal and professional credentials, including personally interviewing the nominee, I believe he is qualified to serve on the DC Circuit Court, and I will vote in favor of his nomination."

Alberto Gonzales, the White House counsel, wrote a blistering letter to Senate Democrats, trying to take apart their objections piece by piece:

"We respect the Senate's constitutional role in the confirmation process, and we agree that the Senate must make an informed judgment consistent with its traditional role and practices," Gonzales wrote. He said, however, that Democrats were going too far and that "a new and shifting standard is being applied to Miguel Estrada."

After thirteen days, Frist called for a vote. The result was 55–44, 5 shy of the 60 required to break a filibuster, but easily enough for confirmation on a simple majority vote. As expected, the four Democrats broke ranks, but all the other votes seemed solidly locked up.

Only one previous judicial nominee, Justice Abe Fortas, had been blocked by a filibuster when he was nominated by President Lyndon B. Johnson in 1968 to be chief justice of the Supreme Court. That nomination was withdrawn and Fortas kept his seat. But Republicans had no intention of withdrawing this one.

"What is this brouhaha all about?" asked Sessions, the Alabama Republican who had won a Senate seat after himself being rejected by the Senate for a federal judgeship. "What is causing us to be subjected to the first filibuster in the history of the United States involving a nominee for a circuit court of appeals judge, or a district court judge for that matter, in the history of this country?" Sessions said it was stunning that Democrats had initiated a rare judicial filibuster against an exemplary man who had "lived the American dream, who has been a success in every category of life, whose integrity has never been questioned, and whose professionalism and skill is doubted by no one."

Frist, in one of his first crises as leader, vowed not to relent, and it put him at loggerheads with Daschle, his Democratic counterpart. Daschle was a heartland Democrat with an amiable style and had remained popular in his conservative state through his dedication to agriculture issues and prominence in Washington. Sparsely populated South Dakota relished the idea it had sent a leader to Washington—even if he was a Democrat. But despite his ability to navigate the political currents back home, he was a partisan leader, albeit one with a talent for making political exchanges sound reasonable in his Midwestern manner.

"We have simply asked that Mr. Estrada fill out his application for this lifetime employment as every other one of his predecessors has," Daschle said about the filibuster, sticking with the Democratic line that Estrada had not been forthcoming enough.

During a May appearance on *PBS NewsHour*, Daschle tried to highlight the fact that the Democrats had approved scores of other Bush judicial nominees. "Well, keep in mind—and I really don't feel that the media has always been as balanced in reporting here, because there's been very little reporting of the one hundred and twenty-two that have already been confirmed," he told his interviewer, Jim Lehrer, referring to others of Bush's judicial picks who had been approved. "We just confirmed a Hispanic judge again today—district and circuit judges. The real story is that the score is one hundred and twenty-two to two. We're willing to settle with that."

But Republicans were not willing to settle. The Senate devoted weeks to the debate, and Frist called vote after vote to shut off the

Estrada filibuster, seven in all. Republicans offered concessions to Democrats to allow further questioning of Estrada, but the vote was always the same. Democrats would not budge. Some talk surfaced of Republicans forcing a rules change to thwart the filibuster—a step that was considered wildly extreme at the time; to tinker with the revered traditions of the Senate bordered on heresy!—but no move was made.

Finally, on September 4, 2003, Estrada withdrew his name from consideration in a letter to Bush. He became the first appellate court nominee blocked by a filibuster. "I believe that the time has come to return my full attention to the practice of law and to regain the ability to make long-term plans for my family," Estrada wrote.

The fight had taken a steep toll on both Estrada and his family. It was having a detrimental impact on his legal practice and made his taking on big cases problematic, because it was unclear how long he would remain in private practice. His wife, Laury Gordon Estrada, distraught by the treatment of her husband, had miscarried during the filibuster.

Republicans expressed outrage at a Democratic victory they felt was outrageous, one achieved through the abuse of Senate rules and by maligning a deserving individual.

"Mr. Estrada received disgraceful treatment at the hands of forty-five United States senators during the more than two years his nomination was pending," Bush said from the White House. "Despite his superb qualifications and the wide bipartisan support for his nomination, these Democrat senators repeatedly blocked an up-or-down vote that would have led to Mr. Estrada's confirmation. The treatment of this fine man is an unfortunate chapter in the Senate's history." (Lest the always existent politics of the moment be forgotten, the White House also released a version of the statement in Spanish.)

Democrats said they hoped the outcome would persuade Bush to nominate more consensus judges. But they were reserved, recognizing that a new line had been crossed and there would be repercussions.

"The real victory for our side would be if George Bush, instead of just nominating nominees through an ideological prism, were to do what the Founding Fathers intended, sit down, talk to the Senate, see if we could come to some agreements on who ought to be judges," Schumer said on *PBS NewsHour.* "Certainly they wouldn't be judges that I agree with on most issues, but sit down and have the advice-and-consent process work. I don't think this is a victory per se at all."

On the same program, Senator Sessions said the filibuster tipped the scales on the separation of powers. "There were fifty-five votes to confirm, which prior to this year, would have confirmed the nominee," said Sessions. "But they blocked an up-or-down vote by carrying out the filibuster rule, and I think that's a very, very grim thing. It should not occur. It shifts the balance of power, weakening the independence of the courts, strengthening the hand of the Congress, and weakening the hand of the president in a constitutional alteration of power that we've never done before, and we should not do now. And I hope there'll be some reevaluation of this on the other side."

While Estrada's fight was done, the bitterness over it lingered and would influence multiple Supreme Court fights in the years ahead as well as the immediate aftermath.

In November 2003, the conservative editorial page of the *Wall Street Journal* published an astonishing find. The newspaper had obtained copies of what were obviously internal memorandum circulated among Democratic senators and staff during the judicial fights that had been raging. The sensitivity was obvious from the candor expressed in the documents.

In one, a memo to Edward Kennedy from a staffer said that a civil rights attorney had encouraged Democrats to hold off on filling any seats on an appeals court that covered Michigan to increase the chances of a favorable ruling in an affirmative action case. That represented an example of trying to use the nomination process to guarantee a judicial outcome.

The most explosive memo was dated November 7, 2001, to Senator Richard J. Durbin of Illinois, a liberal member of the Judiciary Committee with a long-standing interest in judicial confirmations. The staff member reported that a meeting with liberal advocacy groups revealed their major concerns with some of the emerging Bush nominees.

The activists, the memo said, "identified Miguel Estrada (D.C. Circuit) as especially dangerous, because he has a minimal paper trail, he is Latino, and the White House seems to be grooming him for a Supreme Court appointment. They want to hold Estrada off as long as possible."

There it was in black and white. While the Democratic strategy was well known and understood in Washington, it was still shocking to see it written down so explicitly just weeks after Estrada had been forced to withdraw his name. Conservatives pounced, saying the memos illuminated the bad faith of the Democrats and underscored their allegiance to liberal special interests.

"This plunge into the murky deep comes from staff strategy memos we've obtained from the days when Democrats ran the Senate Judiciary Committee from 2001–2002," said the *Journal* in a mocking tone as it disclosed the memos. "Or, rather, appeared to run the committee. Their real bosses are the liberal interest groups that more or less tell the Senators when to sit, speak and roll over—and which Bush judges to confirm or not."

The memos did cause an immediate tumult, but not the one that the newspaper or the source of the documents anticipated. The Democrats who had their files pilfered by Republicans on the Judiciary Committee staff because of faulty computer security practices demanded an investigation. Hatch, the Utah Republican who was then chairing the committee, was embarrassed by the computer infiltration, so he obliged. Much of the media's attention turned to the rummaging through the computer system by Republicans, not the memos themselves. The episode would linger long on Capitol Hill and become an important issue in future hearings. But at the time, it was just a postscript on the Estrada saga.

Over the years, as the judicial wars intensified anew, top Democrats came to regret their decision to filibuster the nomination. Estrada was popular with top Washington lawyers tied to both parties and was much less conservative than some of the nominees who would follow him under President Bush and especially President Trump.

"There was a fear that we were going to lose whatever balance there might have been," Daschle said in 2018. "But I've come to lament the politicization of the courts. I think it has a very negative effect not only on the perception of the courts, but on the courts themselves." He said that rulings had become "predictable" simply by assessing whether a judge was nominated by a Republican or Democrat.

There were other repercussions as well. Daschle, the Democratic leader, in 2004 found himself facing a serious reelection threat in South Dakota against former representative John Thune, a handsome and affable Republican who had barely lost two years earlier to Democratic senator Tim Johnson. Seeking revenge for Daschle's support of filibusters, Frist took the rare step of traveling to South Dakota to campaign against his Democratic counterpart. Thune also hit Daschle for his leadership of the judicial blockade, and conservative advocacy groups used it in their ad blitz against Daschle. It was far from the only issue confronting Daschle as criticism piled up at home. He lost narrowly as Republicans retained the Senate, the first Senate leader to be defeated in half a century.

For Estrada, the confirmation fight was a devastating experience, though he went on to a successful legal career and became known as a top lawyer in Washington. His wife, Laury, died in November 2004 after her own struggle with the confirmation fallout.

In 2010, Estrada, who generally remained out of the public eye and out of the judicial wars, where he was such a test case, weighed in on Elena Kagan's nomination to the Supreme Court in a letter to the Judiciary Committee. They had attended Harvard together and were friends. "If such a person, who has demonstrated great intellect, high accomplishments and an upright life, is not easily confirmable, I fear we will have reached a point where no capable person will readily accept a nomination for judicial service," Estrada wrote.

In 2016, he coauthored a *Washington Post* op-ed during the fight over the Scalia seat that argued the entire judicial nomination process had gone off the rails:

"Republicans and Democrats put the blame on the other for the complete abandonment of rules and norms in the judicial confirmation process," it said. "Both are being insincere—whitewashing their conduct over a long period of time while complaining bitterly about the very same conduct on the part of the other side. Both have chosen, in increments of one-upmanship, to replace a common law of judicial nominations that was based on certain norms with one based on power politics alone."

The brutal op-ed said there was no principle or norm "that either side would not violate itself and simultaneously demand the other side observe as a matter of decency and inter-branch comity."

It was a devastating takedown of both parties by a man who had seen the partisanship up close and extremely personal.

Estrada has refused to revisit his own history or share his perspective on what happened to him and what it meant for the years ahead when it came to judges. "I am not interested in discussing any aspect of my life for public consumption, this period of it included," he wrote in an email declining an interview. "Besides, politics has been politics since time immemorial. Cicero probably did not think that it was a game for the tender or overly-sensitive. Even today, worse things can happen to people than not getting a government job—and have happened to me."

Estrada was no longer in the judicial fight, but others were. After Democrats blocked his confirmation, angry Republicans intensified their discussions about changing the Senate's rules to prevent Democrats from holding up other judges in the future.

12

The Gang's All Here

SENATOR BEN NELSON, the amiable centrist Democrat from Nebraska, was worried. One of the few Democrats to oppose the filibuster of Estrada, he had been increasingly vocal about the need for an acceptable escape from the judicial crisis paralyzing the Senate in the spring of 2005. Now Senator Robert C. Byrd, the West Virginia legend and conscience of the Senate, was striding toward him across the Senate floor.

Republicans, led by Frist, were threatening to use a procedural maneuver to end Democratic filibusters that had bedeviled them for years.

The Estrada fight ended with his withdrawal, but Senate Democrats were persisting in blocking multiple other appeals court nominees put forward by Bush, including Priscilla Owen of Texas, who was in the first tranche of Bush nominees along with Estrada. Owen was perceived as a real threat to abortion rights, given her rulings from the Texas Supreme Court aimed at making it difficult for minors to get an abortion without telling their parents. She was also seen as closely aligned with Karl Rove, Bush's political adviser. Democrats had also dug in deeply against the nominations of William Pryor of Alabama and Charles Pickering of Mississippi. Pryor, a protégé of Jeff Sessions, held well-known antiabortion views and other hard-right conservative stances. Pickering, a onetime Senate candidate who had been named a federal district court judge by George H. W. Bush, was strenuously opposed by civil rights groups for what they saw as a weak record, including giving a young man convicted of cross burning a reduced sentence.

After the Estrada debacle, the Bush administration and Senate Republicans aggressively challenged Democrats over the filibusters, using such tried-and-true attention-getting spectacles as keeping in the Senate overnight to drive home their complaints. Nothing draws photographers like Senate staff rolling out the cots for senators to rest in off the Senate floor, though they are rarely used. Most senators nap in their offices or go to their nearby residences if they run out of gas.

In November 2003, Republicans staged such an overnight marathon called "Justice for Judges." To help elevate the event, Bush gathered at the White House with Owen and two other women appeals court nominees who were in the filibuster sights of Democrats: Carolyn Kuhl and Janice Rogers Brown, both of California.

Overall, Democrats had held up ten different appeals court nominees via filibuster beginning in 2003 over the course of twenty votes, including four on Owen. Bush, frustrated, used his power to make recess appointments in 2004 to finally put Pryor on the appeals court for the Eleventh Circuit and Pickering on the US Court of Appeals for the Fifth Circuit. But the filibusters against others, including Owen, dragged on.

Ben Nelson didn't agree with the filibusters. They were difficult to defend back home in conservative Nebraska. Plus, as a former governor, Nelson saw the value of allowing the executive branch the freedom to install its chosen nominees. He frequently joined with a handful of Democrats who voted unsuccessfully with Republicans to break the impasse. But he also didn't approve of some of the judges Bush was putting forward. The Senate was stuck, and things were getting very ugly. "It left people with little room to do anything," Nelson recalled.

Frist was intensifying his threats to change the rules to eliminate supermajority filibuster power against judicial nominees. While the appeals court judges were important, Republicans wanted to be ready for a possible Supreme Court opening and didn't want Democrats to extend their filibuster strategy to the high court.

Plus, Frist, never short on self-esteem, was weighing a run for president in 2008, and a victory over Democrats on judges would be a nice credential with which to woo conservative voters. He needed to prove he wouldn't be pushed around.

Given the makeup of the Senate, it would now be easier for Frist to win a floor showdown than it would have been in 2003. Republicans gained four seats in the 2004 election and held a 55–45 majority. Frist owned a greater margin to work with in pushing through a potential rules change to the filibuster should a few Republicans balk.

Martin Gold, an expert on Senate procedures and an adviser to Frist, cowrote a law review article entitled "The Constitutional Option to Change Senate Rules and Procedures: A Majoritarian Means to Overcome the Filibuster." It laid out, step-by-step, how to make the rules change with a simple majority vote.

At the time, this was perceived as a wildly radical idea. If there was anything on which the Senate prided itself, it was its reverence for the rights of the minority. Without that sentiment, the Senate was just the House with fewer and more polished members. Senators looked down on the House. Even those who had gotten their starts across the rotunda considered the House the lower chamber.

The brewing procedural tactic was famously dubbed "the nuclear option" by Lott in 2003 when frustrated Republicans first began talking about a way to cut off Democratic filibusters of judicial nominees. Different ideas circulated, but the basic concept was that the majority party could win a ruling that the filibuster was dilatory and out of order or reverse a ruling protecting the filibuster. The result would be a new Senate standard—that a simple majority could end a filibuster rather than the sixty votes inscribed in Senate rules.

To people like Nelson, the former governor of a Republican state and someone who constantly needed to protect his right flank, that kind of arcane chess match represented a drastic step. He believed it would be the end of the Senate because it would limit not only the power of the minority, but also the clout of individual senators, who could tie up the Senate on their own by skillful application of the rules. The phrase "nuclear option" summed up the implications quite nicely for those steeped in the ways of the Senate. (As the title of Gold's law review article suggests, Senate Republicans tried to make the step sound less explosive by referring to it as the "constitutional option," but that never caught on.)

Though a relatively junior member, Nelson's status as a potential swing vote on many issues gave him extra stature. Still, he got nervous when he noticed Byrd determinedly heading his way. Byrd was very formal and extremely protective of the folkways of the Senate. At first Nelson feared he might be in trouble for something he had said during a recent television appearance. Even daring to get engaged in breaking the judicial deadlock could be considered a breach of decorum that would rile Byrd.

"Whenever he started coming toward people, you said, 'Uh-oh, this isn't going to be nice,'" recalled Nelson. "He grabbed my lapel, and I said, 'I am going to get an earful now.'"

Nelson did indeed get an earful from Byrd, but not the one he expected. Byrd encouraged Nelson to move ahead with finding a solution that would avert the showdown. "He said, 'You can do it and I will help,'" Nelson recalled.

The Gang of Fourteen was born.

So-called gangs of lawmakers assembling to find agreement on big policy issues have become common in the Senate, as bipartisan cliques of senators have taken a crack at stubborn subjects such as immigration and health care. But the Gang of Fourteen was something of a new idea at the time, providing the model for multiple, and less successful, future efforts.

Byrd's participation was crucial. He was the senior member of the Senate and a legendary Washington figure, though he had deteriorated both mentally and physically. At times the man who had first entered Congress in 1953 seemed like a visitor from a bygone era, with his formal bearing, archaic speech, and strict personal code. Within a few years, his capabilities would be publicly questioned even as he became a progressive hero for his outspoken opposition to the war in Iraq. But having Byrd on board for anything involving Senate rules was a huge advantage and would bestow significant credibility on the bipartisan effort. In his prime, Byrd was the undisputed master of the inner workings of the Senate, and he still commanded enormous respect from colleagues in both parties.

Nelson then went to Lott, the former Republican leader, who also had a reputation for being able to bend Senate procedure to his favor, to see if he might be interested. Lott had multiple reasons to consider playing a role with the gang. He was still angry at his treatment three years earlier when he had been deposed as leader; he was particularly upset by Frist, who he believed had stabbed him in the back by stepping forward as a potential new leader. The formation of the group was something of an act of mutiny, since the membership would essentially wrest control of the Senate from the leadership when it came to judicial nominations. Lott liked nothing more than a little institutional intrigue and a chance for payback if Frist could be made to look weak. At the same time, he could be the eyes for the rest of the Republicans in keeping his colleagues apprised of what was going on with the rump group. Still, he was in an awkward position because of his history. Rather than officially become a member of the gang, Lott instead played a background role, providing guidance and encouragement.

Nelson knew Senator John McCain of Arizona would not be afraid to challenge his own party. McCain had championed campaign finance reform—anathema to most Republicans—and certainly had no fear of pushing back against Frist and those on the Judiciary Committee who were calling for a floor showdown. Akin to Byrd, McCain saw himself as a protector of the Senate, while he also liked to flex his muscle and demonstrate that he could take on the leadership and win. Plus, he craved the spotlight.

The group quickly took shape, with some of the leading centrist voices in the Senate participating. A crucial addition was the silver-haired John Warner, the central casting Republican senator from Virginia. Warner had played a central role in putting Frist in the majority leader's job but now saw himself as making the future of the Senate a priority.

"He was important in getting others to join us," said Nelson about Warner. "He thought it was the right thing to do." Others drawn to the effort included the centrist Democrats Joe Lieberman of Connecticut; Mark Pryor of Arkansas; Ken Salazar of Colorado; Mary Landrieu of Louisiana; and another elder statesman, Daniel Inouye of Hawaii. On the Republican side, it was a roll call of Republican moderates, with Susan Collins and Olympia Snowe of Maine joining Lincoln Chafee of Rhode Island. Also on board were McCain's close friend and ally Lindsey Graham of South Carolina and Mike DeWine of Ohio.

Part of why the group came together was that certain White House court nominees were proving unpopular on both sides. "Many of the Republicans didn't want them either," Nelson said. "And that is what made the Gang of Fourteen go."

The group began meeting covertly, sometimes in Nelson's office, sometimes in McCain's office, and occasionally in the office of Ms. Collins, as they tried to come up with an approach they could all endorse. Given Byrd's frailty, Nelson once suggested they meet in his quarters, but Byrd, ever the traditionalist, told Nelson no. "He said, 'Mr. Chairman, I come to the chairman.'"

It was a numbers game. The thrust was for the fourteen to agree on a set of conditions under which the group would commit to not filibuster nominees as well as confirm pending nominees who might not be able to secure 60 votes but could easily win 50. With the Senate divided 55–45 in favor of the Republicans, 7 Democrats siding with them would mean 62 votes to break a filibuster—two more than needed. At the same time, 7 Republican votes would mean only 48 votes existed for the nuclear option—two short of what was needed, a number sufficient to take that option off the table.

Nelson, who in his youth worked in a bakery, said the participation of fourteen members was no accident. "I wanted a baker's dozen in case one or two wouldn't be able to do it," he said, upping the baker's count by one. "Fourteen was just insurance."

With almost no press coverage, the group continued to meet and work through drafts of a memorandum of agreement they would send to the leadership of both parties. A review of documents from those private discussions showed that the group's members struggled to define the conditions that would prevent a filibuster. In an early iteration of the agreement, the senators said they "would agree to invoke cloture on future nominees that are not, in our judgment, extremely controversial." That standard, the draft letter said, would mean that "the majority of, and perhaps all future nominees, will receive up or down votes in the United States Senate."

As the meetings progressed and senators fine-tuned the language, they realized they needed to come up with a more definitive standard than "extremely controversial." The meetings then produced another attempt: filibusters would be allowed only in "extraordinary circumstances." Members of the gang knew such circumstances would be in the eye of the beholder—or as McCain said, quoting a famous Supreme Court finding, "It's like pornography—you know it when you see it."

Outside the private gang meetings, pressure was building, and neither party's leadership nor the aligned advocacy groups were happy with what was going on. The entire exercise was a tremendous affront to Frist, a man who liked to remind the people he was talking to that he had held beating hearts in his own hands. If the gang succeeded, it would usurp control from the Senate leader.

Reid and the Democrats were anxious as well, though he was kept apprised of the talks and provided some input along with Schumer.

Democrats wanted to avoid a vote that would end their power to filibuster, but they didn't want the centrists to give away the store either.

As for the advocacy groups, the progressive ones thought Democrats were on the verge of giving up the best tool they had to block
judges. They wanted to force Frist to prove he had the votes to move
forward. On the other hand, conservatives wanted Frist to pull the
trigger and give them the ability to roll over the Democrats once and
for all. Bush still had almost three years left in office and could install
a lot of judges in that time if he was unimpeded by his political opposition.

At the White House, Bush was not saying much about the showdown, though in his State of the Union address a few months earlier
he had declared, to loud applause, that something needed to be done.
"As president, I have a constitutional responsibility to nominate men
and women who understand the role of courts in our democracy and
are well qualified to serve on the bench, and I have done so," he said.
"The Constitution also gives the Senate a responsibility: every judicial
nominee deserves an up-or-down vote."

Vice President Cheney, who by virtue of that job was also the president of the Senate, was ready to back Frist. He made clear that he
would side with the Republicans if they moved ahead with gutting the
filibuster while he was presiding over the Senate.

In late April, Frist delivered a taped message to thousands of Christian conservatives who were taking part in what was called "Justice
Sunday: Stopping the Filibuster against People of Faith." In his remarks, he noted that Reid referred to him as a "a radical Republican. I
don't think it's radical to ask senators to vote."

He soon established a deadline that the Gang of Fourteen would
race to meet. Frist was moving forward with the nomination of Owen,
and a vote to cut off a filibuster against her nomination was set for
Tuesday, May 24. With time running out, the gang gathered for a final
deliberation and a final pep talk from Lott, who slipped in through a
side door. Nelson recalled that when the members all agreed on the

final parameters, an emotional Byrd waved his ever-present handker-chief and praised the group and Nelson. "You saved the Senate."

The deal meant successful cloture votes—and certain confirmation—for a set of long-filibustered nominees: Owen, Brown, and Pryor. Owen was one of the most difficult to come to terms on, and in early iterations of the deal she was part of a group of three who would not be confirmed. In the end, two others were thrown overboard: William Myers III and Henry Saad.

In exchange for guaranteeing the confirmation of the three stalled judges, Democrats received a commitment from the seven Republicans that they would not support any move by Frist to detonate the nuclear option. Future nominations were left to the senators and their own definition of extraordinary circumstances. "Each senator must use his or her own discretion and judgment in determining whether such cir-cumstances exist," the memorandum said.

"The agreement we have reached will allow the Senate to confirm the vast majority of judicial nominations presented to the Senate, while maintaining the spirit of bipartisanship needed to address other issues of concern to the American people. We firmly believe this agreement is consistent with the traditions of the United States Senate that we as Senators seek to uphold," the document read.

The authors had to inform the Senate leaders, and Nelson went to Reid's office along with Lieberman and Pryor to break the news.

Reid expressed satisfaction that the filibuster had survived, but he was not thrilled with the deal, since some objectionable judges would get on the federal bench and others had been left out entirely, meaning the Senate would still have to decide their fate, and they would most likely get confirmed.

Frist, as majority leader, had much more at stake than Reid. The agreement totally undercut him. He said that it fell short of his de-mand that all nominees have the chance for a final vote and later told Republicans that the Republican members of the gang had surren-dered the majority's power.

James Dobson, the influential Christian conservative who headed Focus on the Family, was furious and described the deal as a sellout by moderate Republicans. He expressed "disappointment, outrage, and sense of abandonment" at the result.

The outcome was a real blow to Frist, who had already come under fire for his handling of the Terri Schiavo case, which involved a brain-damaged Florida woman whose treatment had become an ugly cause célèbre among conservatives but was seen as a gross invasion of privacy by much of the country. Frist's presidential hopes would never recover, and he left the Senate at the end of 2006, in compliance with a vow to serve only two terms.

As a result of the deal, Owen, first nominated by Bush in 2001, was finally confirmed on May 25, 2005, on a mainly party-line vote of 55–43, followed within weeks by the confirmations of Brown, Pryor, Richard Griffin, and David W. McKeague.

Among the nominees left out of the agreement, much to Reid's consternation, was a close aide to President Bush: his staff secretary, Brett M. Kavanaugh, part of Kenneth Starr's special counsel team who had prosecuted Bill Clinton's impeachment. Reid tried to round up votes to filibuster Kavanaugh but came up short. He would later be confirmed to the DC circuit court over fierce objections from top Democrats after a three-year wait.

But the immediate crisis was averted, and years of judicial acrimony settled down. In the 2006 elections, Democrats took control of the Senate, shifting the dynamic on judicial fights altogether, as they could pick and choose among Bush's nominees.

Despite disgruntlement among Senate leaders and some of their colleagues, members of the gang were exultant and proud of their efforts to protect the institution.

Outside the Senate chamber in the narrow marble hallway where senators use six elevators to come and go, Warner, the distinguished Virginian, eloquently held forth after the deal was announced on the culture of the Senate, the rights of the minority, the Constitution, and the need to preserve the traditions of such a glorious institution. It was a bravura performance by a Senate showman. I happened to be there, along with Paul Kane, a *Roll Call* reporter who was to join the *Washington Post,* and a *New York Times* colleague, Kate Zernike.

"Quite a speech, Senator," I told Warner. "You ought to write a book."

"A book?" said Warner, a famous playboy of the Senate who had once been married to the movie star Elizabeth Taylor. "If I wrote a book," he mused as he stepped into an elevator, "all anyone would want to know is how Liz was in bed."

We all laughed uproariously. "Well," I said, "maybe that could be a chapter."

"Oh no," said Warner, his eyes lighting up at the memory as the elevator doors closed. "It would be more than a chapter."

Liz Taylor aside, it had been a stirring moment for the Senate, as a group of determined lawmakers had come together to try to save the Senate from itself. They had succeeded in preserving the storied filibuster. Temporarily.

Battle Lines

PRESIDENT OBAMA GOT off to a slow start in filling federal judge-ships. With the country convulsed in a financial crisis when he took office, correcting the economy took precedence for his administration. The White House counsel's office was also focused on trying to fulfill a campaign promise by closing the terror detainee camp in Guantánamo Bay, Cuba, a time-consuming diversion that ultimately failed. Plus, the administration, following the president's own lead, was trying to lower the partisan temperature around the judicial confirmation pro-cess, casting about for a way to select judges whom Republicans could support or at least not block.

Obama named his first nominee, David Hamilton of Indiana, a US district court judge, to a seat on the US Court of Appeals for the Seventh Circuit, on March 17, 2009. The White House had made sure to secure the public backing of Senator Richard Lugar, the veteran cen-trist Indiana Republican, to underscore that the administration was ready to consult with Republicans on judicial picks. Lugar and Obama had a strong relationship from their time on the Senate Foreign Rela-tions Committee and had traveled together internationally.

Hamilton was seen as a moderate, bipartisan choice, and Lugar's backing for a home state pick should have cleared the way for him. Republicans instead blocked him with a filibuster the first chance they got.

"The very first—the very first—nominee to the federal bench that President Obama sent here was filibustered," Senator Leahy recalled later with derision. "Judge Hamilton of Indiana was a widely respected fifteen-year veteran of the federal bench nominated to the Seventh Circuit. President Obama reached out to the longest-serving Republican in the Senate, Senator Dick Lugar, to select a nominee he supported. Yet Senate Republicans filibustered his nomination, requiring a cloture vote before his nomination could be confirmed after a delay of seven months.

"It is almost a case of saying: 'Okay, Mr. President, you think you got elected? We are going to show you who is boss. We are going to treat you differently than all of the presidents before you.' This has never been done before, to filibuster the president's very first nominee. Somehow this president is going to be told he is different than other presidents."

"Different" was Democratic code for their suspicion that Obama was treated disdainfully by Republicans because of his African American heritage. Senators didn't explicitly voice that thought in public, and President Obama steered clear of such suggestions himself, but it was a persistent undertone throughout his tenure.

Conservatives raised objections to Hamilton's early work for progressive groups and his decisions on prayer in public places and abortion that were later overturned. Republican senators were also calling for Obama to renominate some of the judges who were stalled during the last days of the Bush administration as a real demonstration of bipartisanship.

Republicans remembered a striking Obama line from a 2007 speech to Planned Parenthood, in which he took issue with the principle expressed by Chief Justice John Roberts that federal judges should be neutral umpires who simply call balls and strikes. "We need somebody who's got the heart—the empathy—to recognize what it's like to be a young teenage mom," Obama had said. "The empathy to understand what it's like to be poor or African American or gay or disabled or old—and that's the criteria by which I'll be selecting my judges. All right?"

To the Right, it wasn't all right. Conservatives saw Obama's comment as irrefutable evidence that he was looking for activist judges who would rule on emotion more than the law. What Obama was seeking was what the Right considered the very definition of activist judges. Republicans had no intention of making it easy for Obama, no matter what the White House said about finding consensus nominees.

The administration also expended much of its initial judicial energy on a replacement to the Supreme Court for Justice David Souter, who left the court in June 2009. The occasion caused Obama to reaffirm his view that judges needed more than knowledge of the law. "I will seek someone who understands that justice isn't about some abstract legal theory or footnote in a case book," he said. "It is also about how our laws affect the daily realities of people's lives—whether they can make a living and care for their families; whether they feel safe in their homes and welcome in their own nation.

"I view that quality of empathy, of understanding and identifying with people's hopes and struggles, as an essential ingredient for arriving at just decisions and outcomes."

Based on those credentials, Obama nominated Judge Sonia Sotomayor of the US Court of Appeals for the Second Circuit, who would become the first person of Hispanic heritage to take a seat on the high court after her confirmation that August. Sotomayor proved relatively uncontroversial, though she had to backtrack from past comments that a "wise Latina" could make better decisions and bring a better perspective on the struggles of regular people to the bench than a white man without the same experiences.

But Democrats had an almost filibuster-proof majority in the Senate, and complaints about the "wise Latina" statement were nowhere near enough to derail her for what amounted to a rhetorical flourish.

The bigger complication for Sotomayor was that the National Rifle Association (NRA), in concert with Senate Republicans, had begun to take a larger role in court confirmations, given the potency of gun rights as a political rallying point for the Right. The gun group came out against her, and for the first time, it "scored" the vote on Sotomayor's confirmation on its rating of senators, meaning Republicans who voted for her would be penalized in the NRA's analysis of voting records.

Still, she was eventually confirmed, with nine Republicans joining all Democrats in support. A year later, Elena Kagan, the solicitor general whose own appeals court nomination by President Clinton was stalled by Republicans in 1999, was confirmed to the Supreme Court on a slightly more partisan vote. Obama might be struggling to fill the lower courts, but he had quickly placed his mark on the highest one.

The Obama administration eventually accelerated its judicial nominations, given the Democrats' solid majority in the Senate. But when Republicans gained six seats in the party's 2010 election wave, they began to take a harder line against Obama's nominees. The Senate margin had tightened considerably, and though Democrats still held the majority, Republicans were not in a cooperative mood.

In May 2011, Republicans successfully filibustered the nomination to the US Court of Appeals for the Ninth Circuit of Goodwin Liu, a rising progressive judicial star in California who came under fire for his liberal views and frank criticism of Justice Samuel Alito's tough-on-crime approach. With the new margins in the Senate, Liu recognized he had no chance of getting an up-or-down vote and asked that his nomination be withdrawn.

Republicans who had criticized Democrats for filibustering judges in the George W. Bush administration were now turning the tables on Obama and the Democrats. Requiring lower-court nominees to overcome the filibuster even if they were going to be easily approved became routine. In the first five years of the Obama administration, Majority Leader Reid had to file cloture—the motion to cut off filibusters—on more than twenty district court nominees, a previously unheard-of phenomena, since those trial-level judges typically went through with no or very little opposition.

As administration officials sought to fill court vacancies, they ran into deep intransigence from Republican senators, who refused to work with the administration on nominees for their own states, where they could have influenced Obama's choice. Kathryn Ruemmler, the White House counsel at the time, said Republicans such as Senator Ron Johnson, newly elected in Wisconsin, and Ted Cruz of Texas would not even engage with her when she traveled to Capitol Hill to press for judicial candidates. "Some senators wouldn't even forward us names," recalled Ruemmler. "I told them, 'If you send me someone good, I don't care if you are a Republican senator, I will take a look at them.'"

No luck. Adding to the backlog, Senator Leahy, chairing the Judiciary Committee, continued to honor the committee's tradition of requiring "blue slips" to be returned by home state senators before a nominee could move forward. No blue slip, no hearing for a nominee. It was a practice that essentially gave Republicans veto power over judges from their states despite a Democrat in the White House and a Democratic Senate majority. Vacancies piled up.

Those judicial openings had consequences, notably in states with heavy immigration caseloads. The shortage of judges delayed trials, increased workloads, and pushed civil cases to the bottom of the docket. In some parts of the country, federal judges were pleading for relief, in one case with tragic circumstances. John Roll, the federal judge killed during the 2011 Arizona assault that grievously wounded Representative Gabby Giffords and killed five others, had traveled to Tucson to meet with Giffords to thank her for her recent support for declaring a judicial emergency in the state.

In his first term, Obama had failed to get a single nominee confirmed to the US Court of Appeals for the District of Columbia Circuit. The administration was eager to correct that situation, given the predominance on the court of judges appointed by Republicans as well as the court's perceived probusiness slant when it came to adjudicating cases involving federal regulation.

The administration had determinedly pushed the nomination of

Caitlin Halligan, the onetime solicitor general for the state of New York. She was in danger of becoming the Democratic version of Miguel Estrada.

First nominated in 2010 to the seat John Roberts had vacated five years earlier to become chief justice of the Supreme Court, she had been blocked repeatedly by Republicans, who cited her prosecution of a suit on behalf of the state of New York against gun manufacturers. The suit sought to hold gun makers responsible for contributing to a "public nuisance" because of a proliferation of illegal weapons, potentially opening them to suits and criminal charges over gun crimes. The theory ran directly counter to a Republican drive, vigorously backed by the gun lobby, to grant the companies immunity from any gun crimes.

Halligan was acting in her capacity as the lawyer for the state, but the NRA and other gun rights groups exerted tremendous influence over Senate Republicans and were adamantly opposed to her. She was held up by a Republican filibuster in 2011 and her renomination stalled in 2012.

In March 2013, Harry Reid made another attempt to push her across the finish line but again ran into immovable Republican resistance beginning with McConnell, a die-hard backer of gun rights. "Ms. Halligan, as solicitor general of New York, advanced the dubious legal theory that those who make firearms should be liable for the criminal acts of third parties who misuse them," said McConnell, who declared that her view would impose massive liability "against the makers of a lawful product because of the criminal acts of someone else."

Grassley, again teaming up with McConnell, said Reid was wasting the Senate's time bringing up a nominee who could not be confirmed. He rejected the argument that Halligan was simply representing her client in the gun makers case. "I believe a close examination of Ms. Halligan's record indicates she was more than just an advocate," he said. "She was using the full weight of her office to advance and promote a political agenda masked by a legal doctrine that is well outside of the legal mainstream."

Frustrated Democrats knew they could not overcome the opposition but made the case for Halligan based on her strong credentials, her standing in the legal community, and the fact that Obama was at the moment the first president since Gerald Ford not to get a nominee on the influential appeals court.

"I fear my Republican colleagues are treating President Obama differently from other presidents in this regard," said Senator Dianne Feinstein. Again the Obama "difference" was voiced.

The result was preordained. The vote was 51–41, nine votes short of the 60 needed to force a final vote, with only Senator Lisa Murkowski of Alaska breaking with her Republican colleagues. Halligan soon asked Obama to withdraw her nomination, following in the footsteps of Goodwin Liu. Democrats were incensed.

"It was outrageous what happened to her," said Ruemmler. "They did not want us to put anyone on the DC circuit. Full stop. We were back to square one."

In losing that vote, Democrats began coalescing around an aggressive strategy that would ultimately both inflame the Senate and remake the influential appeals court. Democrats had had enough. A momentous showdown seemed inevitable.

Just a few days after the Halligan nomination was killed, Senate Democrats, working closely with the White House, began mapping out a new plan to either force Republicans to relent on the appeals court nominees or face serious consequences. One possibility was for Obama to make several simultaneous nominations, in effect daring Republicans to find specific objections in multiple instances. At the time, the appeals court had four vacancies. Democrats believed Republicans would be hard pressed to come up with legitimate reasons to disqualify four nominees at the same time.

Should Republicans continue to obstruct the nominees, the upshot was clear—Democrats were prepared to change the rules to allow a simple majority to confirm nominees. The nuclear option was back, and being weighed seriously, but this time by Democrats.

One choice for the appeals court was already in the pipeline. At the beginning of 2013, Obama had nominated Sri Srinivasan, who had worked in the Bush administration before becoming principal deputy solicitor general in the Obama administration in 2011.

Srinivasan was a highly regarded legal mind. But his nomination was not met enthusiastically by liberal and labor groups for multiple reasons: his experience in a Republican White House, the direction of some of his arguments, and his representation of bad-actor corporate clients such as Enron. But the Obama administration, determined to fill some of the seats on the prestigious court, firmly put its foot down and informed the groups that it was moving ahead with Srinivasan and that they needed to get on board. For the most part, they did.

With four vacancies on the eleven-member court, McConnell recognized that Republicans could not completely stonewall the White House. Republicans were willing to accept Srinivasan, given his work in a Republican administration. He was confirmed without opposition.

To McConnell and his fellow Republicans, that should have been good enough for Obama. They had acquiesced and granted the president a judge on the important appeals court. They refused to give any more ground. Their fear was that Obama, increasingly reliant on governing through executive order in areas like immigration and the environment, would put as many liberally inclined judges on the court as he could to ensure his edicts were upheld. "The only way the president can successfully bypass Congress is if he stacks the court with ideological allies who will rubber-stamp his executive orders," contended Grassley. "There is no big secret here. The other side hasn't been shy about this strategy."

Grassley and other Republicans griped that the administration was trying to "pack" the DC court for its political purposes.

The White House dismissed that idea as comical, since it was only trying to fill existing vacancies, not trying to add to the court as FDR had done before he was thwarted in the 1930s. The White House was far from satisfied with the confirmation of Srinivasan, the first South

Asian named to a federal appeals court. Reid, Schumer, and Obama saw it as only a first step and intensified their push to fill as many of the remaining vacancies as possible. To them, multiple simultaneous nominations were the answer.

In June, the fight began in earnest as Obama arrived in the Rose Garden accompanied by three new appeals court nominees and a bold new determination to get them on the bench. Just bringing the appellate nominees into the Rose Garden, a locale typically reserved for Supreme Court picks, highlighted the seriousness with which the administration was approaching the conflict. The president made clear he believed he had been mistreated by Republicans.

"My judicial nominees have waited three times longer to receive confirmation votes than those of my Republican predecessor," Obama said. "Let me repeat that: my nominees have taken three times longer to receive confirmation votes than those of my Republican predecessor. These individuals that I nominate are qualified. When they were given an up-or-down vote in the Senate—when they were finally given an up-or-down vote in the Senate—every one of them was confirmed. So this is not about principled opposition. This is about political obstruction."

The nominees were chosen for maximum effect. Nina Pillard, a professor at Georgetown University, was considered the most progressive of the three. She had worked in the Clinton administration and for the NAACP Legal Defense Fund. Patricia Millett was the more moderate pick, a veteran appellate lawyer who had represented both the Clinton and Bush administrations before the Supreme Court and whose husband was a retired military officer. The third was Robert Wilkins, an African American whom Obama had nominated for the federal district bench in DC and who had been confirmed without opposition in the Senate. If Republicans were going to erect roadblocks to this trio, they were going to have to defend filibusters against three highly regarded nominees—two women and a minority candidate who had already won overwhelming approval.

"They have broad bipartisan support from across the legal community," Obama said. "The nonpartisan American Bar Association have given them—each of them—its highest rating.

"These are no slouches," he said to Rose Garden laughter. "These are no hacks. They are incredibly accomplished lawyers by all accounts."

The fight was on.

14

Going Nuclear

As the three nominees entered the confirmation pipeline, Republicans came up with another argument to try to head them off—that the DC circuit court was not that busy and didn't really need the extra help.

Grassley, who ridiculed the workload of the appeals court and said that the new judges would have nothing to do, introduced legislation that would reduce the number of judges there by—not coincidentally—three slots. The legislation had no chance of being approved but helped drive home his argument.

"The objective data clearly indicate the DC circuit caseload is very low and that the court does not need any additional active judges," said Grassley, who, as usual, found a past example from Democrats, who in 2006 blocked a Bush nominee to the court, Peter Keisler, citing a low workload. Keisler quickly became a rallying cry for Republicans against the Obama picks. Republicans were also arguing that the fight over judges was an attempt by the Democrats to distract from problems with the implementation of the new health care law. In typical Senate fashion, Republicans were throwing up a variety of challenges to the Democrats in the hope of finding one that would take flight.

Reid probably didn't need more motivation to challenge Republicans. But he got some in mid-August when the DC circuit court—the center of the judicial fight—ruled that the administration was violating the law by not pursuing a required review of Yucca Mountain in Nevada as a potential nuclear waste dump.

For Harry Reid, Yucca Mountain was nonnegotiable. He had spent years fighting federal efforts to create a nuclear facility there and, using his tremendous clout, had essentially defunded the effort. Now the court that Republicans were trying to keep tilted toward conservatives was saying the project should be kept alive. The 2–1 decision was written by a judge with whom Reid was very familiar: Brett Kavanaugh. The dissent was by another well-known judicial name in Washington: Merrick Garland.

Given his ability to choke off funds for the project, Reid downplayed the court's decision, but he was deeply unhappy with it. "All of the sudden Harry Reid was on fire," said one Democratic activist who was working with Reid on the makeup of the courts. "Now he knew the importance of the federal judges."

Despite all the back-and-forth, the three Obama judicial nominees were slowly making their way through the process and were headed for floor votes.

Millett, considered the most confirmable nominee, was at the front of the line and reached the Senate floor on October 31, 2013. Republicans were also that day blocking the nomination of Mel Watt, a Democratic congressman from North Carolina, to be head of the Federal Housing Finance Agency. Such opposition was a relative rarity, since lawmakers usually received a semblance of professional courtesy when nominated for an administration job.

The tone was set when John McCain, one of the leading members of the Gang of Fourteen, came to the floor to announce his opposition to both Watt and Millett. "I believe that neither candidate should be affirmed by the Senate at this time," said McCain, who recounted his own experience in the Gang of Fourteen, which defined "extraordinary circumstances" as a reason to block nominees. McCain did not delineate what he saw as those circumstances in these two cases, but he did urge Democrats not to change the rules to end the sixty-vote threshold to cut off filibusters against nominations.

"We will destroy the very fabric of the Senate," he warned.

Democrats argued that Millett was a superbly qualified lawyer with a wealth of civic interests from teaching Sunday school to visiting the hospitalized and homebound. They said a blockade of the nomination would lead to repercussions. "Patricia Millett is an outstanding nominee who deserves to be treated on her merits," said Leahy, rejecting McCain's position. "No argument has been lodged against her that would rise to the level of an extraordinary circumstance."

Then Leahy, known to be an avid institutionalist wary of tampering with Senate rules and traditions, warned his Republican colleagues of the potential fallout. "If the Republican caucus finds that despite her stellar legal reputation and commitment to her country that somehow a filibuster is warranted, I believe this body will need to consider anew whether a rules change should be in order," he said. "That is not a change that I want to see happen, but if Republican senators are going to hold nominations hostage without consideration of their individual merit, drastic measures may be warranted."

The attempt to force a final vote on Millett's nomination then went down, 55–38, five votes shy of the 60 needed. Two Republicans, Collins and Murkowski, bucked the filibuster and voted with Democrats.

Pillard was next, with her nomination falling to a filibuster on November 12, putting Republicans in the position of having blocked the nominations to the DC circuit of three of the nation's elite women lawyers—Halligan, Millett, and Pillard. Democrats sought to drive that point home. "If Republicans vote in lockstep to continue their filibuster against Nina Pillard, then Senate Republicans will have blocked three outstanding women in a row from being confirmed to what is considered the second-highest court in our country," said Leahy.

Grassley took offense at that line of attack.

"That argument is offensive, but predictable," he said. "We've seen this before. When the other side runs out of legitimate arguments, their last line of defense is to accuse Republicans of opposing nominees based on gender or race. It's an old and well-worn card. And they play it every time. The fact of the matter is that I've voted for seventy-five women nominated to the bench by President Obama, as well as a host of other nominees of diverse backgrounds."

Grassley then went further. He and other Republicans had been regularly taunting Democrats over their threats to detonate the nuclear option, suggesting that Reid, the majority leader, either didn't have the nerve or the votes to do so. In July, McConnell had said Reid would be remembered as the worst Senate leader in history if he forced through a rules change, and Grassley baited him anew in November.

"That brings me to the constant threat from the majority about changing the rules on the filibuster," Grassley said. "All I can say is this: Be careful what you wish for."

He went on: "Remember, it was the Democrats who first used the filibuster to defeat circuit judges. It was the Democrats who first used caseloads to defeat circuit judges. So, if the Democrats are bent on changing the rules, go ahead. There are a lot more Scalias and Thomases out there we'd love to put on the bench."

Such comments had not gone unnoticed in Harry Reid's leadership suite off the Senate floor.

"Durbin walks into my office one morning and says, 'They are mocking you out there, Grassley and [John] Cornyn,'" Reid recalled. "They said the same things at different times. 'He is a big bluff.' 'He's saying he is going with the nuclear option.' 'He couldn't do it if he wanted to.' 'He doesn't have the votes.'

"I will tell you what they didn't know," Reid continued. "I didn't have 'em. But they pissed me off, so I went and got the votes."

It wasn't going to be easy. With a five-vote margin, Reid needed to get nearly everyone on board. Most Democrats, angry over the Republican tactics, which they attributed to a sheer desire to thwart Obama, were ready to make the change, having seen McConnell force needless cloture votes on nominations. Since Democrats had held the Senate majority since 2006, many Democratic members had never even served in the minority, so they had little experience with the value of Senate rules in protecting the minority and keeping lawmakers relevant.

Some of the more senior members, notably Carl Levin of Michigan, were going to be hard sells. Levin revered the rules of the Senate and could not be easily persuaded by his peers. Patrick Leahy also fell into that category, but he had suggested he was ready to act.

Levin, a beloved member of the Senate with a reputation for integrity, undertook a personal crusade to persuade Democrats not to move forward with the nuclear option. He was a lame duck, having already announced he would not seek a seventh term in 2014, but his long tenure and position as chairman of the Armed Services Committee made him someone Democrats would not easily dismiss.

"I understood the frustration that Harry Reid was presented with, but I thought it was a mistake," recalled Levin. He believed changing the rules would backfire and that Democrats should instead force Republicans to stay on the floor to conduct their filibusters rather than move to other business once the vote to cut off the filibuster failed. Levin thought that Republicans could be worn down.

Levin argued against nuking the filibuster at a party lunch, hoping in particular to sway two of Reid's other toughest targets: the California senators Barbara Boxer and Dianne Feinstein. Both worried that eliminating the sixty-vote threshold could come back to haunt them if a future Republican president nominated someone to the Supreme Court who would gut abortion protections. Democrats might then have little recourse to stop an objectionable nominee.

The Californians also feared that changing the threshold on nominations could eventually lead to eliminating the right to filibuster legislation, allowing a Republican majority to force through legislation limiting or eliminating abortion rights.

"Boxer and Feinstein were hard," acknowledged Reid. A compromise was reached. If he went forward, he agreed to exempt Supreme

Court nominees from the new rules, theoretically protecting the right of the minority to block high court picks if they could muster forty-one votes.

Wilkins, the third appellate court nominee, was next. On Monday, November 18, Senate Republicans successfully filibustered his nomination. The stage was set. At a closed party lunch the next day, Feinstein, one of the most reluctant to change the rules, told her colleagues that she thought the time had come to move forward despite the potential that Democrats could pay a future price. Republicans, she said, had gone too far, overreaching with their opposition to all three judges.

Still, many harbored doubts that Reid would move forward with such an explosive action. A man who had argued in recent years about the potential damage of changing Senate procedure was probably not going to be the one to do it. Maybe he was, as the Republicans believed, a big bluff.

But he wasn't. Three days later, Reid opened what would turn out to be one of the most significant days in Senate history.

"There has been unbelievable, unprecedented obstruction. For the first time in the history of our republic, Republicans have routinely used the filibuster to prevent President Obama from appointing his executive team or confirming judges," Reid said. "The need for change is so very obvious. It is clearly visible. It is manifest. We have to do something to change things."

Reid went through the pending filibusters against Obama's three appeals court nominees, the filibuster against Mel Watt and the successful filibuster of Halligan, noting that Republicans had blocked four of Obama's five nominees to the DC circuit while Democrats had approved four of President Bush's six nominees to that same court.

"The change we propose today would ensure executive and judicial nominations an up-or-down vote on confirmation—yes, no. The rule change will make cloture for all nominations other than for the Supreme Court a majority-threshold vote—yes or no. The Senate is a living thing, and to survive it must change, as it has over the history of this great country. To the average American, adapting the rules to make the Senate work again is just common sense. This is not about Democrats versus Republicans. This is about making Washington work—regardless of who is in the White House or who controls the Senate."

Of course, it was, at that moment at least, strictly about Democrats versus Republicans. Republicans pushed back, though they would need Democratic help to thwart Reid. Despite the combustible nature of the action, the Senate was solemn as members sat at their desks digesting the significant moment before them. McConnell took the floor.

He angrily reiterated his claim that Democrats were mainly trying to divert attention from politically crushing failures with the new health care law. He charged that Democrats were about to "break the rules to change the rules." He delivered his most punishing line with a reference to the discredited claim by Obama that his new health care law would ensure that if you liked your health care plan, you could keep it. McConnell equated that to earlier pledges by Reid not to tamper with the Senate rules to push through judges.

Reid, he remarked, "may just have well said: 'If you like the rules of the Senate, you can keep them,'" repeating it for emphasis at the laughter and encouragement of his amused Republican colleagues.

He blamed Democrats for starting the fight a decade earlier through "serial filibustering" of President Bush's circuit nominees, beginning with Estrada. "This business of filibustering circuit court judges was entirely an invention of the guys over here on the other side, the ones you are looking at right over here," he said, referring to Reid and Schumer. "They made it up. They started it. This is where we ended up."

McConnell, in what would prove to be clever foreshadowing, also told Democrats that they were fooling themselves if they believed they could maintain the supermajority filibuster for Supreme Court nominees once Republicans were in power again.

"Get this," he said. "They think they can change the rules of the Senate in a way that benefits only them. They want to do it in such a way that President Obama's agenda gets enacted but that a future Republican president could not get his or her picks for the Supreme Court confirmed by a Republican Senate using the same precedent our Democratic friends want to set. They want to have it both ways. But this sort of gerrymandered vision of the nuclear option is wishful thinking."

He called on long-serving Democrats to join Republicans in beating back what he called an exercise in raw political power. He then delivered what might have been his most memorable line. "I say to my friends on the other side of the aisle," McConnell concluded ominously, "you will regret this, and you may regret it a lot sooner than you think."

While the term "nuclear option" sounded dramatic, what followed was anything but. Through a series of highly scripted procedural motions, Reid called back the Millett nomination for reconsideration.

When the new vote on her nomination again failed to break the Republican filibuster, Reid raised a point of order with Leahy, who as the senior Democrat, was presiding. Biden, the vice president, was not in the chair. Reid inquired whether the Senate standard to break filibusters on nominations except for the Supreme Court was a majority. The answer was no—as Reid and everyone in the hushed chamber knew quite well. Reid then called for a vote to overrule the ruling of the presiding officer. It passed on by a margin of 52–48. Three Democrats sided with Republicans—Carl Levin and Senators Joe Manchin III of West Virginia and Mark Pryor of Arkansas, both representing conservative states.

It was that simple. By a majority vote, Democrats had changed the rules governing filibusters, and nominees no longer had to overcome the sixty-vote threshold. It took just over two hours. No mushroom cloud arose in the chamber, but the impact was undeniable.

"Under the precedent set by the Senate today, November 21, 2013, the threshold for cloture on nominations, not including those to the Supreme Court of the United States, is now a majority," said Leahy from the presiding officer's perch. "That is the ruling of the chair."

The Senate then took up the Millett nomination. The Republican filibuster was overcome by a simple majority—a first in Senate history—and she headed toward confirmation in the days ahead, along with Representative Watt and dozens of others held up by Republican tactics.

As the day's events sunk in, Republicans were aghast, but some Democrats cheered the outcome, saying it was long overdue.

"I have waited eighteen years for this moment," exulted Senator Tom Harkin, a progressive Democrat from Iowa and a longtime proponent of reducing the power of the filibuster. Harkin acknowledged that both parties were at fault in the escalating warfare over nominations throughout the years but that it had reached an unacceptable level under McConnell and the Republicans.

"Who cares who started it?" he asked. "It is time to stop. Even if I accept the fact that Democrats started it—maybe they can prove that we did. It is possible way back when. It has escalated. It turned from a punch here to a punch there to almost extreme fighting. It has reached the point where we can't function."

Levin, one of the Democratic opponents, believed it was a disaster.

"Overruling the ruling of the chair, as we have now done, by a simple majority is not a one-time action," Levin said after the vote. "If a Senate majority demonstrates it can make such a change once, there are no rules which bind a majority, and all future majorities will feel free to exercise the same power—not just on judges and executive nominations but on legislation.

"If it can be changed on judges or on other nominees, this precedent is going to be used, I fear, to change the rules in consideration of legislation," Levin continued. "Down the road—we don't know how far down the road, we never know that in a democracy—but down the road the hard-won protections and benefits for our people's health and welfare will be lost."

Under the change, not only Millett ascended to the bench but Pillard and Wilkins as well, followed by dozens of other judicial and executive branch nominees who might have stalled without the action driven by Reid. A misstep by Ted Cruz that kept the Senate in session at the end of 2014, after Republicans had won the majority beginning in 2015, allowed the Democratic-led Senate to install two dozen additional Obama nominees before Democrats ceded power a few weeks later.

But the wisdom of changing the rules would come under question, especially after the 2016 election. Chuck Schumer, Reid's lieutenant at the time, was one of a number of Democrats who later expressed regrets, a sentiment that Reid thought was Schumer's weak attempt to escape responsibility for a decision he supported.

Other former senators believed Reid had acted hastily out of pique.

Reid and his allies insisted it was the correct move no matter the future implications, arguing that Republicans would have done the same thing at their first opportunity—though that was impossible to know. Their mistake, they said, was not doing it sooner and not abandoning the Judiciary Committee's "blue slip" practice that let Republicans hold open home state judgeships.

"If I had to do it over again, five hundred times I would do it," Reid said. "They gave me the reason. We could not get people on the DC circuit. We were having decisions go wrong because there were so few people on the court."

Recalled Levin, "There was a short-term advantage; we got a couple of judges through. But it was a bad precedent. Once the majority can just change the rules at will, there are no rules."

Reid was convinced he was right. But his nuclear effort was to play out in the years ahead in ways that were utterly predictable and extremely consequential.

15

Dumbledore

DESPITE THE UNPRECEDENTED circumstances surrounding the Scalia vacancy, the White House was following its well-established process for vetting and nominating a Supreme Court justice. Members of Obama's team had been through it twice before with the selections of Sonia Sotomayor and Elena Kagan. The personnel in the administration had changed, but the steps to a nominee were well traveled.

Merrick Garland, sixty-three, was the front-runner, mainly because of his respect in Republican circles and Washington's legal community. In desperate need of Republican support, Obama's team naturally looked at Garland, a highly regarded former prosecutor who had been on the US Court of Appeals for the District of Columbia Circuit since 1997 and its chief judge since 2013.

He had won significant Republican backing—including from seven Republicans still in the Senate—when he was first confirmed, was revered by colleagues, and was a regular presence at court events and judicial investitures in Washington. Despite ideological differences, members of the legal elite ran in similar social circles and attended the same legal functions. It was very clubby.

While Garland wasn't exactly campaigning for a Supreme Court seat, he was a highly visible personality who was well liked and respected in that rarified legal world. He would clearly draw support from both the Republicans and Democrats who inhabited it. He was known to have yearned for a seat on the court for years, and his carefully constructed career, like those of many ambitious Washington players, seemed designed to put him in position for one. But time was passing. If Garland was ever going to get on the court, this was probably his last opportunity.

But Obama was going to be Obama and deliberate over his choices.

"It was not a sham process," said one senior White House official who was closely involved. "It was thorough and it was serious. I think it served the president well. You don't cut corners, you don't play politics. We were ready with three at the end."

Besides Garland, the other two top candidates were Sri Srinivasan, named by Obama to the DC appeals court three years earlier, and Paul Watford, an African American who sat on the San Francisco–based federal appeals court. Other names were in the mix as well, including two women. One of them, Jane Kelly, was a former public defender from Iowa who was now on the federal appeals court based in Saint Louis. Her Iowa roots were considered potentially attractive to Grassley, who had supported her confirmation in 2013. But her record as a defense attorney was also rife with targets attractive to anyone who wanted to derail her.

Reid, the Democratic leader, as usual had his own thoughts and moved to stir things up. He tried to get the name of Brian Sandoval, the centrist Republican governor from Nevada and a former federal judge who supported abortion rights, into the mix. Reid liked Sandoval, and he thought it would also be nice to get a popular Republican out of the political picture for life. He figured that Republicans would be hard pressed to reject one of their own.

But they weren't. McConnell had his team deliver the word to Sandoval that it would be very painful for him should he get into the conflict. Other Republicans, following McConnell's edict, said they had decided not to move ahead on anyone no matter who it was. Reid's trial balloon was quickly punctured when Sandoval hurriedly asked that his name be withdrawn—if it was ever really in play at all.

All the alternatives to Garland were younger and, apart from Srinivasan, were perceived to be more liberal, offering the possibility of rallying the more progressive side of the party. Srinivasan, a veteran of Republican and Democratic administrations, was treated with skepticism by some progressives for his record and perceived bias against labor, though he had sided with the Obama administration on some appeals court decisions.

Obama and his inner circle had one overarching concern when it came to the other candidates—they feared that their reputations could be destroyed by the confirmation process, derailing promising careers and even the possibility of a high court seat down the road. Garland would be a more difficult target, and he was already in the later stages of his own celebrated public service.

Obama was not being paranoid. As the nomination neared, Senator Cornyn, the number two Republican, warned that whoever the president selected would be treated as a "piñata." The remark drew condemnation from Democrats during the daily war of words that had broken out on the Senate floor. It was a ripe opportunity for Harry Reid.

"Think about that," Reid said about Cornyn's comment as he took to the Senate floor to castigate the Republican on March 8. "They don't know who the nominee is. They don't know anything about the person, but they already have in their mind that they are going to beat this person like a piñata. These are his words, not mine. Direct quote: 'I think they will bear some resemblance to a piñata.' Think about that. He is saying Republicans are going to do all they can to hurt this person's reputation, to beat on them, like a piñata."

Angered by Reid's assault, Cornyn followed him to the floor and said it was Democrats who had perfected the art of personal attacks on judicial nominees. "I am not going to be preached to by the Democratic leader," Cornyn retorted. "By the Democrats who have been responsible for filibustering judges, creating a new verb in the English language—'Borked'—when they blocked Robert Bork's appointment to the US Supreme Court, when the Democratic leader invokes the

nuclear option, breaking the Senate rules for the sole purpose of packing the DC Circuit Court of Appeals with like-minded judges so that
the president wouldn't have to worry about judges who might question
overreaching his authority under the Constitution by issuing executive
orders or otherwise circumventing the role of Congress," Cornyn continued. "This is a playbook that has been written by the Democratic
leader and our colleagues across the aisle. Do they expect us to operate
under a different set of rules?"

Cornyn made clear he and his Republican colleagues were not going to break and move forward with filling the seat, no matter who was
anointed in the White House Rose Garden. "We do know it would be
improper to allow a lame-duck president to forever change the balance
on the Supreme Court for perhaps the next thirty years, as he is heading out the door," Cornyn said.

The prospect of a Republican assault on the nominee essentially made
the selection of Garland a certainty, given the White House's view.

"I remember a meeting where we were going through the nominees," said another top Democrat closely involved in the process, "and
the president said, 'Republicans are going to try to ruin whoever this
is, and the only one they can't ruin is Merrick Garland. Our chances
of getting anybody through are less than fifty-fifty, so I don't want to
ruin these careers.'"

Considering his extraordinary record of public service and recti-
tude, Merrick Garland's reputation would indeed be hard to ruin. He
could be blocked but he would be hard to vilify.

Born in Chicago and raised in the northwest suburbs, Garland was
a model student who ended up at Harvard and Harvard Law and then
went on to top clerkships, including with the acclaimed judge Henry J.
Friendly on the US Court of Appeals for the Second Circuit in New
York and then for Justice William J. Brennan Jr. of the Supreme Court.

During his college years, Garland interned for Abner Mikva, an
appeals court judge and former House member from Illinois who was
legendary both as a legal mind and a dispenser of political wisdom.

Mikva became a mentor of Obama's as well, another tie between him and Garland as the president weighed his choice.

After working for the Justice Department during the Carter administration, Garland went into private practice for the law firm Arnold & Porter, mainly practicing corporate law. Wanting a return to public service, he became a prosecutor in the US attorney's office for the District of Columbia, handling local corruption and crime cases, including the prosecution of Mayor Marion Barry for crack cocaine possession.

Garland went to work at the Department of Justice for the new Clinton administration in 1993. There he became integral to two high-profile prosecutions that added to a tough-on-crime reputation that contributed to his centrist image—that of the Unabomber, Ted Kaczynski, and Timothy McVeigh, who bombed the federal building in Oklahoma City.

Immediately after the bombing, which killed 168 people, including many children at a day care center, Garland volunteered to be sent to the site and would remain there for weeks to oversee the investigation. His efforts, including the decision to seek the death penalty for McVeigh, won him plaudits from Republicans, including Senator James Inhofe, who would later support his nomination to the federal appellate court.

Garland also pleased the media when he demanded that reporters be allowed to attend a preliminary hearing for McVeigh, who was being held at a military base whose commanders initially sought to bar reporters. "I told them, 'We're not going to have the first investigation of domestic terrorism and conspiracy in secret,'" Garland recalled during a speech at Harvard Law School in August 2016. "So they went out and let the press in."

Garland's work in the government wasn't his only contribution to the District of Columbia. With little fanfare or recognition, the judge tutored students at an elementary school in a usually overlooked corner of the city for nearly twenty years.

Another attribute of Garland's also stuck out to White House insiders: his love of the Harry Potter books by J. K. Rowling. During the Harvard speech, he noted that one of his daughters was having trouble reading before she delved into the Potter series. "The thing that got her over the hump was being read the 'Harry Potter' books," he said, according to an account of the speech in the *Harvard Gazette*. "And then having her read the 'Harry Potter' books to us." His appreciation later led to Rowling speaking at the college. "I recommended that J.K. Rowling get an honorary degree, which she did—thus paying her back," Garland, in a rare boast, confessed proudly.

To some in the White House, Garland's wisdom, kindness, devotion to doing the right thing, and work with students reminded them of Albus Dumbledore, the all-knowing headmaster at Hogwarts. Some came to refer to him lightheartedly among themselves as Dumbledore, because they thought the comparison fit him so perfectly and helped them to conceive of how best to sell him.

Good reasons existed to go with the other candidates who might excite Democratic activists more than a Potter-loving sixty-three-year-old white man seen as a centrist. Garland wasn't really going to fire up anyone outside Washington's legal establishment. "There was a lot of pressure from the Left," said one Obama White House official. "If you wanted to get somebody on the court, he was probably the best pick. He was hard to argue with. But if you wanted to make a statement, he wasn't it."

Obama didn't want to make a statement. He wanted his best chance at getting someone on the court over a seemingly impenetrable Republican roadblock. His staff was ready to roll out Srinivasan or Watford if Obama went that way, but Garland it was. To Democrats who thought it was a mistake, it was another case of Obama letting his law professor side triumph over his political operative side.

On the morning of March 16, Obama sought to build some excitement and enthusiasm for his nominee with a widely distributed email stating that he would be announcing his court pick at eleven a.m. that day. "I'm confident you'll share my conviction that this American is not only eminently qualified to be a Supreme Court Justice, but deserves a fair hearing, and an up-or-down vote," he wrote in the note. Even before he had named his candidate, Obama was trying to show that he had fulfilled his duty to seek the advice of the Senate, and it was now going to be left to the Senate to do its job.

The White House then began to inform its allies in the Senate and in the progressive community whom the president intended to nominate, and the stage was set for a major announcement. Learning that it was Garland, some top Democratic aides on Capitol Hill tried to argue, wondering if it was still too late for the president to pick a more energizing choice.

Shortly after eleven o'clock on a sunny mid-March day, Obama entered the Rose Garden with Garland and Vice President Biden to make his best case yet for Republicans to consider his candidate—he was nominating a man who, the last time he was before the Senate, won a majority of Democratic and Republican votes.

"I said I would take this process seriously—and I did," said Obama as he ran through the impressive catalog of Garland's life. "I chose a serious man and an exemplary judge, Merrick Garland. Over my seven years as president, in all my conversations with senators from both parties in which I asked their views on qualified Supreme Court nominees—this includes the previous two seats that I had to fill—the one name that has come up repeatedly, from Republicans and Democrats alike, is Merrick Garland."

To Obama, he had delivered to Republicans what they had so many times in the past said they wanted: a consensus judge who had earned the respect and trust of both parties.

"To suggest that someone as qualified and respected as Merrick Garland doesn't even deserve a hearing, let alone an up-or-down vote, to join an institution as important as our Supreme Court, when two-thirds of Americans believe otherwise—that would be unprecedented," Obama said, referring to polls. "To suggest that someone who has served his country with honor and dignity, with a distinguished track record of delivering justice for the American people, might be treated, as one Republican leader stated, as a political 'piñata'—that can't be right."

Obama then demanded that Republicans give Garland a hearing and a vote.

"If you don't, then it will not only be an abdication of the Senate's constitutional duty, it will indicate a process for nominating and confirming judges that is beyond repair," said Obama, overlooking his own role in the unsuccessful filibuster against Alito. "It will mean everything is subject to the most partisan of politics—everything. It will provoke an endless cycle of more tit-for-tat, and make it increasingly impossible for any president, Democrat or Republican, to carry out their constitutional function. The reputation of the Supreme Court will inevitably suffer. Faith in our justice system will inevitably suffer. Our democracy will ultimately suffer, as well."

It was an apt description of the state of the judicial nomination process.

Obama then introduced a clearly emotional and teary Garland, who called the nomination "the greatest honor" of his life, with the usual caveats for marriage and children.

Slightly more than one month after Scalia's death, Obama had chosen the nominee predicted by many—notably Ron Klain. But as Klain himself had predicted, Republicans had a head start in the clash that would prove hard to erase.

After the ceremony ended, Obama began making calls to Capitol Hill, urging Republicans who had backed Garland before and agitated for his nomination six years earlier when Obama last had a Supreme Court seat to fill. The president's plea fell on deaf ears.

Orrin Hatch was quickly on the floor explaining how he—and most fellow Senate Republicans—would not change their position even with Garland as the nominee. "I think highly of Judge Garland," Hatch acknowledged. "But his nomination doesn't in any way change current circumstances. I remain convinced that the best way for the

Senate to do its job is to conduct the confirmation process after this toxic presidential election season is over. Doing so is the only way to ensure fairness to the nominee and preserve the integrity of the Supreme Court."

In the four weeks since Scalia's death, Republicans had ample time to polish their argument against filling the seat, and Hatch and others deployed a new wrinkle. Their claim that the American voters needed to weigh in had struck many as hollow, since Obama had been elected to a four-year term in 2012. Now Republicans offered a new rejoinder.

"The 2012 election, however, was not the only one with consequences," Hatch said. "The 2014 election, for example, had tremendous significance for the Senate's power of advice and consent. The American people gave control of the Senate, and therefore control of the confirmation process, to Republicans."

To bolster his case, the senator was armed with a *New York Times* editorial from 1987 that made the same argument defending the Democratic effort to block Bork. Hatch happily cited an excerpt.

"The President's supporters insist vehemently that, having won the 1984 election, he has every right to try to change the Court's direction," the editorial said. "Yes, but the Democrats won the 1986 election, regaining control of the Senate, and they have every right to resist."

Hatch didn't mention that Democrats that year did not deny Bork either a hearing or a floor vote on his confirmation as Republicans were now planning to do with Garland.

Hatch was not alone. Despite Obama's plea, most Republicans were not moved in the slightest by the pick, and many of them immediately made clear that they were not interested in meeting with Garland in the traditional courtesy sessions that would begin the day following the announcement. Even Jim Inhofe, the Oklahoma Republican who had supported Garland in the past following his work on the federal building bombing, said he would not vote for Garland, who called him immediately after the nomination and asked him for a meeting.

"I made it very clear to him," Inhofe told MSNBC's Chuck Todd on the daily version of *Meet the Press*. "I said, 'I want to make sure you understand, there's no misunderstanding. I will not vote—I will not support you or any other nomination of this president, because that would be breaking new ground, and I'm not going to do it. And it doesn't matter if Obama would nominate George W. Bush. I would still not do it.'"

Inhofe had come to the conclusion that considering a presidential Supreme Court nominee with ten months left in a president's term would be "breaking new ground."

Republicans believed that such face-to-face courtesy meetings, recorded by the reporters and photographers who would stake out the visits, would risk giving the impression that they were considering Garland. Plus, Garland could potentially sway a few to back him.

In his own phone call with Garland, McConnell informed the newly minted nominee that the judge need not waste his time trying to get on the majority leader's schedule. "Rather than put Judge Garland through more unnecessary political routines orchestrated by the White House, the Leader decided it would be more considerate of the nominee's time to speak with him today by phone," McConnell's spokesman, Don Stewart, said in a statement. "And since the Senate will not be acting on this nomination, he would not be holding a perfunctory meeting, but he wished Judge Garland well."

There were a few defections. Those Republicans facing potentially difficult reelections—Mark Kirk, Kelly Ayotte, and Pat Toomey—joined Susan Collins and suggested that they might meet with Garland. And Jeff Flake and Orrin Hatch said that perhaps Garland could get a hearing and vote in the lame-duck Senate should Hillary Clinton win—and the dreaded prospect that a more liberal nominee be forthcoming.

That line of thinking quickly disappeared after McConnell and others pushed back and said that would not happen under any circumstances. The White House wasn't interested in fostering any lame-duck talk either, for fear it would give any wavering Republican an easy way out.

Neither was John McCain, the self-fashioned protector of the Senate's traditions and image, budging after Garland's selection. Of course, McCain was also running for reelection and was worried about conservative unrest in Arizona. He embraced the argument that the elections of 2014 had somehow nullified Obama's 2012 election and presidential power.

Republicans familiar with Garland from their years in Washington liked him personally. His prosecutorial reputation was solid and reassuring to them as far as it went. But they weren't really worried about the outcome of the few criminal matters that reach the Supreme Court except perhaps in the case of the death penalty, which Garland clearly supported.

They were concerned with the cultural and regulatory issues that would come before the court. And while Garland's opinions may have carried a more centrist sensibility, Republicans were convinced he would side with the government far more often than not. His middle-of-the-road reputation was not persuasive if they could hold on until after November on the off chance a Republican could fill the seat left open by the death of their hallowed conservative. "Barack Obama calling someone a moderate doesn't make him a moderate," McConnell was to say later. "From a conservative point of view, I don't think you could have a worse nominee then Merrick Garland."

The Obama administration's careful and meticulous review of nominees had gained little. And it wasn't just Republicans.

On Capitol Hill, while Senate Democrats publicly lauded the choice and generally saw it as the best chance to break the Republican blockade, there was also private grousing about the blandness of Obama's selection in the middle of an intense partisan war. Given how stubborn Republicans had been, it seemed to many that there was very little chance that they would crack just because the White House had sent up a man who had won GOP support before.

As an alternative, progressives in the party preferred a woman or a minority or someone who conceivably was both. Such a candidate could not only stir more excitement on the left but it would also allow Democrats to paint Republicans as insensitive to race and gender—an undertone of the party criticism three years earlier when it attacked Republicans before deploying the nuclear option. That theme could fit nicely into Clinton's presidential campaign. And though they might be unsuccessful in breaking the Republicans, a stonewalled woman or minority nominee could drive up voters' enthusiasm for Democrats, who were worried that they would not be able to replicate the African American turnout that had twice delivered the White House to Obama. But Obama and his team went with the more conventional choice.

As staff in the office of Richard Durbin, the number two senator and a key ally on the Judiciary Committee, listened in on a conference call from the White House revealing the pick, a groan went up when it was revealed that Obama had gone with Garland.

Progressive groups were also dismayed that Obama went with such a middle-of-the-road choice.

"It's deeply disappointing that President Obama failed to use this opportunity to add the voice of another progressive woman of color to the Supreme Court, and instead put forward a nominee seemingly designed to appease intransigent Republicans rather than inspire the grassroots he'll need to get that nominee through the Senate gauntlet," Charles Chamberlain, the executive director of Democracy in America, said in a statement.

Garland was beginning his quest on Capitol Hill facing not just staunch resistance from Republicans but skepticism from Democrats and activists who were not all that enthusiastic. Still, they figured that if Garland didn't get through, then President Hillary Clinton would have the chance to make a more exciting choice.

16

Stalemate

EVEN AS THEY awaited the identity of the nominee, people inside and outside the White House were putting together a campaign on what would become Garland's behalf. The administration and its allies did not plan to do nothing while Republicans simply refused to take up the nomination. Obama remained a popular president among Democrats and independents.

In February, a core group was formed that featured seasoned political operatives with deep connections and experience with the Obama administration. Among the leaders of the outside effort was Stephanie Cutter, an Obama administration and Senate veteran, who had headed up the push to confirm Sotomayor. Also a veteran of the 2004 presidential campaign of John Kerry and the staffs of Ted Kennedy and Harry Reid, she was a deputy campaign manager for Obama in 2012 and played a significant role in other administration issues, including health care.

Others being brought in to coordinate the communications strategy included Katie Beirne Fallon, the former White House director of legislative affairs; Anita Dunn, a former White House communications director; Paul Tewes, the former 2008 Iowa state director of Obama's campaign; and Julianna Smoot, a top fundraiser and another veteran of the 2012 presidential campaign. It was a strong, plugged-in team with big ideas and an ambitious fundraising goal to achieve them. A confidential strategy memo spelled out the campaign and the motivation behind it.

"There's a reason they are blocking the President's eventual nominee," the memo read. "It's part of a larger effort—funding by decades of investment by the Koch brothers and other wealthy conservatives to overturn progressive policies and accomplishments." The memo warned of a national conservative network "using the courts to attack nearly every facet of the progressive agenda and overturn decades-old victories we have long thought settled.

"We need to fight back," it declared.

The strategy was to first create a political environment to force Republicans to cave and hold a hearing and vote on Garland, and then convince at least five Republicans to break ranks and support Garland on the floor. Second, the activists would use the overall fight to knock off Republicans in November and regain control of the Senate and the White House. The memo called for an eye-popping $36 million in spending, the vast majority—$26 million—to go to television advertising, with another $3.5 million for staff.

The key targets were Republicans up for reelection—Ayotte of New Hampshire, Portman of Ohio, Kirk of Illinois, Johnson of Wisconsin, and Toomey of Pennsylvania as primary targets, with Richard Burr of North Carolina and Roy Blunt of Missouri as secondary targets. The strategy called for "putting direct pressure on targeted members of the Senate that includes organizing for town meetings, delegation meetings, and driving large numbers of calls to Congress using patch-through, dedicated 800 numbers and emails to members."

It was standard stuff but the kind of activity that can rattle politicians who don't like their phone lines being jammed by angry callers or their town halls being populated with aggressive protesters. The angry and effective Tea Party protests during the summers of 2009 and 2010 had made a deep impression on lawmakers of both parties.

Also on the target list was Grassley. As chairman of the Judiciary Committee and up for reelection in the politically divided state of

Iowa, Grassley was an especially inviting target who could be made into a symbol of the entire conflict. If Democrats could get Grassley to relent, it would be a huge step forward.

Grassley was an intriguing figure who had undergone an evolution in recent years. Elected to the Senate in 1980 after three terms in the House, Grassley had earned a reputation for conducting independent oversight of the administrations of both parties. He was inspired at the start of his Senate tenure by a meeting with Ernie Fitzgerald, a famous Pentagon whistle-blower who in 1968 testified about $2 billion in cost overruns in an Air Force transport plane program and was later fired at President Nixon's personal direction. His treatment led to whistle-blower protections that Grassley, as a self-avowed protector of taxpayer interests, embraced.

Grassley was culturally conservative from his Iowa upbringing, but he was also known for his willingness to work across the aisle, particularly with Senator Max Baucus, the centrist Montana Democrat who served with Grassley on the Finance Committee. They worked for years together on health care, tax law, and trade bills, as control of the committee went back and forth along with shifts in the Senate majority.

But the Republican political climate in Iowa had been shifting for decades as well, with the religious Right rising and eventually taking over the state party. The archconservatives' control was cemented with Obama's election in 2008. Grassley's bipartisan efforts no longer were something to admire among many Iowa Republicans—they were to be disdained and rejected.

The 2009 health care debate was a prime example. Grassley himself had always championed the private-market approach of the emerging Obama health care plan, preferring it to a government-run program, which he saw as socialized medicine. As they had in the past, Grassley and Baucus teamed with a group of four other lawmakers in another of the Senate's "gangs" to try to reach a compromise that could be enacted with bipartisan support. But a deal proved elusive, and as the talks dragged on, Democrats came to believe that Grassley was stalling. He had, after all, championed some of the fundamental elements of the Obama plan, including the so-called individual mandate—the requirement that Americans would have to buy health insurance or pay a penalty.

At the same time, Republicans had begun to realize that blanket opposition to Obama and his policies was paying off politically, as conservatives rallied around them and the Tea Party movement was born. Grassley faced pressure from within his ranks to call off the bipartisan effort. Baucus recalled that soon after one joint appearance together, Grassley called him to tell him that they would have to keep their distance or Grassley could find himself facing a serious primary challenge.

Democrats became alarmed when Grassley, touring his state during the first summer of raucous public hearings blasting the health care proposal, didn't defend the Democratic legislation against spurious Tea Party accusations that the bill contained "death panels" to ration care. Grassley even suggested that his then–critically ill colleague Ted Kennedy would have been denied cancer treatment due to his age—a reference he later said he regretted.

By the fall of 2009, the compromise effort collapsed, and bipartisan Chuck Grassley faded from the scene to instead become an arch critic of the health care bill he had helped design. Grassley also underwent a change of heart about federal bureaucrats. Gone were the whistleblowers with the courage to come forward with tales of waste and mismanagement. Now they were tyrants.

"Today, we are ruled more and more by excessive regulation and executive fiat," Grassley said in a 2018 speech to the Heritage Foundation. "Worse, we've done little to prevent our system of separated powers from yielding itself to the sweeping authority of federal agencies, or what many call the administrative state.

"We've moved from a government by and for the people, to a government by the bureaucrats and for the connected insiders," he said.

With Grassley seen as a main impediment to Garland, Harry Reid and Democratic activists set out to make as much trouble for him as they could. Reid was determined to find a serious opponent for Grassley, and he thought he had one.

Patty Judge, a former state agriculture commissioner who had been elected statewide, decided to jump into the race against Grassley. She appeared formidable given her experience, name recognition, and the fact that she, like Grassley, had real farming credentials in ag-loving Iowa. (Two years earlier, a highly touted Democratic Senate candidate had lost to Joni Ernst after seeming to disparage Grassley as a "farmer from Iowa who never went to law school.")

At seventy-two, Judge was a little old for a first-time Senate run, but she was still a decade younger than the then-eighty-two-year-old Grassley. The icing was that her name was Judge, a coincidence that would constantly remind voters what the race was all about. She made clear that Grassley's obstruction of the Supreme Court nominee would be a central element of her campaign.

"I don't like this double-speak," Judge told the *Des Moines Register* in February 2016. "I don't like this deliberate obstruction of the process. I think Chuck Grassley owes us better. He's been with us a long time. Maybe he's been with us too long."

The Washington backing of Judge was considered intrusive and heavy handed back in Iowa and upset some local activists, who saw it as interference in state elections. But she won a four-way primary in June. "I am the Judge that Chuck Grassley can't ignore," she said at her victory party.

Back in Washington, and to Grassley's mounting consternation, Reid and his Democratic colleagues were vociferously pounding the Iowan on the Senate floor. "Instead of exercising his once respected independence, my friend the senior senator from Iowa is taking his marching orders from the Republican leader and refusing to give President Obama's Supreme Court nominee a meeting, a hearing, or a vote," said Reid as part of a coordinated attack on Grassley from the floor on March 3.

Durbin, joining Reid, offered a word of caution to Republicans. "Fair warning to my Senate Republicans," he said. "They say the American people should decide. They will decide—they will decide in November that the Republicans in the Senate should do their job."

The attacks were clearly getting to Grassley. "Give me a break," he retorted to his colleagues. "We made a decision based on history and our intention to protect the ability of the American people to make their voices heard."

Democrats had no intention of giving him a break and instigated protests back home in Iowa for the duration. Reid, who loved playing mind games with his opponents, took particular joy in slamming Grassley. The Iowan's staff, unaccustomed to such relentless criticism, felt under siege both back home and in Washington. Grassley was seething.

Astonishingly, both Grassley and Hatch, two of the most senior members of the Senate and on the Judiciary Committee, seemed caught off guard by the uproar surrounding the Republican position.

"I didn't have any qualms about it, because I didn't think it would be a big deal," Grassley said later about his decision to thwart Obama— and, by extension, Garland. "But I found out when I started having my town meetings that it was a big deal." The Reid attacks went too far, he felt.

"I remember for the next three or four months, he every morning was giving a speech about me and having *Des Moines Register* articles or this or that up there just tearing me apart all the time," Grassley recounted. "I thought it was very uncustomary for a fellow senator to be so personal."

Hatch also believed the furor was unwarranted. To him, the delay in the confirmation was simply temporary and political. Like most Republicans, he anticipated Clinton would win and either Garland or another Democrat would ultimately be sitting on the court in place of Scalia. "At that particular time, I was pretty sure Democrats were going to win, so I didn't think it was that big of a postponement for them," Hatch said. "They would get whoever they wanted."

Hatch, the Republican who had lobbied for Garland's nomination in 2010, said he even traveled to Garland's quarters in the federal court building near the Capitol to explain his position. "I went down to his chambers and talked to him," Hatch recalled. "He understood. He knew that we were in a position where there wasn't a lot we could do. It was an unpleasant time and an unpleasant situation."

Democrats intended to make it as unpleasant as possible. With the nomination of Garland, Democrats and their activist allies began a social media campaign with the hashtag #DoYourJob, demanding that Republican senators give Garland a hearing and vote. Planned Parenthood, one of the groups advocating for Garland, noted that every Supreme Court nominee since 1875 had received a hearing and a vote within 125 days of nomination except for those who were withdrawn. "Tell GOP Senators to #DoYourJob!" the group declared in boldface on its website the day Garland was announced.

The outside efforts being coordinated by the former Obama aides were organized under the umbrella of the Constitutional Responsibility Project, which created a website, WeNeedNine.org, to make the case that the Republicans were hobbling the court by holding the seat open. The group sought to spur a wave of grassroots activity in the states of the senators considered most susceptible to election-year pressure. They helped turn out Garland supporters to confront the senators at appearances and town hall meetings during the spring break.

Conservative groups, of course, were also working hard against Garland and to bolster Republican senators in their potentially politically risky stance.

The well- and secretly funded Judicial Crisis Network produced a television ad assailing Garland that ran in multiple states, portraying him as weak on gun rights and a new court vote for late-term abortions, two claims certain to inflame conservative voters. "Merrick Garland, a liberal judge from a liberal president," the narrator intoned ominously in a television ad entitled "He's No Moderate."

The National Rifle Association weighed in heavily against Garland, seeing him as a potential fifth vote to reverse a landmark 2008 Scalia-drafted ruling that the Second Amendment guarantees an individual's right to keep a firearm at home for self-defense. Garland had not been directly involved in ruling on gun rights cases, but the powerful lobbying group suspected him of being a potential foe because he had voted to have the DC appeals court convene en banc to rehear a case overturning the district's extremely strict gun laws. The request was rejected, but that one thin example was enough for the NRA and gun rights advocates to dig in against Garland. That was significant in holding Republicans together, since none dared run afoul of that group.

At the same time, the National Federation of Independent Business, the small-business lobby, for the first time jumped into the political fight over the court, saying its review of Garland's record on regulatory issues showed that he overwhelmingly ruled in favor of the government in the cases that had come before him.

The advocacy effort wasn't aimed just at bucking up Republicans; it was also helpful in keeping strays in line. The most public victim was Senator Jerry Moran, a low-profile Republican from Kansas. If anyone could be expected not to rock the boat, it was him. Moran was the definition of a Republican team player.

Yet at a late March town hall meeting during a state swing, Moran amazed everyone in Washington by making news and breaking with McConnell. "I would rather have you complaining to me that I voted wrong on nominating somebody than saying I'm not doing my job," Moran told a small group of his constituents in tiny Cimarron, Kansas. "I can't imagine the president has or will nominate somebody that meets my criteria, but I have my job to do," Moran said. "I think the process ought to go forward."

The backlash wasn't immediate, since his position took time to filter back to DC. But when it came a few days later, it was ferocious. A national Tea Party group said it would explore recruiting a primary challenger, and the Judicial Crisis Network began preparing ads. The mild-mannered Moran—who had overseen the party's effort to win the Senate in 2014 as chairman of the National Republican Senatorial Committee—was suddenly persona non grata. After consulting with Grassley, he quickly sought to make clear he was no friend of Judge Garland and that if there was a hearing it would only show how bad the nominee was.

"As I have said since the vacancy was created, I believe I have a duty to ask tough questions and demand answers," Moran said in a statement. "I am certain a thorough investigation would expose Judge Garland's record and judicial philosophy and disqualify him in the eyes of Kansans and Americans."

The minimutiny was over, and the message was delivered to the rest of the rank and file: Break from the party pack at your political peril.

While both sides were engaged in a public conflict, a private effort to derail Garland was under way as well. Republicans were combing through Garland's life to find some disqualifying behavior that would quiet Democratic calls for a hearing and vote. Personal issues had nearly cost Clarence Thomas his seat, and what is known politely as opposition research—or more impolitely as "oppo"—had become a routine element of major confirmation showdowns.

The problem was that with Garland's sterling record of public service and civic involvement, there didn't seem to be much "there" there. Republicans were struggling. One piece of oppo they peddled was a 1976 review of *The Fantastiks* that Garland had written for the *Harvard Crimson*.

Garland pretty much panned the production but praised the songs, including "It Depends on What You Pay," a number that later became known as "the rape song." The song was very politically incorrect and was updated in revivals of the play. Republicans hoped to make the case that Garland had laughed off the idea of sexual assault. They pushed the story on media outlets and were especially eager for the *New York Times* to report on the review because they knew that if the *Times* wrote about it, it would carry added credibility and might force others to follow up. But news organizations were not biting on an attempt to hold Garland accountable for that review forty years later. It seemed minor and far out of context. Republicans were frustrated.

"I guess I am struggling on how can this not be a big story?" an upset Republican operative emailed. "It's very simple—he called a song about rapes hilarious." The operative pointed to past comments by Todd Akin, a Missouri congressman who lost a Senate race to Claire McCaskill in 2012 after he said that "legitimate rape" didn't lead to pregnancies. "Remember Todd Akin? And he wasn't a nominee for a lifetime appointment."

The White House was aware of the oppo but also realized that if that was the best Republicans had, they were not going to get far in tarnishing Garland from a personal standpoint.

Democrats were particularly delighted by any high-profile backing for Garland from the conservative legal world, and they embraced the support of Kenneth Starr, the former solicitor general and special counsel who relentlessly pursued Bill Clinton. After the nomination, Starr had praised Garland and then in April he took his support another step. "Good government calls for us to have a hearing and vote up or down," Starr said at the Baylor Law School.

Republicans were not as quick to jump on Starr's finding this time. The White House remained stymied. In response, Obama headed out to the University of Chicago Law School, where he once taught, to try to make a dignified appeal for Garland, who, like Obama, considered Chicago his hometown. Obama loved the opportunity to present his academic side. During his appearance, he recounted the entire history of the judicial wars and acknowledged some Democratic culpability.

"In fairness, Democrats are not blameless on this," he said. "If you talk to Republicans, they'll also often point to the Bork nomination as where this all started. And there have been times where Democrats used the filibuster to block what Republican presidents or conservative legal theorists viewed as eminently qualified jurists."

But this was an entirely new level of obstruction, in his view.

"I will say that there has not been a circumstance in which a

Republican president's appointee did not get a hearing, did not get a vote, and as a general proposition, they have been confirmed even where there have been strong objections," said Obama. He said that Republicans had "decided that placating our base is more important than upholding their constitutional and institutional roles in our democracy in a way that is dangerous."

Obama, in a question-and-answer session with students, was questioned on the diversity of the court and his role in expanding it. He lauded his overall efforts and defended his pick. "I appointed a Latino woman and another woman right before that, so, yeah, he's a white guy, but he's a really outstanding jurist. Sorry."

Republicans were well prepared for Obama's visit and had their rebuttals ready, including the fact that Obama himself had tried to filibuster Alito—a position that, like Biden's speech in 1992, was always deployed by Republicans as evidence that Democrats were hypocrites.

"Barack Obama is the first president in history to take action to deny a Supreme Court justice a vote and the last person who should be lecturing Republicans," a spokesman for the Republican National Committee said.

This is where the fight was. Democratic activists would issue regular compendiums of editorial endorsements, hold protests at Senate offices in the states of targeted Republicans, and arrange conference calls with former Garland clerks to sing his praises. But Republicans were not budging.

There was a momentary blip of optimism when Judiciary Committee Republicans said they assumed that the nominee would fill out a required questionnaire, but Republicans did not send him one drafted specially for him, as would be normal in such proceedings.

A few more Republicans joined Collins and Kirk in agreeing to hold meetings. The two Republicans from Oklahoma, a state that owed a debt to Garland, met with him together. They immediately said they would not back a hearing or a vote.

"During our time with Judge Garland, we extended Oklahoma's

gratitude for the many weeks he spent in our state working for justice for those who lost loved ones from the Oklahoma City bombing," the senators said in a joint statement. "Judge Garland was aware going into this meeting that we will not support any Supreme Court nomination during this presidential election year."

Grassley finally met with Garland for breakfast in the Senate dining room, not the setting where senators usually quiz nominees on their judicial views. Grassley was meeting him, but it was a social interview, not a Supreme Court one.

For Grassley, it was a pleasant interaction but not transformative. Two years later, he could still not talk about Garland without raising the "Biden rule" as the reason to block his dining partner. (Grassley also noted that he picked up the tab.)

"If you were just voting on the personality of the person, you couldn't find a better person to support," he said. "But it was a basic difference of judicial philosophy that backed up everything I said."

In addition to the refusal of Republicans to break, Democrats and their allies were discovering another problem—lack of money. As they traveled the country trying to beseech dependable donors to underwrite the effort behind Garland, there was little response. "It was pretty clear early on the money wasn't going to be there," said one disappointed fundraiser.

Big donors wanted to spend their money on the presidential and Senate campaigns, not an effort to win the court seat that increasingly looked like it was going to be unsuccessful and could await a Democratic White House. The grand plan to spend $36 million now looked like a pipe dream, and the effort eventually drew in less than $10 million.

The donors were focused elsewhere, on the bigger picture. Hillary Clinton would win the election and either Garland or another nominee would take Scalia's seat on the court. Put the resources where they would best pay off—and be recognized and appreciated.

The List: Part II

TRUMP HAD PROMISED a public list of judicial prospects. Now Don McGahn, Leonard Leo, the Federalist Society, and the Heritage Foundation had to produce one for public consumption. A few of the names were already obvious. Trump had mentioned William Pryor of Alabama and Diane Sykes of Wisconsin the night of Scalia's death and the South Carolina debate, so they were certain to be on it.

McGahn and his conservative allies began a process he would follow throughout the coming months: consult with federal judges and former court clerks to identify candidates who would meet their conservative criteria and evaluate their potential.

Earlier in the campaign, during the Iowa Caucuses, Jonathan Bunch, a top official of the Federalist Society, had gotten in touch with McGahn to talk about judicial screening and to see if the Trump campaign was interested in any assistance. McGahn told him that no, the campaign was fine and was already working with someone with experience in Supreme Court judicial selection: John Sununu.

It was the most inside of inside judicial nomination jokes. Sununu was the White House chief of staff who had recommended David Souter as a court pick to President George H. W. Bush. To conservatives, Souter was the epitome of an unvetted Republican nominee who turned out to be a liberal. McGahn could hear the Federalist Society intermediary practically gasping on the phone.

McGahn heard recommendations from colleagues. Working late one night, a partner at Jones Day suggested McGahn look at Thomas Hardiman, a Pittsburgh-based appeals court judge who, like McGahn, had graduated from Georgetown University Law Center. Another colleague, James Burnham, pushed Gorsuch's name forward. Gorsuch's writings, Burnham told McGahn, reflect "everything you've been saying only better written and smarter."

They began collecting other names and assembled a short list of federal appeals court judges named by George W. Bush and state supreme court justices who had made it onto the radar of the conservative movement. It came together quickly. Then they waited for Trump to decide when to release it to the public.

And waited. Trump was a little gun shy. The list of foreign policy advisers he'd announced at the *Washington Post*'s editorial board meeting in March had attracted ridicule and only intensified the establishment's concern that Trump was nowhere near ready to deal with the nation's grave national security threats. Trump wanted to avoid a repeat of such an embarrassment at a critical stage of his campaign.

McGahn thought Trump might want to go public before the May 3 Indiana primary, since Trump had a chance to effectively clinch the nomination in that state. The list could help seal the deal. It had always been envisioned as an effective tool against fellow Republicans. But no instructions were forthcoming. Trump triumphed in Indiana and Cruz dropped out, leaving only Ohio governor John Kasich as a primary foe, one with little chance of success in a primary season that saw Republican voters moving hard to the right.

A few weeks later, Trump was suddenly ready to go with the list. The timing came as a shock to McGahn and others. The original rationale for the list was to reassure conservative voters to help him hold off Cruz and others. Now that Trump was moving into the general election, the list could provide ammunition to be used against him by Democrats.

Nonetheless, McGahn was ready to move forward.

"You sure about this?" Trump asked over the phone, still wounded by the immediate backlash to the list of foreign policy advisers.

McGahn said he was and offered to issue it under his own name if Trump was nervous. Trump declined.

"This better not get fucked up," Trump said and hung up.

On May 18, the Trump campaign made history by becoming the first presidential campaign to issue a list of prospective court nominees, guaranteeing the president would pick from that list. Eleven judges were named, eight men and three women. All were white. Six were federal appeals court judges, five were state supreme court judges. (As it turned out, neither of Trump's nominees were actually on the first list.)

Sykes and Pryor were there, of course, along with Hardiman, the Pennsylvania judge recommended by a colleague. The other appeals court judges were Raymond Kethledge of Michigan, Steven Colloton of Iowa, and Raymond Gruender of Missouri. The five state high court judges were David Stras of Minnesota, Joan Larsen of Michigan, Allison Eid of Colorado, and Utah's Thomas Lee, the brother of Senator Mike Lee. Another state jurist was Don Willett of Texas, known as a prolific tweeter sometimes at the expense of Trump, a fact that would no doubt inhibit his chances once it came to Trump's attention.

It was a very Trumpian assembly in one respect: it was a beyond-the-Beltway collection of names meant to emphasize the candidate's outsider status. It was also light on the Ivy League credentials typical of the current members of the court—and an academic background that Trump, it was later shown, favored in his Supreme Court judges.

Still, many conservatives were thrilled. This was a collection of anti-abortion, hard-line conservatives that they could only dream of getting on the high court. The criticism that followed the disclosure of Trump's foreign policy advisers would not recur in this case, foreshadowing the fact that the entire judicial selection and confirmation process would operate much differently and more effectively than most aspects of the Trump operation.

Grassley, the Judiciary Committee chairman who conceivably would handle the confirmation of any Trump nominees, was effusive—and the fact that a judge from his home state of Iowa was on the list wasn't lost on him. He also flicked at the ongoing blockade against Garland, noting that disclosing the possible nominees added to the knowledge that voters would have in making their presidential choice.

"Mr. Trump has laid out an impressive list of highly qualified jurists, including Judge Colloton from Iowa, who understand and respect the fundamental principle that the role of the courts is limited and subject to the Constitution and the rule of law," Grassley said. "Understanding the types of judges a presidential nominee would select for the Supreme Court is an important step in this debate so the American people can have a voice in the direction of the Supreme Court for the next generation."

Liberal advocates and Democrats were aghast. The candidates on the list were anathema to them. Trump was running as a Republican, to be sure, but in the past, he had been pro-choice and had regularly even defended Planned Parenthood as a resource for women.

"Donald Trump's list of potential Supreme Court nominees are a woman's worst nightmare," said Ilyse Hogue, president of NARAL Pro-Choice America. "Their records reveal a lineup of individuals who would likely overturn *Roe v. Wade* if given the chance, gutting what's left of abortion access in this country and heaping punishment on women."

The one troubling development for Trump was that while some conservatives praised the list, they suspected that Trump would not follow through; rather, they saw it as an attempt to trick Republican voters. Hurtling toward the party's nomination, Trump still had not won over some of the conservative movement's elite. "Like every clause of every sentence uttered in every breath Donald Trump takes, this is all subject to change," said Erick Erickson, an influential conservative blogger. "He will waffle, he will backtrack, and he simply cannot be believed."

Despite such gripes, Trump was happy.

"My list of potential U.S. Supreme Court Justices was very well re-
cieved," he said on Twitter, with a characteristic misspelling. "During
the next number of weeks I may be adding to the list!"

Trump was right. The first list was far from the final word. Trump
and his advisers wanted to expand on it. As the candidate struggled
to solidify conservatives in what was now a race with Hillary Clinton,
they began considering other, younger prospects. Gorsuch was already
squarely on the radar to fill the Scalia vacancy. McGahn had kept
him off the first list to spare him extra scrutiny, but knew he needed
to place Gorsuch on the list before the election if he was to get on the
court. Trump's aides acknowledged that both the first list and later the
expanded version had plenty of "filler" names who had no real chance
to ascend to the court but would help diffuse the spotlight on the real
prospective candidates.

By this point, Gorsuch was emerging as a strong choice for the
first vacancy in the minds of McGahn, Leo, and others after exhaustive scrutiny of his voluminous opinions. "He checked out," said Leo.
"It became apparent to me during that process that this guy was the
sleeper candidate.

"He had very strong views and he was not skittish about presenting
those and making those known."

On September 23, with the critical first presidential debate approaching, the Trump campaign issued a list of another ten judges,
this one with Gorsuch prominently mentioned. Also included was
Senator Mike Lee, Republican of Utah, who had remained a Trump
critic, like other prominent members of Utah's Mormon leadership.
In fact, the solidly Republican state was in danger of tipping toward
Clinton. Steve Bannon, who had come on board to rescue Trump's
endangered candidacy, added Lee's name to the list in a naked attempt
to appease Lee as well as his friend in the Senate Ted Cruz.

His own inclusion on the list didn't immediately revise Lee's view
of Trump. "This does not change Sen. Lee's mind about Trump in
any way whatsoever," the senator's office said in a statement. But it did

result in backing for Trump from Cruz, who had refused to endorse Trump at the party convention in Cleveland, stunning the audience there and leaving the Trump team outraged at what they saw as a betrayal.

Cruz credited the expanded list for his decision to finally embrace the man who suggested his father might have been involved in the Kennedy assassination and had insulted his wife. "We know, without a doubt, that every Clinton appointee would be a left-wing ideologue," he wrote. "Trump, in contrast, has promised to appoint justices in the mold of Scalia.

"For some time, I have been seeking greater specificity on this issue, and today the Trump campaign provided that, releasing a very strong list of potential Supreme Court nominees—including Sen. Mike Lee, who would make an extraordinary justice—and making an explicit commitment to nominate only from that list."

The party was abandoning some of its deep-seated reservations about Trump as the election neared and the idea of allowing Clinton to fill the vacancy sunk in. The list was clearly helping Donald Trump persuade previously reluctant conservative Republicans to coalesce around him. One more iteration would emerge, but it was months away. For now, the list was set, and the election headed toward the finish line.

18

Upset

THE CAMPAIGN BEHIND Garland kept on, but it proved increasingly hard to maintain the interest of the media or the public. Both were much more absorbed in one of the most tumultuous presidential campaigns in history, one pitting the first woman major-party nominee against a brash billionaire reality television star liable to say anything at any time.

Garland's predicament became part of the background noise of the election year. Garland might be seen going into the occasional Republican office, but there was not much more to say after the Republican senator visited said no hearing or vote would be happening.

The White House held daily conference calls with Capitol Hill staff on the day's events, but to the aides on the congressional end of the call the activities sounded repetitive, and staffers started to roll their eyes at the predictable schedule. There was no shift in strategy, and the Hill aides were frustrated with what they saw as the White House's complacency. "There was a 'We got this' attitude," one Hill official complained.

On the conservative side of the fight, a few Republicans, increasingly certain that Trump would be the nominee and that he would surely lose, began lobbying for Republicans to move ahead with Garland, arguing he would be the best the party would get. But the argument didn't get very far and those voices were quieted.

Garland was in stasis. He kept going to his chambers at the appeals court, where he continued to handle his administrative duties. He didn't preside over cases, since it was conceivable that cases from the appeals court docket could wind up at the Supreme Court, where he still hoped to sit. He might then have to recuse himself over conflicts. He went regularly to an office in the Eisenhower Executive Office Building adjacent to the White House that was being used as a war room. He even went through the "murder boards," the mock hearings that all nominees are subjected to as part of the preparation for the showdown with the Judiciary Committee—a showdown that he would never face.

He continued to tutor at the Washington grade school, J. O. Wilson Elementary, and in June delivered the commencement address there, predictably tearing up. True to his White House nickname, he quoted his favorite headmaster in urging the students to stay close with friends and even be willing to tell them when they were wrong. "As Professor Dumbledore told the Hogwarts class at the end of their school year, 'It takes a great deal of bravery to stand up to your enemies, but as much to stand up to our friends,'" he said.

He also delivered the commencement speech at his own high school outside Chicago, Niles West. At that appearance he quoted another character from the Potter books, Hermione Granger, "one of my favorite people." The White House would set up and publicize such favorable settings, but Garland never discussed the impasse over his own nomination.

The White House returned Garland's 141-page questionnaire, bolstered by reams of documentation, in early May, hoping it could spur Republicans to act. But it did not. With attention diminishing, Democrats were pressed on whether they should do something unconventional such as book him on the *Today* show or conduct a faux hearing with just Democrats present—a tactic the minority party has used in the past on policy matters to capture media attention when the majority wouldn't cooperate. Top Democrats weren't interested.

"I think some would probably like us to do some sort of a pretend hearing. That gets them off the hook," Leahy, the senior Democrat on the Judiciary Committee, said. "But the Senate is not a pretend office."

All sorts of ideas swirled at the White House, but everything was dismissed as below the dignity of the Senate, the court, and Garland himself. "He didn't want to do anything silly," said one person advising him.

All the while, Trump's raucous presidential campaign was in constant turmoil. He may have excited Republicans with his Supreme Court list, but he harbored other judicial views that alarmed some conservatives. With his self-styled Trump University, a real estate and wealth creation class, under fire in federal court as a rip-off, Trump suggested he couldn't get a fair hearing from the presiding judge, an Indiana-born American of Mexican heritage named Gonzalo Curiel, because of Trump's disparaging comments about Mexicans.

It sparked an outcry, including from Speaker Paul Ryan, who called it the "textbook definition of a racist comment." Mark Kirk, the embattled Republican senator from Illinois, said he could no longer support Trump because of that comment and others. As usual, Trump wouldn't back down. He said his comments had been misconstrued and did not represent an attack on all people of Mexican heritage—just the one causing him problems.

"I do not feel that one's heritage makes them incapable of being impartial, but, based on the rulings that I have received in the Trump University civil case, I feel justified in questioning whether I am receiving a fair trial," Trump said in a statement.

It was the precursor of many attacks by Trump on judges and circuit courts that stood in his way, a pattern that alarmed both members of the judiciary and those who believed it showed that Trump considered the judiciary subservient and susceptible to political pressure. It also exposed a raw motivation for promising to install conservative judges—he believed those judges would side with him and his

Mitch McConnell, the Senate Republican leader known for his obstructionist tactics, quickly decided on that day in February 2016 when Justice Antonin Scalia died that he would prevent President Barack Obama from filling the Supreme Court vacancy, setting in motion an earth-shattering series of political events. *Al Drago/New York Times*

President Barack Obama walks out of the White House with Judge Merrick B. Garland of the US Court of Appeals for the DC Circuit to introduce him as the nominee for Scalia's seat. Garland, a highly regarded jurist with a centrist reputation, never got so much as a hearing because of unshakeable Republican resistance. *Doug Mills/New York Times*

Miguel Estrada is sworn in for his Senate confirmation hearing in September 2002 after his nomination by President George W. Bush to the US Court of Appeals for the DC Circuit a year earlier. Democrats aggressively filibustered Estrada's nomination, setting off the contemporary era of judicial warfare. He asked that his nomination be withdrawn in September 2003 after Republicans failed to break the blockade despite a concerted campaign. *Paul Hosefros/New York Times*

Senate Majority Leader Bill Frist, with President George W. Bush and Texas state supreme court justice Priscilla R. Owen, one of multiple Bush nominees who had been blocked by Democrats, touching off a furious partisan debate. A bipartisan deal in 2005 among the so-called Gang of Fourteen led to Owen and others being confirmed and temporarily averted an effort to weaken the filibuster, delaying that showdown for another eight years. *Doug Mills/New York Times*

Republican presidential candidate Donald Trump speaks at a news conference on March 21, 2016, during the final stages of construction of the Trump International Hotel, the converted Old Post Office building on Pennsylvania Avenue in Washington. This was the first time Trump disclosed that he intended to make public a definitive list of people whom he would nominate to the Supreme Court if he was elected president. *Photo by Al Drago*

Democratic senator Chuck Schumer of New York speaks during a February 2016 rally demanding that Senate Republicans give a Supreme Court nominee to replace Justice Scalia a fair hearing and a vote. Merrick Garland was nominated the next month but never got either as Democratic efforts on Garland's behalf failed to break through. *Photo by Al Drago*

Don McGahn, the White House counsel for the first two years of the Trump administration, looks on as Judge Neil M. Gorsuch, President Trump's pick for the Supreme Court vacancy, talks with Senator Chuck Grassley, the chairman of the Judiciary Committee. Former Republican senator Kelly Ayotte, Gorsuch's "sherpa" through the Senate, is also present. Grassley's refusal to consider Obama's nominee opened the door for Gorsuch's nomination. *Al Drago/New York Times*

In his February 2017 meeting with Democratic senator Richard Blumenthal of Connecticut, Gorsuch said he found the president's attacks on federal judges disheartening and demoralizing. That bit of candor prompted an angry reaction from the president and sparked fears among Republicans that he might withdraw Gorsuch's nomination. *Al Drago/New York Times*

Neil Gorsuch is sworn in by Supreme Court Justice Anthony Kennedy on April 10, 2017, as President Trump looks on. Gorsuch's wife, Marie Louise, is holding the Bible. It was the first time a sitting justice had sworn in one of his former clerks to join him on the high court. Democrats failed to raise enough doubts about Gorsuch to weaken strong support from Republicans, who changed Senate rules to overcome a Democratic filibuster. *Al Drago/New York Times*

"Say hello to your boy," President Trump told Justice Anthony Kennedy when they talked and shook hands at the 2017 State of the Union address. "Special guy." The president was referring to Kennedy's son Justin, who had worked with Trump as a banker. The White House undertook a subtle campaign to make Kennedy feel comfortable in leaving the court with Trump in office, opening a second seat for Trump to fill in the first two years of his tenure. *Martin H. Simon/Redux*

Don McGahn, the White House counsel, watches as Brett Kavanaugh meets with Texas Republican senator Ted Cruz in Washington in July 2018. From the first days of the Trump administration, McGahn wielded enormous influence over the selection of judicial nominees. He favored Kavanaugh from the start as the pick for a second opening on the court even though Kavanaugh's extensive Washington pedigree and strong ties to the Bush family clashed with the outsider image Trump liked to cultivate. *Al Drago/New York Times*

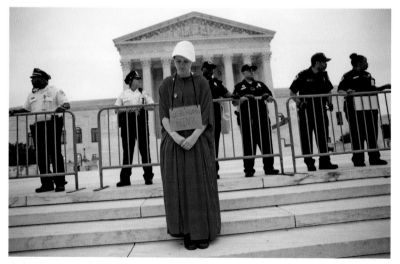

A demonstrator dressed as a character from *The Handmaid's Tale* protests outside the Supreme Court building in October 2018. Kavanaugh's nomination drew strong resistance from women and abortion rights groups even before he was accused of an attempted sexual assault during his high school years. His raucous confirmation hearings were repeatedly interrupted by shouts from opponents in the audience who were removed by Capitol police. *Tom Brenner/New York Times*

Republican senator Susan Collins of Maine is pursued by reporters after leaving the secure room where a single copy of the FBI report on Judge Brett Kavanaugh was being held. Collins was a crucial vote on the troubled nomination as one of two centrist Republican women. The White House kept in close contact with her throughout the contentious nomination fight, seeing her vote as decisive. Her position was certain to provoke a political backlash no matter how she voted. *Erin Schaff/New York Times*

Christine Blasey Ford is sworn in on September 27, 2018, to testify about her sexual misconduct allegations against Judge Brett Kavanaugh. Her compelling testimony delivered in a packed hearing room had many believing Kavanaugh's nomination was dead and would have to be withdrawn. Kavanaugh testified separately after her. *Erin Schaff/New York Times*

An angry Brett Kavanaugh testifies before the Senate Judiciary Committee on September 27, 2018. Following Ford's gripping appearance, McGahn told Kavanaugh that he needed to "reboot the room" and push back forcefully on his Democratic questioners as they had rehearsed in preparation for his appearance. Kavanaugh's fiery defense of himself helped win Republican support but gave Democrats more reason to oppose him, saying he had displayed a temperament unsuited for the court. *Erin Schaff/New York Times*

After a follow-up FBI investigation produced no new corroboration of Ford's accusations, Brett Kavanaugh was narrowly confirmed to the Supreme Court. He was ceremonially sworn in on October 8, 2018, in the East Room of the White House by retiring justice Anthony Kennedy as Kavanaugh's family and President Trump watched. It was the first time a justice would be replaced by a former clerk, and Kavanaugh's confirmation, combined with Gorsuch's, cemented a new conservative majority on the court. *Doug Mills/New York Times*

views, and woe unto those who did not. It helped fuel a determination to remake the courts if he got the chance, because sitting judges were nothing more than partisans with an agenda. He much preferred his partisans.

With the nomination about to be formally bestowed, Republicans rolled into Cleveland for their convention, still somewhat shocked that Trump was about to become their standard bearer. McConnell, in a convention address dedicated mostly to vilifying Hillary Clinton, found time to remind a cheering audience what was really at stake.

"On that sad day when we lost Justice Scalia, I made another pledge that Obama would not fill his seat," McConnell said. "That honor will go to Donald Trump next year."

Trump, in his dark and foreboding acceptance speech, promised that the "replacement for Justice Scalia will be a person of similar views and principles. This will be one of the most important issues decided by this election."

To the Republicans at the convention and around the country, Trump had never made a more honest statement. They knew that the court was a top reason for voting for him despite widespread doubt. Trump even gave a special shout-out to the single group that might be most influenced by the court—and would have seemed most likely to look askance at Trump because of his personal history. "I would like to thank the evangelical community, who have been so good to me and so supportive," he said.

It was an entirely different story for the Democrats at their convention in Philadelphia following the Republican event. For a Harry Potter fan, Merrick Garland became the judicial version of He Who Must Not Be Named. In a deliberate strategy, Clinton, Obama, and their fellow Democrats avoided any direct reference to Garland and the ongoing Senate blockade of his nomination. "He was not mentioned once at the Democratic convention, certainly by any of the major speakers," said Leo, the Federalist Society leader. "Not mentioned once."

The sole reference to the Supreme Court in Clinton's speech was related to campaign finance laws and the court's *Citizens United* ruling, when she said that "we need to appoint Supreme Court justices who will get money out of politics and expand voting rights, not restrict them." She also dinged Trump for his attack on the judge of Mexican ancestry overseeing the Trump University case. Obama said nothing in his remarks, which were part valedictory, part Clinton endorsement, and part Trump-bashing.

It was a graphic illustration of how Democrats just put less emphasis on the court and its political power than Republicans.

A convention is one of the few moments when a disengaged public tunes in to politics, and the Garland fight might have garnered some attention. But Democrats had decided it was best to keep him out of and away from the political fray that was a national convention. "We didn't want to politicize him," explained one top Obama aide. "Maybe that was the wrong call. We didn't want to turn him into a political football. We needed to keep him as pristine and clean as possible, and that meant not inserting him into the public debate at the convention."

Others believed that the Democrats didn't want to remind the public of a presidential failure when the baton was about to be passed. It was a time to celebrate Obama's success and his assumed successor. Whatever the reason, the decision would haunt Democrats as a missed opportunity.

As the Democrats met in Philadelphia, Trump was touring the country holding rallies. The presidential opposition traditionally goes dark during the other party's nominating convention out of courtesy and the fact that most of the media attention is on the convention. But not Donald Trump. At events in Iowa he made the choice as clear as he could for Republican voters nervous about him and his temperament but also worried about the makeup of the court. It was a remarkable statement from a presidential candidate, and it revealed Trump's awareness of the doubts about him.

"Here's the story," Trump told a conservative crowd in Cedar Rapids, Iowa, on July 28. "If you really like Donald Trump, that's great. But if you don't, you have to vote for me anyway. You know why? Supreme Court judges, Supreme Court judges. Have no choice. Sorry, sorry, sorry.

"The next president of this country, remember, could have as many as four or five, which would be a lot, that would be an all-time record," Trump continued, noting that if "Crooked Hillary" picked the judges, "you are going to end up with another Venezuela."

Trump then went on to explain the genesis of his now well-known list, saying he understood the concern of some that he might install liberal judges. He also said that past Republican presidents "didn't do well" either. It was a pointed but veiled reference to Chief Justice John Roberts, the George W. Bush appointee who in the mind of many conservatives was a liberal traitor because he had upheld the new health care law. Trump liked to joke that it could be called Robertscare.

"You look at what happened with Obamacare," he reminded the enthusiastic crowd. "Our conservative judge, twice, kept Obamacare. We could have killed Obamacare.

"You have to do it for the reason," he said, urging the audience to support him despite any reservations.

It was brutally honest in its own way and the most naked connection Trump could make between his own election and the future of the Supreme Court. The message was "You might loathe me, but you will like my justices."

Following the convention season, Democratic attention in Washington turned back to Garland. Valerie Jarrett, a senior adviser to the president, gathered about twenty activists in the White House. What, Jarrett demanded, were they doing to get Merrick Garland confirmed?

That didn't sit too well with some of the attendees, including Nan Aron, the liberal judicial activist, who spoke last. She didn't hold back, saying she had just watched a well-organized political convention in

Philadelphia at which the name Merrick Garland hadn't come up once. Imagine, she said, if that was a Republican president being ignored by a Democratic Senate. It would have been the talk of the convention.

As the Senate returned from an extended summer recess and the campaign trail, Democrats tried to regain some momentum on Capitol Hill for Garland, who had now set the record for the longest wait ever for a hearing by a Supreme Court nominee. The seven-week summer break, the longest for the Senate in decades, had done no favors for the Garland campaign or his nomination. Democrats urged the White House to dispatch Garland back to the Capitol, where he could get some press attention.

The nominee made a highly publicized visit with Leahy, the top Democrat on the Judiciary Committee. Vice President Biden also visited the Senate again on Garland's behalf; senators rallied at the Supreme Court with Garland's clerks to demand he receive a hearing; and they took to the floor to angrily remind Americans of the situation.

Reid aimed at his favorite target—Chuck Grassley—reading a critical letter to the editor published in the *Des Moines Register*. Leahy lashed out at McConnell and the Republicans.

"Perhaps the Republican leadership was hoping that Americans had forgotten about the unprecedented obstruction of a Supreme Court nominee. But I can assure you that Americans—and certainly Vermonters—have not forgotten," Leahy said. "They have not forgotten the fact that Senate Republicans have refused to hold a hearing for Chief Judge Garland, and they have not forgotten this unprecedented step in not allowing a hearing. They have not forgotten that some senators still have not even afforded Chief Judge Garland the courtesy of a meeting."

It all had the whiff of desperation and resignation. It was September, the Senate would soon be out until the election. Republicans had held out to this point. There was little reason to think they would surrender now.

Some Democrats began to see the Garland affair as a potential

campaign issue to regain the Senate, the odds of which were looking favorable. Republican Mark Kirk in Illinois had little chance to
win, and Democrats were also optimistic about their chances in New
Hampshire and Wisconsin, where the former senator Russ Feingold
was trying to avenge his loss to Ron Johnson six years earlier.

With a little luck, and a Clinton victory, Democrats could punish
Republicans for their obstruction and regain the majority. One race
that had moved away from them, however, was Grassley's. Despite the
battering, he seemed secure. Opponent Judge, and Judge Garland, had
not been enough.

The presidential campaign itself was experiencing earth-shattering
twists and turns. On October 7, the *Washington Post* made public
the *Access Hollywood* tape containing Trump's lewd comments about
women. Then, on October 28, James Comey, the director of the FBI,
sent a public letter to Congress, telling top lawmakers he was ordering
a reopening of the investigation into Clinton's use of a private email
server after earlier clearing her of charges. It was a stunning development that froze Clinton's campaign. Her lead in the polls slipped and
her momentum stalled.

But she remained the favorite against Trump. And as the election
grew closer, the Republican focus began to shift in an ominous direction when it came to the court. Some leading Republicans began
suggesting that perhaps letting the people decide—the standard set
by McConnell back in February—shouldn't really be the standard
after all.

McCain, campaigning for reelection, was the first, saying that
Republicans would stand united against any Clinton nominee. Then
Cruz chimed in, offering his view, that "there is certainly long historical precedent for a Supreme Court with fewer justices." Finally Richard Burr, a usually reasonable North Carolina Republican, was caught
on tape saying that if reelected he would "do everything I can do to
make sure four years from now, we still got an opening on the Supreme
Court."

Republicans were now suggesting that they would try to hold the Scalia seat open another four years to prevent President Hillary Clinton from filling the vacancy. It was incredible to many in both parties. Susan Collins attributed the new view to preelection tensions over what she called the most bizarre presidential campaign of her lifetime.

"I certainly understand that the court has become much more ideological than is desirable for that institution, and that is why there are those who have taken what I believe to be an untenable view," she said. "We don't even know who her Supreme Court nominees are going to be, so how could we possibly draw a line in the sand? I certainly hope we don't go down that route."

Collins was right about one thing—anxiety was rising over the presidential campaign as Election Day approached. The night before, a top Republican strategist revealed that the view in the Senate was that Clinton would win and Democrats would recapture the majority, a prediction that Speaker Paul Ryan also said had been presented to him. McConnell had gambled on the court seat but lost.

He and his colleagues and advisers gathered on Election Night at the headquarters of the National Republican Senatorial Committee a few blocks from the Capitol to monitor the results. Expectations were low, but as the night progressed, McConnell's spirits improved.

"Are we gonna make America great again tonight?" he asked fellow attendees at one point. By the end of the night, McConnell had achieved a monumental victory, one that would forever secure his legacy as the most skilled obstructionist ever in the Senate.

"The Supreme Court ended up being the single biggest issue in leading Trump to get ninety percent of the Republican vote," McConnell said as he later weighed the outcome. "It ended up helping him win the election."

McConnell acknowledged that his decision to blockade the nominee was a gamble that had paid off, for his side at least. "We gained a chance," he said. "The other way we had no chance. It gave us a chance and it worked out in a very significant way. It ended up not costing us a single seat. Not one of our people lost over this issue, and if anyone was going to, it would have been Grassley. It petered out as an issue against us and ended up being a plus in the presidential race to help us."

McConnell not only preserved a Supreme Court seat, he elected Donald Trump president.

19

Postmortem

As McConnell and his allies celebrated the remarkable outcome of Election Day, aides to Chuck Schumer scrapped their planned Election Night press release, in which Schumer would have called for the quick consideration of Garland by the Senate. His nomination was dead. He would not reach the Supreme Court. Months of effort had failed to shame Senate Republicans into at minimum granting Garland, one of the most esteemed legal minds in the country, a hearing for a Supreme Court nomination made with almost a year left in Obama's term.

Not only did Republicans not relent under pressure, they retained the Senate and saw a Republican president elected. They were not punished for their actions, they were rewarded. They could hardly believe their good fortune.

There was absolutely no doubt that the court vacancy, which held many dubious Republicans behind Trump despite his clear weaknesses and flaws, had been a major factor in the outcome. Twenty-one percent of voters said that Supreme Court appointments were the primary factor in their presidential choice, and 56 percent of those who held that view favored Trump, compared with 41 percent backing Clinton, according to exit polls. In such a close election, the court was a decisive factor, and it helped Republican Senate candidates as well. "That Supreme Court vacancy was golden," said Senator Roy Blunt, the Missouri Republican and former House majority leader and a man with a deep understanding of his party's politics and beliefs.

McConnell couldn't have known at that moment in the Caribbean when he decided to block Obama's nominee, whoever it was, that his decision would have such consequences. The most significant one was that Americans who had grave doubts about an untested and unconventional Republican nominee weighed their choices and decided they preferred the vacancy to be filled by him rather than Hillary Clinton. Divorces, bankruptcies, lies, abusive talk and behavior toward women, racially charged language and sentiments, a misunderstanding of the role of the courts, and more, none was enough to shake Trump voters with a court seat on the line.

Tony Perkins, head of the Family Research Council, an archconservative Christian Right group, summed it up in a glowing introduction of McConnell at the group's Values Voter Summit in the fall of 2018. He credited McConnell with one of the "most courageous political acts that has ever been done in the history of the United States Senate.

"What that decision did is it kept the issue of judges and the centrality of the US Constitution to our republic at the forefront of the presidential election and in the minds of the American voters," Perkins said. "It helped frame the presidential election, and it has now, ladies and gentlemen, put our nation on a path of restoring this constitutional republic."

Lavish praise indeed.

Democrats were crushed. The prospect of a Trump presidency was unfathomable to most of them, and the fact that a Supreme Court seat Obama had every right to fill would now be in the hands of Trump was deeply depressing, disturbing, and heart wrenching. The chance to tip the balance of the court—even before the Clinton loss—had been within Obama's grasp, only to be snatched away by McConnell and a Republican Senate that had for eight years done everything in its power to impede the Democratic president. White House aides were numb and teary.

The recriminations began. Did Obama make the wrong pick? Should he have gone with a more liberal candidate, a woman or a minority who could have excited activists and led to added pressure on Republicans? Was it a mistake to not be more confrontational and unconventional and put Garland in front of the public at mock hearings or on television? Was Obama personally aggressive enough? The hashtags hadn't gotten the job done either.

"I think the fact of the matter is the Democrats didn't have their heart in it," said Leonard Leo, referring to the Garland nomination's inability to rouse the party and the base. "There were a number of people on the left who thought Obama choked in the selection of Garland as the nominee."

Many Democrats on Capitol Hill still believe Obama and his team blew it, that they should have gone with another nominee. It was unconscionable to them that the White House had found a way to lose both the policy fight by failing to advance Garland and the political fight by losing the election. The White House was drawn to Garland by his supposed backing from Republicans like Hatch, but they were never going to relent. A more progressive candidate could have served as a rallying symbol in the election.

Other Democratic allies don't fault the selection of Garland.

"I actually thought it was smart," said Nan Aron of the Alliance for Justice. "Many people disagree and say it should have been someone who could galvanize several constituencies to go to bat for them. But having lived through many, many of these fights—It was an election year and groups had their eyes on electoral work rather than helping a Supreme Court nominee."

As they assessed the outcome, the Democrats involved said they did what they could in a way that they thought best served the president and the nominee. Complicating their task was the fact that the money for a huge television campaign just never materialized; donors had other interests.

"Should Barack Obama have stormed the Judiciary Committee?" asked Eric Schultz, a White House communications operative and former Schumer aide who was a key player in the Garland fight. "What more could have been done?

"When we looked back, nobody could name something, a lever we didn't pull, something we should have done," he said.

Other questions remained. Would McConnell have set a vote on Garland in the lame-duck session had Clinton won? He definitively says no.

"I never seriously considered doing that. I thought if we do that it would mean, we made it all up, we really didn't mean it when we said the next person who is elected ought to fill the vacancy. I think that is the kind of thing that gives politicians a bad name."

On top of that, it seems unlikely that McConnell would have been willing to give Obama a third justice no matter what, given his opinion of the president. Not to mention those Republican senators who had already been threatening to hold the vacancy open indefinitely.

Some argued that Obama should have exercised his constitutional power to put Garland on the court through a so-called recess appointment, but the opportunity for such a move had been significantly narrowed by the court itself two years earlier and would fly in the face of Obama's by-the-book philosophy. Garland, with his desire to preserve his reputation and integrity, probably would have turned thumbs down on that idea as well. It never gained any traction at the White House.

What about Clinton? Would she have named Garland or gone with a younger, more liberal choice? Arguments for both exist. Picking a more exciting, more progressive alternative would have quickly put her stamp on the court—while also rebuking Republicans for what they did.

But renominating Garland would have had its own benefits. It would be the least complicated way to quickly fill the seat while expending little political capital, allowing the new president to focus on other matters. It would have been portrayed as an olive branch to Republicans. And it would have rewarded Garland for enduring such a partisan ordeal with grace.

The Clinton campaign itself hadn't decided what it would do, according to one of her closest advisers. "We never got that far," said John Podesta, who served as chairman of the campaign.

Garland returned to the Old Executive Office Building war room on December 14 for a farewell to the Obama aides who had tried but failed to shepherd him to the Supreme Court. The judge, who had been emotional at his nomination, was teary once again as he thanked the staff and expressed his appreciation for the countless hours they'd devoted to his cause. Though he was not successful, he told them he relished the experience as part of the arc of his career. He was effusive in his gratitude, and for one aspect of the months of political jousting in particular—that he had emerged professionally intact, his reputation unscathed. He would return to being chief judge of the US Court of Appeals for the District of Columbia Circuit, the second-most-important court in America. It was not the Supreme Court, but it was not a bad consolation prize.

"His worry was not that he would never be confirmed," said one attendee, "his worry was that he would be dragged through the mud, and he was very thankful that never happened to him or his family."

Still, it had to be a bitter pill for a man worthy of the high court who was denied his professional and personal dream because of a political fight totally beyond his control. He never discussed his experience publicly. Not even Dumbledore could summon enough magic to overcome the deep partisanship that had engulfed the nation's judicial politics. The future of the Supreme Court was now in the hands of Donald Trump.

20

Gorsuch

Trump's shocking election was followed by an equally shocking transition, as Chris Christie, the governor of New Jersey, who had been heading up the effort, was fired by Trump along with other leading officials. As a federal prosecutor in New Jersey before his governor days, Christie had sent the father of Jared Kushner, Trump's son-in-law and close adviser, to prison, and Kushner—the driving force behind Christie's firing—had exacted his family's payback. Christie's services were no longer needed now that a Trump administration was going to be an unexpected reality.

Within a few weeks of the election, chaos reigned as both prominent Americans and foreign heads of state cold-called into Trump Tower in New York to try to connect with the president-elect. No one seemed quite sure of what was transpiring, but Trump himself sought to calm mounting alarm about his preparedness to take over the country's highest office in two months.

"Very organized process taking place as I decide on Cabinet and many other positions," he tweeted. "I am the only one who knows who the finalists are!"

After his swearing-in on January 20, 2017, the furor only intensified following a dark inaugural speech in which Trump lamented "American carnage" at a moment that is traditionally inspirational. A giant women's protest march thronged through Washington the next day, with its crowds easily exceeding the numbers at the inauguration it-self. The president immediately issued executive orders trying to undo Obama administration programs and threw the nation's airports into chaos with a promised travel ban to forbid entry of refugees and immi-grants from certain majority-Muslim countries. Uncertainty prevailed at all levels.

Except one. The filling of the Scalia vacancy on the court was pro-ceeding smoothly and right on schedule. In the days after the elec-tion, Republicans were ebullient, recognizing that Trump would reap the benefits of McConnell's stonewall of Obama. The mid-November convention of the Federalist Society at the Mayflower Hotel in Wash-ington was a celebration of Trump's triumph and the recognition that the group, with its role in shaping Trump's Supreme Court list, was ascendant. Attendees remember Judge Pryor, a potential replacement for Scalia, being treated like a rock star at the event. But it was not to be. Gorsuch was the prohibitive in-house favorite.

Well before the nomination became public, McGahn and his staff had assembled a fifteen-page, hour-by-hour breakdown of how the confirmation process would unfold over the next four months. It was minutely detailed. "I leave nothing to chance," McGahn was fond of saying.

"SCOTUS TASKS AND TIMING," the confidential memo was headed. "Week of January 30th Announcement (the dates below as-sume January 31 Announcement)." The nomination, as it would turn out, was made that night.

Though the memo was written while speculation still swirled in Washington about the identity of the nominee, it made clear the choice was all but made. On the memorandum's schedule for Febru-ary 1 were back-to-back courtesy visits by the nominee to home state senators Cory Gardner and Michael Bennet, both of Colorado. Gor-such was the only potential candidate from Colorado. He was assur-edly the pick.

The memo also made explicit that the Trump White House would not let a Democratic filibuster derail any nominee. Under the Democratic rules change of 2013, moving ahead with the confirmation of a Supreme Court nominee would still require sixty votes to break a filibuster. McConnell had warned at the time that Republicans would simply change that remaining barrier to a simple majority if they regained control. McGahn understood and shared that view.

One of the last entries on the memo made clear the final plan. "If we do not get 60 votes, WHC, OLP, and WH OLA will work to meet with leadership to plan a possible Senate rules change, which requires 51 Senate votes—or 50 plus VP." That is, should Democrats choose to filibuster, the White House counsel, the Office of Legal Policy, and the White House Office of Legislative Affairs were more than prepared to demolish that effort.

Gorsuch was already well into the process. After the January 5 meeting with McGahn at his law office and then with the other members of the screening committee in the transition headquarters, Gorsuch met on January 14 with Trump and McGahn in New York. McGahn told Trump that Gorsuch was hands down the best choice.

A tall, impressive man from a longtime Colorado family, Gorsuch had deep Washington ties as well from the period in the 1980s when his mother, Anne, was the first woman administrator of the Environmental Protection Agency. He spent his high school years in the nation's capital, graduating from Georgetown Preparatory School, before going on to Columbia and Harvard Law, where one of his classmates was Barack Obama. He had multiple prestigious clerkships, including with Justice Kennedy, worked briefly in the Justice Department under President George W. Bush, and had been confirmed without opposition to the US Court of Appeals for the Tenth Circuit in 2006. He was sworn in by his former mentor, Justice Kennedy.

The Gorsuch family had gone through a searing experience while in Washington. His mother, a conservative Colorado state lawmaker, was selected by Ronald Reagan in 1981 to head the EPA. She had already earned a reputation as a hard-charging opponent of federal energy and land use policies in Colorado and embraced the name given to a fractious, like-minded group of state lawmakers—the House Crazies. At the EPA she imposed budget cuts and regulatory rollbacks, and she ran afoul of the agency's staff. She would be forced out in less than two years under the pressure of multiple investigations into the agency's handling of a pollution cleanup program. It was an ignominious exit from Washington and one that had to have left a bitter memory with her high school–age son. Washington had destroyed his mother's reputation.

In her memoir, Gorsuch recalled the disappointment expressed by her son, saying he told her that she "should never have resigned."

"You didn't do anything wrong," Neil Gorsuch told his mother. "You only did what the president ordered. Why are you quitting? You raised me not to be a quitter."

"It scarred him," said one of the officials involved in his Supreme Court selection. To an administration populated by officials determined to tear down Washington's regulatory powers like the EPA, it was just the kind of scarring they appreciated.

Though he was nearly certain to be the pick, Gorsuch was not the only candidate being interviewed. The administration's search committee also talked to six others: Thomas Hardiman, William Pryor, Diane Sykes, Raymond Kethledge, Don Willett, and Amul Thapar, a federal district court judge in Kentucky and a favorite of McConnell's. The White House wanted to make sure that McConnell's pick got some love from the White House, given the majority leader's importance in the confirmation process.

Pryor, Alabama's former attorney general, was portrayed as one of the front-runners at the time, and some in the administration even pushed that story line, in part to deflect attention from Gorsuch as the White House was nearing an announcement. It made sense, since Pryor was one of the names Trump had first mentioned as a possible nominee during the Republican debate the night Scalia died. Pryor, though, was in an odd political situation. He was seen by the Left as an archconservative who strongly opposed abortion rights. But he had also prosecuted Roy Moore, the chief justice of the Alabama Supreme Court, for Moore's refusal to remove a two-ton facsimile of the Ten Commandments from his courthouse. By forcing Moore out as chief justice, Pryor had angered the Far Right, which was leery of some of his appellate court decisions as well.

Pryor, Hardiman, and Gorsuch met with Trump in New York on January 14, just days before the inauguration. Judge Kethledge was left off the list for a face-to-face interview. Bannon thought him too impressive and was worried that Trump might favor him over Gorsuch, upending the underlying strategy.

So Gorsuch it was. Trump accepted McGahn's recommendation as the overwhelming choice, and the president called Gorsuch in Colorado on January 30. He and his wife, Louise, were soon in a military jet on their way to Washington, where they would be secluded until the big unveil.

The disclosure of a Supreme Court nominee was a major moment for the already struggling Trump administration. This was a Washington rite that was usually done with pomp and dignity, and those surrounding Trump wanted to do it properly to show they were capable of performing the basic functions of the presidency. Filling the Scalia vacancy held open by McConnell was the very reason many conservatives had voted for Trump in the first place. This was a big deal.

It was not without one final wacky aspect, however. Though Gorsuch was the pick, the media did not know that and was keeping its eyes and cameras on the whereabouts of other candidates, including Hardiman in Pennsylvania. When Hardiman got in his car in Pittsburgh about noon that day and began driving east, it set off a frenzy of speculation that he was on his way to DC for the White House ceremony. Something of an "O. J. Simpson in the white Ford Bronco" moment ensued, as reporters tried to map his vehicular progress. The White House, not wanting to spill the beans about Gorsuch, played along to enhance the drama. But Hardiman was on an unrelated in-state trip and already knew he wasn't headed for the court. The White House would never have taken the chance of a traffic backup on the Pennsylvania Turnpike or an accident spoiling its big moment.

Later that evening of January 31, just as McGahn's memo had predicted, Trump convened a ceremony in the White House to announce his first Supreme Court choice. He referred quickly to his now famous list of nominees, saying he had initiated what "may be the most transparent judicial selection process in history."

"Months ago as a candidate, I publicly presented a list of brilliant and accomplished people to the American electorate and pledged to make my choice from among that list," he said. "Millions of voters said this was the single most important issue to them when they voted for me for president."

He also wanted credit for keeping the nominee's identity quiet, given the bountiful leakiness of his administration so far.

"So was that a surprise? Was it?" he asked proudly.

In introducing Gorsuch, he praised his "outstanding legal skills, a brilliant mind, tremendous discipline" and expressed how seriously he had taken replacing Scalia. He singled out the presence of Maureen Scalia, the wife of the late justice, at the ceremony. "She is really the ultimate representative of the late, great Justice Antonin Scalia, whose image and genius was in my mind throughout the decision-making process."

It was obvious that McGahn's emphasis on the opinions written by Gorsuch had made an impression on Trump. "Not only are we looking at the writings of the nominee—and I studied them closely," Trump said, in what was no doubt an extreme exaggeration, "but he is said to be among the finest and most brilliant" of judicial writers in a "long, long time."

Gorsuch followed with a bland ode to the federal judiciary and a promise to "do all my powers permit to be a faithful servant of the Constitution and laws of this great country."

He paid tribute to the "towering" judges—Scalia and Robert

Jackson—who had occupied the seat he would now try to fill and complimented the institution that would now review his nomination.

"As this process now moves to the Senate, I look forward with speaking with members from both side of the aisle, to answering their questions and to hearing their concerns. I consider the United States Senate the greatest deliberative body in the world, and I respect the important role the Constitution affords it in the confirmation of our judges."

That wasn't always the case, however. In 2002, Gorsuch had written an opinion piece tearing into the Senate for its handling of judicial confirmations during the early years of the Bush presidency.

"Today, there are too many who are concerned less with promoting the best public servants and more with enforcing litmus tests and locating unknown 'stealth candidates' who are perceived as likely to advance favored political causes once on the bench," he wrote. "Politicians and pressure groups on both sides declare that they will not support nominees unless they hew to their own partisan creeds. When a favored candidate is voted down for lack of sufficient political sympathy to those in control, grudges are held for years, and retaliation is guaranteed."

He also lamented the treatment of a couple of judges in particular. "Some of the most impressive judicial nominees are grossly mistreated," he wrote. "Take Merrick Garland and John Roberts, two appointees to the US Court of Appeals in Washington, DC. Both were Supreme Court clerks. Both served with distinction at the Department of Justice. Both are widely considered to be among the finest lawyers of their generation."

Still, he wrote, "Garland was left waiting for 18 months before being confirmed over the opposition of 23 senators. Roberts, nominated almost a year ago, still waits for a hearing—and sees no end to the waiting in sight. In fact, this is the second time around for Roberts: he was left hanging without a vote by the Senate at the end of the first Bush administration. So much for promoting excellence in today's confirmation process."

Times and opinions change when you are the nominee needing to clear the Senate. Aides quickly let it be known that the first person Gorsuch called after the nomination ceremony was Merrick Garland, "out of respect."

Given his reputation as an antiregulatory crusader, Gorsuch's nomination was met with exhilaration by Republicans, who gleefully pointed out his easy confirmation a decade previously.

"When [Gorsuch] was confirmed to the Tenth Circuit Court of Appeals," said John Cornyn, the number two Republican in the Senate, "he was confirmed by the Senate on a voice vote. In other words, he was essentially voted [in] unanimously, including people like Senator Schumer, the Democratic leader, who was here at the time, and others of our colleagues across the aisle. So I think it's going to be really important for the American people, as they hear the inevitable criticism of this nomination, that they remember the senators who were here at the time Judge Gorsuch was confirmed to the Tenth Circuit."

While Gorsuch wooed the Senate, he probably was not as effusive in his expressing his appreciation and gratitude to Trump as he might have been—an omission that proved troublesome later.

Schumer wasted no time in making his opposition clear, an opposition fueled in part by the tumult of the opening days of the Trump administration and the sentiment that the courts might need to be a final line of defense against the administration. He issued a tough statement just minutes after the nomination ceremony. "A little more than a week into the Trump presidency, the new administration has violated our core values, challenged the separation of powers, and tested the very fabric of our Constitution in unprecedented fashion," he said. "Now more than ever, we need a Supreme Court justice who is independent, eschews ideology, who will preserve our democracy, protect fundamental rights, and will stand up to a president who has already shown a willingness to bend the Constitution."

Schumer's most important statement was his next one. "The Senate must insist upon sixty votes for any Supreme Court nominee, a bar that was met by each of President Obama's nominees," he said. The challenge was thrown down. The minute the nomination was made, the Democratic leader had declared Senate Democrats would require Gorsuch to clear the filibuster hurdle.

At the White House, that news thrilled McGahn. If the Senate was going to have to change the rules on Supreme Court nominations, he would much prefer it happen on this nomination, when the ideological balance of the court was not at stake and Gorsuch was such a qualified candidate. In the event of a Democratic blockade, wary Republicans could be much more easily persuaded to change the rules. It would be harder to do so when the tilt of the court was in play and centrists like Susan Collins and Lisa Murkowski might balk at changing the rules for a nominee perceived as hostile to abortion rights. Republicans couldn't believe Democrats were going to go to the mat on Gorsuch.

Schumer and his fellow Democrats were under tremendous pressure from their constituents to stand up to Trump, and the new party leader, in one of his first major tests, felt he could not give an inch on Gorsuch, particularly after the Republicans' refusal to allow Garland so much as a hearing. To most Democrats, Gorsuch's nomination was illegitimate, a seat stolen from both Garland and Obama. They were drawing a line against a nominee they considered hostile to their constituencies.

As Gorsuch began making his courtesy visits in the Senate the day after his nomination. Trump had a message for Republicans if Democrats dug in. "If we end up with that gridlock, I'd say, 'If you can, Mitch, go nuclear,'" the president told reporters at the White House. "Because that would be an absolute shame if a man of this quality was caught up in this web."

Those weren't the only comments Trump was making about the judicial process. He was angry that a federal district court judge in Washington State had temporarily blocked the new travel ban, inciting Trump to return to his campaign practice of attacking federal judges he saw as biased against him and his policies.

"The opinion of this so-called judge, which essentially takes law-enforcement away from our country, is ridiculous and will be overturned!" Trump tweeted on February 5 as Gorsuch was on Capitol Hill. "If something happens blame him and court system. People pouring in. Bad!"

That provided an opening for Democrats to try to test the willingness of Gorsuch, who was showing signs of not wanting to be controlled by his administration minders, to be independent of Trump. The senator who first took advantage was Richard Blumenthal, the Connecticut Democrat who sat on the Judiciary Committee and was himself a former Supreme Court clerk.

In their meeting on February 8, Blumenthal told Gorsuch that there was an "elephant in the room" in the form of Trump's persistent attacks on the federal judiciary. Gorsuch replied that, as a judge, he found the attacks disheartening and demoralizing—words that were later confirmed by the team around Gorsuch. From their perspective, the comments could help win some Democratic votes.

At the White House, officials were aghast and attributed the Gorsuch shot at Trump to poor guidance from Kelly Ayotte, who had just lost her New Hampshire Senate seat and was serving as Gorsuch's guide through the personalities of the Senate—a "sherpa," in senatorial parlance.

The comments created an emergency at the White House. Trump was already concerned about appointing Supreme Court justices who might turn out to be less conservative than advertised. How would he respond to criticism and disloyalty from a man whom just days earlier he had glowingly recommended for a post at the pinnacle of America's judiciary?

McGahn got a frantic late-night phone call from Reince Priebus, Trump's chief of staff, saying the president was going to be unhappy and might want to withdraw Gorsuch. McGahn told others working the nomination that he was afraid he might be fired over Gorsuch's comments. White House aides wanted Gorsuch to retract or walk back the remarks. The perfectly executed Supreme Court nomination was about to blow up.

From the perspective of Gorsuch and his allies, the nominee had a solid counterargument to make. In the ragged first days of the administration, the Supreme Court nomination was the best thing the troubled White House had going by far. Withdrawing the nomination would be a huge embarrassment.

Trump eventually responded as he would in so many cases—by pretending the episode had been misrepresented by the media. He also lashed out at his communications staff.

The president denied that he had been ready to kill the nomination and argued that Blumenthal had misconstrued Gorsuch's comments in the private meeting—though Gorsuch's handlers had confirmed them at the time. Even top White House officials were never certain how far the president had been willing to go. But the crisis passed, and Gorsuch moved into the intense preparation that McGahn's memo had spelled out far in advance.

The interaction with Blumenthal, though, illustrated Gorsuch's desire to be viewed as independent, someone not tied to Trump. He wanted Democratic support to legitimize his nomination, coming as it did from Trump after the nearly yearlong blockade of Garland. He particularly wanted the blessing of Senator Michael Bennet, the Colorado Democrat caught in a tough political spot between the home state nominee and his own party.

Given that the Trump administration hadn't had much time to staff up, the White House brought on some seasoned Republican political and public relations operatives to help prepare Gorsuch for his time before the Judiciary Committee. Among those enlisted to help were Rob Collins, who had directed the successful 2014 Republican effort to win the Senate majority, and Ron Bonjean, a popular public relations professional who had accomplished the rare Washington feat of serving as spokesman for the top Republicans in both the House and Senate. He was also widely known for an annual Christmas bash at which he would bring in a mystery guest, usually a washed-up Hollywood actor, to make cocktail conversation and take selfies with celebrating political staffers and journalists.

Gorsuch, who had been inhabiting the insular world where federal judges reign supreme, began to get frustrated with the entire process. He was irritated that he would have friendly, and—he thought—productive meetings with Democrats, only to hear them come out and say they intended to oppose him. He also bristled at his Washington advisers. Gorsuch was accustomed to running his own show and didn't like being told how to act or what to say. He eventually called in a large circle of former clerks who took time off from their jobs and headed to Washington to help their mentor and protect him from Washington groupthink. "Gorsuch didn't trust the Washington people around him and wanted to bring in clerks that he trusted from over the years," said one Republican who worked on the nomination.

Among those on the Gorsuch team was Mike Davis, a partisan bulldog and former Iowan who had clerked for him and had political experience from the George W. Bush White House. Davis added to Gorsuch's comfort level.

Unfortunately, Gorsuch had not disclosed his plans for reinforcements to his Washington advisers, and soon the two groups were circling each other, clashing over how to proceed. It took time for relations to shake out.

Tempers flared during the traditional mock hearings, as Gorsuch argued with the questioners and pressed back on suggested answers. He often warned the White House that he could always "pick up his bat and ball and return to Colorado," where he could remain a prominent federal appeals court judge for the rest of his life while the president would lose one of his few notable accomplishments to date.

"Neil basically said, 'I am my own man, I am going to decide how to answer these questions, and you guys just leave me alone,'" recalled one senior person involved in the prep work. He said Gorsuch's thought was that "I don't need you to tell me what I think, and if you don't like what I think I can go back to Colorado."

Tensions were raw but eventually settled down as the Washington advisers and the collection of former clerks found their respective roles. Both sides began to feel better about the prospects, with the hearing set to begin in mid-March.

One Horse-Sized Duck

DEMOCRATS WERE DISTURBED and distracted by the ongoing chaos of the Trump takeover as the Gorsuch hearings before the Judiciary Committee approached. Progressive advocates worried that Democratic senators had so far not laid a glove on the nominee. In retrospect, Democrats realized they were ill prepared for the Gorsuch proceedings.

They had struggled to define him, and the media's focus was fully on the Trump frenzy. The nomination was not getting the attention it normally would. One area where Democrats seemed to make some headway was on the issue of workers' rights, highlighting a case in which Gorsuch had sided against a truck driver who was fired for leaving his disabled vehicle and its load in potentially life-threatening sub-zero weather. The trucker won his appeal and Gorsuch came off as coldhearted in what became known as the case of the frozen trucker.

Gorsuch also encountered another last-minute snag. A former woman student of his at the University of Colorado law school said that the judge, a part-time instructor there, had suggested that women sometimes manipulate law firms to get maternity benefits but then leave after the child is born. Such a sentiment would have implications for Gorsuch's views on women, an important aspect of the hearing given concerns about abortion rights and discrimination.

But as the judge's confirmation hearing began in the large Hart Senate Office Building room equipped for special high-profile events, the nominee appeared in little trouble. Democrats would either back him or Republicans would change Senate rules and install him over their objections.

A few of Gorsuch's advisers lingered around the back of the hearing room as reporters and the public funneled in for what is always one of the most intriguing shows in Washington—a full-blown Supreme Court confirmation showdown. As they awaited the start, one Gorsuch strategist was pressed on the idea that Gorsuch was eager to be confirmed so he could take his seat on the court and exact his revenge on Washington for how it had treated his mother decades earlier.

One of the officials smiled knowingly. "That's our theory too," he said.

The hearing got under way but didn't get far before Senator Feinstein, the top Democrat on the committee, revisited a very sore subject. "We are here today under very unusual circumstances. It was almost a year ago today that President Obama nominated Chief Judge Merrick Garland for this seat," she said. "Unfortunately, due to unprecedented treatment, Judge Garland was denied a hearing, and this vacancy has been in place for well over a year. I just want to say I am deeply disappointed that it is under these circumstances that we begin our hearings."

It would be far from the last time Garland's name would come up during the hearing for a seat that Democrats believed rightfully belonged to him.

McGahn had arrived proudly with Gorsuch and intended to monitor the entire hearing. But other events interrupted. Over in the House, the FBI director, James Comey, had picked the same day to inform the Intelligence Committee that the agency was investigating whether members of Trump's campaign had conspired with Russia to interfere with the presidential election the previous year. It was another crisis for the White House. Gorsuch would have to continue without McGahn, his sponsor, looking on and consulting.

In her opening remarks, Feinstein noted Gorsuch's dissent in the truck driver case and his call to strip bureaucrats of some of their power to write rules to carry out the broad legislative mandate of Congress. "Such a change in law would dramatically affect how laws passed by Congress can be properly carried out," she warned.

Under Senate tradition, Gorsuch was introduced at the hearing by his home state senators, Republican Cory Gardner and Michael Bennet. For Bennet, a Democrat with national ambitions, it posed a dilemma.

Democrats were lined up against Gorsuch, but it would be bad form for Bennet to repudiate a judge from Colorado with the potential to be on the Supreme Court for decades. Gorsuch had bipartisan support in Colorado's business and political community. Perhaps more important, Gorsuch was a favorite of Philip Anschutz, the conservative Denver billionaire who'd once hired Bennet and given him business opportunities when he arrived in Colorado. Anschutz had then backed Bennet politically. Bennet, a younger Democrat from the New West, was playing a long game, hoping to become part of a national ticket at some point or at least a major Democratic figure.

In his introduction, Bennet noted that Gorsuch "exemplifies some of the finest qualities of Colorado, a state filled with people who are kind to one another, who, by and large, do not share the conceit that one party or one ideology is all right and the other all wrong." But he also noted that Gorsuch was a nominee solely because of the Republican mistreatment of Garland.

"The Senate's failure to do its duty with respect to Judge Garland was an embarrassment to this body that will be recorded in history and in the lives of millions of Americans. And it is tempting to deny Judge Gorsuch a fair hearing because of the Senate's prior failure. But, Mr. Chairman, two wrongs never make a right. The Supreme Court is too important for us not to find a way to end our destructive gridlock and bitter partisanship. In my mind, I consider Judge Gorsuch as a candidate to fill the Garland seat on the Supreme Court."

As questioning began the next morning, Grassley sought to defuse one of the most explosive elements: whether Gorsuch would be able to take on Trump, the president who had promoted him for the court opening.

"I would like to have you describe, in any way you want to, what judicial independence means and specifically tell us whether you would have any trouble ruling against a president who appointed you," Grassley said.

Gorsuch, supremely self-assured and confident in his expertise before this rapt panel of politicians, batted such concerns away. "That is a softball, Mr. Chairman," he said, his tone oozing with certainty acquired in years of talking to juries. "I have no difficulty ruling against or for any party other than based on what the law and the facts in the particular case require, and I am heartened by the support I have received from people who recognize that there is no such thing as a Republican judge or a Democratic judge. We just have judges in this country."

That set the tone for the hearing. Like most of his recent predecessors in the same seat, he refused to deal in specifics on cases concerning abortion and gun rights, saying it could prejudice his involvement in future cases.

If he indicated his agreement or disagreement with past precedents, Gorsuch said, "I am signaling to future litigants that I cannot be a fair judge in their case because those issues keep coming up. All of these issues, as you point out, keep coming up."

Another thing he had no answer for was a question by Senator Leahy on if he thought Garland had been treated fairly by the very committee he was now testifying before.

"Senator, as I explained to you before, I cannot get involved in politics," Gorsuch replied, citing "judicial canons" prohibiting it. "I think it would be very imprudent of judges to start commenting on political disputes between themselves or the various branches."

It was quickly clear that Gorsuch, though deeply knowledgeable about the law, was not going to give any answers that would complicate his ascension to the high court. He peppered his answers with folksy "goshes" and "gollies" for good measure. It was the standard jousting match, in which the nominee has the easy out of saying he cannot respond to a matter that might come before the court. Gorsuch did jump, though, at the opportunity to respond to the claim that he had shown sexism while teaching his law school class in Boulder.

He said the question about taking advantage of maternity benefits arose from a standard legal ethics textbook that he taught in his class and that the idea of the question was to have the students reason through how they should handle such situations—situations Gorsuch said he found disturbing.

Gorsuch was breezing. As the hearing wore on, amused Republicans practically abandoned serious questioning and asked Gorsuch questions about sports, the practice of kids trying to ride sheep in rodeos, and his experiences with Byron "Whizzer" White, the former justice from Colorado who was a storied college and professional athlete and played basketball with clerks on the court inside The Court.

"How is his jump shot?" asked Ted Cruz.

Jeff Flake probably took the cake with his question, offering one sent to him by a family member as the hearing veered into absurdity. "My son, Dallin, a teenager, said, 'Ask him if he would rather fight a hundred duck-sized horses or one horse-sized duck,'" Flake said.

"You got me," said Gorsuch.

One last bit of intramural drama took place. As Gorsuch was being questioned, the Supreme Court, located just one block away, reversed a ruling based on a 2008 opinion Gorsuch had issued in a separate legal fight over the responsibility a school district had in providing programs for autistic children. Chief Justice Roberts wrote the unanimous decision, which again made Gorsuch seem hard-hearted in setting low expectations for special education. A person close to the Supreme Court said that the justices debated the timing but that Roberts decided to go ahead, believing it would make the high court look good—though at Gorsuch's expense. Roberts was essentially hazing Gorsuch at his big moment in the Senate spotlight.

"A number of the other justices thought it was very impolitic," the source said. "There were a couple of justices who were pretty pissed off at Roberts. It was not a good way to start the relationship." It was embarrassing for Gorsuch, and Roberts had obviously timed it to be so, since there was no real reason the court had to issue the ruling that day.

Senator Durbin confronted Gorsuch with the ruling just before a lunch break, and it was probably Gorsuch's worst moment—both his legal judgment and his humanity had been found lacking by the court he was supposed to join.

Gorsuch sought to explain.

"If anyone is suggesting that I like a result where an autistic child happens to lose, it is a heartbreaking accusation to me, heartbreaking. But the fact of the matter is, I was bound by circuit precedent.

"I was wrong, Senator. I was wrong because I was bound by circuit precedent, and I am sorry," he said.

For someone as confident and proud as Gorsuch, it had to be difficult. He was very angry over the turn of events.

Gorsuch may have been coasting through his hearing, but some of his prospective future colleagues wanted to see a little humility. Still, the hearing was effectively over, with Democrats unable to do much damage.

22

Nuclear Winter

ALMOST SINCE THE Gorsuch nomination was made, a small group of senators had been in talks to try to avoid a showdown that would allow the Senate to change the rules on filibusters against Supreme Court nominees. Bennet was particularly determined to do what he could, because he didn't want to be caught in a conflict in which he either would have to filibuster a home state nominee or break with most of his fellow Democrats. Like many others, Bennet also believed the constant one-upmanship in the judicial fights was destroying the Senate.

Hoping to build a new iteration of the Gang of Fourteen that had averted the nuclear option in 2005, Bennet turned to two of the remaining members of that group: John McCain and Susan Collins. Other Republicans such as Thom Tillis of North Carolina and Bob Corker of Tennessee expressed modest interest. On Bennet's side, he was working in concert with Senator Chris Coons of Delaware, a more centrist Democrat on the Judiciary Committee and another senator worried about the future of the Senate.

The idea was fairly simple—Democrats would provide the sixty votes needed to clear the way for an up-or-down vote on Gorsuch if the Republicans would agree not to support a rules change on the next nominee if the person represented a sharp change in the ideological makeup of the court. Bennet and Coons sought to rally their colleagues and offered various proposals. But things had changed since 2005. Democrats had already upended the rules to their advantage in 2013; Republicans thought it was only fair that they get a chance to do the same.

McCain told Bennet that he respected the attempt but didn't sense the same resolve in the Senate to avert the conflict. "There was a feeling that it was just not doable," recalled Bennet, who said McCain told him that "it doesn't feel to me like we are going to make it happen this time."

Bennet said that there seemed to be an easy acceptance by the two leaders, McConnell and Schumer, that a change in the rules was unavoidable. Schumer needed to show that Democrats would do whatever they could even if they could not prevail. McConnell wanted revenge for 2013 and to show Democrats that he had been right that year when he predicted Democrats would come to regret the power play. The two leaders never even met to discuss the idea of resolving the fight without a change in rules, a fact that perplexed Bennet.

"It is absolutely incredible that it was not in the job description of either the majority or the minority leader to have a discussion of whether we wanted to surf over this cliff before we did," said Bennet, who considered the 2013 nuclear option to have been a gigantic mistake. "It was all done in good faith, but we never got close to making a deal."

Though a deal seemed out of reach, that didn't mean that Republicans and conservative activists weren't worried. They were determined to change the rules now rather than risk waiting until the second confirmation, when Democrats might be able to prevail. Leonard Leo and other activists did what they could to sabotage any agreement.

"The last two weeks of the fight before the cloture vote, our hair was on fire," said Leo, who reached out to Republicans daily to keep them from weakening and not make any agreement over the filibuster. "We had a heck of time keeping everyone together."

The floor vote was imminent. Schumer, the Democratic leader, offered to meet with Republicans and Trump to discuss a new nominee to head off the climactic rules change, but that idea was a nonstarter.

One last hiccup emerged when Gorsuch was accused of plagiarizing some of his academic writings, but, like the complaint of sexism in the law class, it didn't really gain traction. Given events to come, the plagiarism charge seemed almost quaint.

On April 6, 2017, the Senate convened to consider the Gorsuch nomination, and everyone knew what was ahead. McConnell opened the debate by reciting a history of the court fights, blaming the Democrats for most of the turmoil and delivering a vow: "This will be the first and last partisan filibuster of a Supreme Court nomination," McConnell said, stating clearly that he intended to use the same procedure Reid had used nearly four years earlier to overturn the procedure on lower-court nominees.

As expected, the attempt to cut off debate then failed on a 55–45 vote. Four Democrats, including Bennet, voted with the Republicans. McConnell then successfully set in motion the process to set the threshold for cutting off the filibuster of a Supreme Court nominee at a simple majority. It was approved. The Senate's second nuclear war in four years was over. McConnell high-fived Cornyn.

Gorsuch was confirmed the next day on a 54–45 vote. It was April 7, the exact day McGahn's memo predicted that he would be approved, before Gorsuch was even nominated.

Gorsuch would not have been named to the court had it not been for McConnell. The new justice seemed to recognize that fact with a September 2017 visit and speech at the McConnell Center at the University of Louisville—a center near and dear to the Senate leader's heart. Nothing prohibited Gorsuch from appearing with McConnell. But to many, making such a high-profile speech with McConnell as one of his first public events outside the court smacked of returning the favor—as did a later speech at the Trump International Hotel in Washington.

In Louisville, Gorsuch touted his ability to interpret the law impartially no matter the outcome. "Sometimes the good guy loses and the bad guy wins," Gorsuch said. "But that is what the law demands."

23

Giving the Slip to the Blue Slip

GORSUCH'S CONFIRMATION WAS a triumph for Trump and his new team, but it was only the beginning as far as McGahn, McConnell, Grassley, and the Federalist Society were concerned. They had plans well beyond the Supreme Court, which hears relatively few cases each year. It was in the lower courts, particularly the federal appeals courts, where far-reaching precedent could be set outside the high-profile legal arena of the Supreme Court. The appeals courts would be a crucial venue for upholding conservative ideals and weakening liberal policy and government power.

In agreeing to become White House counsel, McGahn had reached a unique agreement with Trump, one that granted him tremendous power. McGahn had insisted that if he were to take the job, he would have almost unfettered authority to pick candidates for the federal courts for approval and nomination by the president. It was a significant change in White House practice, but McGahn had delivered for Trump with his consultation on the judicial list and earned his confidence over their months together. Trump granted his request with no resistance.

Previous administrations reviewed and picked judges via judicial recommendation committees, exhaustive review, and consultation with the Justice Department. McGahn wanted to dispense with all that, markedly speeding up the process and giving him a degree of control unknown to past White House counsels. The stage was set for a swift Trump administration assault on scores of vacancies on the federal bench, many open due to Republicans' refusal to fill seats while Obama was president.

Under the rules change of 2013, a Republican president, in concert with a cooperative Republican Senate, could install dozens and dozens of federal judges if the Senate was simply willing to devote the time to the task. No Democratic votes would be needed to approve a single judge with the threshold set at a simple majority vote. Still, the underlying process would chew up a considerable amount of the Senate's floor time, a valuable commodity considering the Senate's relatively short workweek since senators typically arrive Monday evening and depart Thursday afternoon.

McConnell, seeing the federal courts as a major element of his legacy and basking in the conservative approbation of holding the Scalia seat open, was certainly willing to devote the time and effort. There just wasn't that much else to do, given the polarization of the Senate and little agreement on legislation, which in nearly all cases still required sixty votes to advance. The filibuster remained in place for legislation.

But to guarantee McConnell was on board, the first appellate court nominee that Trump put forward, on March 21, 2017, was Amul Thapar, the conservative Kentucky district court judge who was a favorite of the majority leader. Thapar had also been interviewed for the Scalia vacancy as a courtesy to him and to McConnell, though he was not a serious contender for the post. Eager to cement a bond with McConnell, Trump and McGahn pushed Thapar forward for the appeals court after Gorsuch got the Supreme Court opening.

By elevating him from the district court, Trump kept Thapar in line for possible future Supreme Court consideration while simultaneously stroking McConnell. Thapar would be confirmed in May 2017 just as McGahn and the Trump administration were beginning to accelerate the push to fill more than 120 vacancies on the bench.

Trump's list of Supreme Court candidates was proving to be valuable not just for the high court, but for the lower-court vacancies as well. The first wave of appeals court nominees named in May included two state supreme court justices who had been on the high court list—David Stras of Minnesota, who had clerked for Clarence Thomas, and Joan Larsen of Michigan, a former Scalia clerk. The initial set of nominations also included Amy Coney Barrett, a law professor at Notre Dame Law School with a rock star reputation in conservative legal circles.

Republicans hailed the first judicial foray from the White House, with Cornyn saying Trump had a "tremendous opportunity" to fill the courts with judges with glittering conservative credentials and records.

Democrats and their liberal allies were alarmed, accusing the Trump administration of moving forward without the traditional consultation with senators of both parties. They threatened roadblocks. "They are not going to get any cooperation unless they bring us into the process," Durbin, the Illinois Democrat, said. "The Republicans taught us a lesson. You can delay things with impunity."

Democrats didn't hold many cards, but they still had one weapon to thwart determined Republicans. Despite multiple changes in Senate rules, Democrats could still hold up judicial nominees through what was known as the blue slip process—a remaining bit of Senate arcana.

The blue slip referred to an actual blue slip of paper on which senators registered their approval or objections to judicial nominees from their home states; they could also signal their objection by refusing to return a blue slip altogether. In fact, it was the recalcitrance by Republicans to return blue slips during the Obama years that led to many of the judicial openings that the White House and Senate Republicans were now so giddy about filling.

Pat Leahy, the Democratic Judiciary Committee chairman, enforced a strict blue slip rule—no slip, no hearing—and the vacancies piled up as Republicans refused to hand back blue slips on the president's nominees. Some in the Obama White House joined counsel

Kathryn Ruemmler in embracing the idea of relaxing the policy to enable the administration to push through more nominees. This drew a stiff rebuke from Leahy, who would brook no White House meddling in committee business. Then the Obama administration's pursuit of Republican blue slips backfired when, in a deal with the two Senate Republicans from Georgia, the administration nominated a Republican choice adamantly opposed by House and Senate Democrats for his antiabortion, pro–Confederate flag record. The nomination died.

The obscure Judiciary Committee practice dated back to 1917 and was essentially a way for home state senators to protect their patronage rights over judicial picks. The blue slip originated to force the White House to consult with senators on nominees who would be interpreting the law in their states and to make sure their political allies got the powerful, highly respected positions. Senators had good reason to hang together on the subject. If the White House was willing to go against the wishes of one, it would probably be willing to go against the wishes of another. So when home state senators objected, other senators would support them on the grounds they might later need similar protection themselves. The question of who sat on the federal court in a state was seldom of enough importance to cause political waves for senators in other states, so they could support their colleagues at little risk. But the blue slip was considered mainly advisory during that period.

Then in the mid-1950s, James O. Eastland, the Mississippi Democrat and segregationist, took over the Judiciary Committee. He began enforcing a strict blue slip policy but had a special purpose in mind. With the Supreme Court beginning to hand down civil rights rulings that would need to be interpreted and enforced by other federal courts, the identity and political views of federal court nominees suddenly took on new importance for Eastland and others in the South. He wanted more control over the makeup of the judiciary, and the blue slip was a way to ensure it. Like the Dixiecrat use of the filibuster to block civil rights legislation, the blue slip became another procedural tool of conservative Southern Democrats opposed to federal civil rights intervention. Eastland remained chairman for nearly two decades, and the blue slip became ingrained as a Senate tradition.

Still, the policy was not chiseled into the Senate's rules and was totally dependent on the discretion of the committee chairman. Upon Eastland's departure, successive chairmen treated the blue slip differently and allowed some leeway. Joe Biden, for example, overruled objections from fellow Democrats and allowed some judges to move forward despite blue slip issues. Orrin Hatch also allowed some deviation.

But enforcing blue slip approval was much more the rule than the exception, and Democratic chairmen refrained from considering judges who did not have home state Republican approval. The Congressional Research Service found that since 1979, only three judicial nominees out of hundreds were approved after receiving a negative blue slip from one senator; none were approved with negative blue slips from both. Obviously, exceptions were few and far between.

With Obama's election, Republicans were unnerved enough in 2009 by the prospect that Democrats might drop the blue slip practice that all GOP senators signed on to a letter urging the new president to respect the tradition when it came to naming judges. "Despite press reports that the Chairman of the Judiciary Committee now may be considering changing the Committee's practice of observing senatorial courtesy, we, as a Conference, expect it to be observed, even-handedly and regardless of party affiliation," all forty-one Republican senators wrote Obama in March. "And we will act to preserve this principle and the rights of our colleagues if it is not."

Despite the Republican fears, Leahy was a strict constructionist when it came to blue slips and adhered faithfully to the policy, costing Democrats opportunities to install judges. But with Trump as president and scores of court openings around the nation, Senate Republicans would not be so devoted to the blue slip now that it was their turn in the majority. The last barrier to advancing judges over objections from the minority was about to fall.

The first real hint came from McConnell during an interview with the *New York Times* for its *New Washington* podcast in September 2017. The Senate leader was at first reluctant to provide his view on the blue slip, noting that it was the purview of the Judiciary Committee chairman, who at that time was Grassley. But then McConnell volunteered his own opinion. "My personal view is that the blue slip, with regard to circuit court appointments, ought to simply be a notification of how you're going to vote, not the opportunity to blackball," McConnell said.

With that comment, the majority leader sent a clear signal to Grassley that he should not allow Democrats to use the blue slip as a veto over Trump's nominees for much of the country. It should be strictly advisory for nominees for appeals courts, which often had jurisdiction over multiple states. The issue was geographic. Though Republicans had the majority, the Senate was narrowly divided. And given the way multistate appeals courts were dispersed, Democrats could block appointments in a wide swath of the country if they failed to return blue slips.

The huge—and liberal—US Court of Appeals for the Ninth Circuit was a prime example. The court's jurisdiction covered California, Oregon, Washington, Hawaii, Idaho, Montana, Nevada, Alaska, and Arizona. Of those states, California, Washington, Oregon, and Hawaii were each represented by two Democrats, while Montana and Nevada had one Democratic senator apiece. Under a strict interpretation of the policy, Republicans might not be able to confirm any appeals court nominees for those states. And there were plenty of other circuits where Democrats loomed large. McConnell was not about to miss his moment because of some arcane Senate tradition that was virtually unknown to the public. If he could withstand the heat from blocking Garland, eliminating the blue slip would be a cinch.

Grassley, hoping to maintain some semblance of independence, was in no rush to tear up the blue slip. While he noted there had historically been exceptions to the rule, he continued to resist pressure from his colleagues, the White House, and the Federalist Society to abandon the practice. He tried to work with Democrats and Republicans, personally visiting their offices to obtain their signatures. The White House was ordered to record all contacts with senators over nominations so he could produce evidence of consultation before he overrode any objections. Grassley was ever cognizant of being seen as a fair chairman and cared what his colleagues thought of him, despite his need to appease his base as well.

He had some success getting Democratic buy-in for a handful of circuit judges from some of the states represented solely by Democrats—Illinois, New York, New Mexico, and Hawaii among them. He also got the Democratic senators Debbie Stabenow and Gary Peters of Michigan to go along with the nomination of Joan Larsen for the Sixth Circuit Court of Appeals, a victory for Grassley considering that Larsen, a former state supreme court justice, had been on Trump's Supreme Court list.

It was with Justice David Stras of Minnesota that the first sign of blue slip trouble surfaced. Stras, the former Thomas clerk and a member of the Federalist Society, was also on the high court list. But with that vacancy filled, Trump nominated him for a seat on the US Court of Appeals for the Eighth Circuit. As his nomination moved through the early stages, Senator Al Franken, the former *Saturday Night Live* writer and performer turned progressive activist and then Minnesota senator, announced he would not be returning a blue slip on Stras, who as a supreme court justice in Minnesota had been popularly elected.

"I have grown concerned that, if confirmed to the federal bench, Justice Stras would be a deeply conservative jurist in the mold of Supreme Court Justices Clarence Thomas and Antonin Scalia, justices who the nominee himself has identified as role models," Franken said in a statement. As a member of the Judiciary Committee, Franken had been praised for his tough questioning of Gorsuch during the nomination hearing and was gaining credibility on judicial nomination issues despite his lack of a law degree. That he wasn't a lawyer helped him simplify issues and get to the heart of the matter rather than focus on legal procedure and technicalities.

The fight was on. A conservative judicial group immediately placed a TV ad assailing Franken for obstructing Stras.

"Justice David Stras earned more votes and a higher percentage of the vote statewide than Senator Al Franken did," said Carrie Severino, counsel to the Judicial Crisis Network. "Franken is trying to block the Judiciary Committee from even reviewing Justice Stras's sterling record, and his refusal to return the blue slip for Justice Stras is unacceptable. By not returning his blue slip, Senator Franken is choosing Washington politics over the people of Minnesota."

Franken, a darling of the Left who was even being mentioned as a possible presidential candidate, won the backing of liberal advocacy groups for trying to stand in the way of Stras by employing one of the few alternatives available to Democrats.

But an unrelated, explosive news story gave Grassley an opening to roll over Franken. In November 2017, Franken became the latest high-profile man to come under scrutiny for sexual misconduct after a photo surfaced showing a grinning Franken groping a sleeping woman companion on a 2006 USO tour. The moment was at the start of the #MeToo movement, when women worldwide began to fight back against ingrained sexual harassment and assault. More accusations followed against Franken from women who said the senator had groped and tried to kiss them without consent. Franken was in deep trouble. Republicans demanded an ethics inquiry, and Democratic women senators were deeply unhappy at the prospect of having to defend Franken. At the same time, Democrats were trying to win a special Senate election in Alabama, one in which the Republican candidate, Roy Moore, was accused of taking advantage of teenage girls in the past. Democrats didn't want to look like they were protecting one of their own. Franken was on the defensive.

On the very day that the Minnesota Democrat issued his first statement and apology for his behavior, Grassley announced that he would convene a hearing for Stras despite Franken's refusal to provide a blue slip. It could not have been a coincidence. Franken was under siege and in no position to fight back.

Grassley did his best to make it appear that he was not abandoning the blue slip courtesy—at least for partisan reasons. He simultaneously announced that he would also conduct a hearing for Kyle Duncan, a nominee to the Fifth Circuit who was being opposed by Senator John Kennedy, a Louisiana Republican who was gaining an increasingly visible role on the Judiciary Committee.

"Let me be clear: I will maintain the blue slip courtesy," Grassley said, but he also made it clear that by that, he meant he would treat it as advisory and weigh other factors in deciding to move ahead. He certainly wasn't maintaining the standard followed by Leahy, though just a few years earlier Grassley had joined his colleagues in demanding that Obama and Leahy do so.

Grassley then made a point that was becoming clear to many of those inside and outside the Senate following the judicial fights. The blue slip had been such a potent weapon mainly because it had been backed up by the threat of a filibuster on the floor. In the rare cases where the committee chairman had decided to ignore a blue slip objection, the offended senator could then try to defeat the nomination through a filibuster. Other senators, worried about their own prerogative, would then support their colleague in case they needed the same help later. But the filibuster against nominees had been fatally weakened in 2013, and now the blue slip was exposed, vulnerable, and headed for the Senate scrap heap.

"The Democrats seriously regret that they abolished the filibuster, as I warned them they would. But they can't expect to use the blue slip courtesy in its place. That's not what the blue slip is meant for," Grassley said.

Besides Franken's very serious political troubles, his cause with Stras had been harmed by the fact that his home state Democratic colleague,

Senator Amy Klobuchar, a former prosecutor and more senior member of the Judiciary Committee, had returned a blue slip on Stras. It gave Grassley credibility in claiming Stras had some Democratic backing and that Franken was acting as a partisan. "I won't allow senators to prevent a committee hearing for political or ideological reasons," Grassley said. "Using the blue slip for these purposes is not consistent with historical practice."

Franken, in an astounding political fall, announced on December 7 that he would resign. Stras was confirmed by the Senate the next month, on January 30, becoming the first appeals court judge in decades to be confirmed without positive blue slips from both senators from a state.

"Democrat and Republican chairs have stuck to the blue slip rule despite the tensions in this body," Schumer said. "So this is a major step back, and another way that the majority is slowly, inexorably, gnawing away at the way this body works and making it more and more like the House of Representatives. It's not a legacy, if I were the leader or a member of that party, that I would be proud of."

Republicans were proud of it. They were winning, and the change in the tradition didn't seem to bother them. Grassley said it was Leahy's own choice to so strictly interpret the blue slip and that he was not bound by his predecessor, particularly considering the Democratic decision to nuke the filibuster on nominees. But his position was in stark contrast to the one he had taken in 2015 in an op-ed in the *Des Moines Register*.

"Over the years, Judiciary Committee chairs of both parties have upheld a blue-slip process, including Sen. Patrick Leahy of Vermont, my immediate predecessor in chairing the committee, who steadfastly honored the tradition even as some in his own party called for its demise," he wrote. "I appreciate the value of the blue-slip process and also intend to honor it."

In an interview, Grassley conceded he had increasingly deviated from blue slip enforcement but said he was justified. "Maybe I've just had a few more exceptions than other people have had," Grassley said. "But then the process of the Senate has changed a lot since Reid went ahead with his nuclear option. They used to argue for the nuclear option that forty-one senators shouldn't be able to hold up a nominee, so they change it to fifty-one," he said, referring to simple majority approval. "So now, after making that argument, then they want to say one senator not returning a blue slip can hold somebody up? As far as I'm concerned, that is legitimate when you have everything in one state. But when you have several states in a circuit and when one state doesn't fill up its slots, then that makes all the work for the others."

The judicial spigots were now almost fully open, and Trump, through the determination of McGahn, McConnell, and Grassley, intended to let the nominees flow.

24

The Trump Judiciary

As the Trump administration moved into its second year, the machinery of installing conservative federal judges was humming along. The president himself could hardly believe his good fortune.

"You know, when I got in, we had over one hundred federal judges that weren't appointed," Trump told a crowd in Richfield, Ohio, in March 2018, referring to the number of vacancies left by Obama. "Now, I don't know why Obama left that. It was like a big, beautiful present to all of us. Why the hell did he leave that?" Trump asked to roaring applause. "Maybe he got complacent."

Obama had not gotten complacent. Lack of any sort of cooperation from Republicans had thwarted the president for years. Then when Republicans took control of the Senate in 2015, hardly any judicial nominees advanced. Trump would take nearly any opportunity to cast aspersions on Obama and ridicule his predecessor. He was exultant about the number of openings on the federal bench.

"Now we have about one hundred and forty-five federal district court judges. We have seventeen court of appeals judges," he said. "Think of one hundred and forty-five district judges. That's world-changing, country-changing, USA-changing. And we're going all out."

While he was wrong about Obama, he was right about the implications of being able to fill all those slots now that both the filibuster and the blue slip were so badly weakened and Democrats had no real way to prevent a crush of conservative judicial confirmations.

"We were left a present," a giddy Trump told his supporters, calling it a "gift from heaven. We were left judges. They're the ones that judge on your disputes. They judge on what's fair on the environment and what's not fair; where they're going to take your farms and factories away and where they are not. Amazing. It was the gift. Thank you very much, President Obama. We all appreciate it. Thank you. What happened? How did he do that?"

McGahn was the White House powerhouse on judges, but Trump was getting a better sense of the role of the federal courts. He had already been thwarted in some initiatives by federal judges willing to push back against his policies, so he knew they could stop him. He knew about the power and the influence of the courts in interpreting federal policy, and he was reveling in his ability to put people on the courts who, at least from their records, shared an anti-regulatory, anti–government intervention view of the world.

Unlike many others who might privately hold such beliefs, Trump spoke about the courts and judges in stark political terms. Judges like to portray themselves as somehow above politics, saying they don't wear *R*s or *D*s on their robes. Cases regularly popped up of judges appointed by Republicans who crossed up conservatives or someone appointed by Clinton or Obama who joined in conservative opinions. But the outcome of many cases could also be easily predicted based on the party of the president who appointed the judge.

The Supreme Court was increasingly being split into blocs, pitting the minority Democratic appointees against the majority Republican appointees. In the case of Garland, for instance, Republicans had been confident that while he projected a more moderate temperament and point of view, he would still regularly side with the other justices who had been nominated by Democrats in his decisions.

Trump cut through much of the high-minded malarkey about the neutrality of judges with a single tweet.

"We need more Republicans in 2018 and must ALWAYS hold the Supreme Court," he tweeted in the run-up to the midterms. To Trump, the Supreme Court was like a legislative body that was simply the product of politics.

Republicans were thrilled about their record in confirming judges in 2017. It was one of their singular achievements, since their legislative record was thin, as the party finally passed a significant tax cut only under pressure at the end of the year and had failed miserably to repeal the health care law despite seven years to prepare for the opportunity. Judges were a high-water mark, and McConnell made sure to emphasize it at every turn. "Senate Continues Historic Judicial Confirmation Process," screamed the headline on a press release from McConnell's communications operations.

By mid-December, the Senate had confirmed twelve new appeals court judges, the most of any president ever in his first year. Some Trump judges were being put on the bench despite being rated as not qualified by the American Bar Association, which once had significant influence over the judicial confirmation process. Its role was being diminished by Republicans except when it worked in their favor, such as in the case of the Gorsuch nomination.

Republicans were breaking other Senate norms in their rush to get judges on the bench, including stacking multiple nominees at one hearing, a practice that had been avoided in the past because it split the attention on the nominees and shortened the time available for lawmakers to question them.

The rapid pace did produce some embarrassing mistakes. As the judicial assembly line rolled to the end of 2017, a handful of federal district court judges had to withdraw due to a lack of qualifications and other factors.

One, Brett Talley, a thirty-six-year-old nominee for a district court seat in Alabama, had failed to disclose on his nomination papers that his wife was chief of staff to McGahn. Talley had been unanimously rated unqualified by the ABA and had some other interesting elements in his background, including being an author of horror stories and a paranormal investigator. He had also written some highly partisan blog posts and had defended the Ku Klux Klan. He had advanced out of the Judiciary Committee on a party-line vote, but his problems compounded, and Grassley urged the White House to pull back the nomination.

Perhaps the poster boy for the rushed nomination process was Matthew Petersen, a former colleague of McGahn's at the Federal Election Commission. McGahn was eyeing Petersen, who had been educated in Utah, for a district court seat in that state and had persuaded Senators Orrin Hatch and Mike Lee, the two Utah Republicans, to go along. But a district court seat for the District of Columbia became available, and McGahn instead had Trump nominate Petersen for that opening, a move that exposed Petersen somewhat since he would have no Senate patrons for his nomination. (The District of Columbia has no representation in the Senate—and it would be Democratic if it did!)

Petersen appeared before the Judiciary Committee on December 13 and ran into a buzz saw in the form of Senator Kennedy from Louisiana, who seemed to be taking it upon himself to expose the shortcomings of some of the administration's judicial nominations. In a series of questions that constituted one of the most painful inquisitions in Senate memory, Kennedy highlighted Petersen's total absence of trial experience—a shortcoming that could complicate the performance of a federal district court judge.

The exchange disclosed that Petersen, a regulatory lawyer, had never tried a case to a verdict in any court, had never taken a deposition on his own, was not at all familiar with rules of trial procedure or evidence, and could not define motion in limine, a basic motion to exclude evidence in civil and criminal trials.

"I would probably not be able to give you a good definition right here at the table," he said as Kennedy humiliated him.

Petersen, who also worked as a committee counsel in the Senate and House, sought to defend himself. "I understand the challenge that would be ahead of me if I were fortunate enough to become a district court judge," he told Kennedy. "I understand that the path that many successful district court judges have taken has been a different one than I have taken."

But the damage was done. It was a brutal takedown, and the video of the questioning went viral after Senator Sheldon Whitehouse tweeted out a link.

"MUST WATCH: Republican @SenJohnKennedy asks one of @real DonaldTrump's US District Judge nominees basic questions of law & he can't answer a single one," Whitehouse tweeted. "Hoo-boy."

On December 16, Petersen sent a letter to Trump withdrawing his nomination.

"I write to inform you that I am withdrawing from consideration to be a United States District Judge for the District of Columbia. While I am honored to have been nominated for this position, it has become clear to me over the past few days that my nomination has become a distraction and that is not fair to you or your Administration," Petersen wrote. He sought to justify his performance, saying that the district's federal court was focused on the kind of administrative and constitutional law in which he had expertise through his work in Congress and on the FEC.

"I had hoped that my nearly two decades of public service might carry more weight than my two worst minutes on television," he wrote. "However, I am no stranger to political realities, and I do not wish to be a continued distraction from the important work of your Administration and the Senate." He remained at the FEC.

Kennedy, interviewed by a New Orleans TV station, said Petersen should not have been nominated for the influential position in the first place. "Just because you've seen *My Cousin Vinny* doesn't qualify you to be a federal judge," Kennedy said. "And he has no litigation experience. And my job on the Judiciary Committee is to catch him. I would strongly suggest he not give up his day job."

Kennedy, a former Democrat who was quickly becoming a highly quotable member of the Senate, seemed to be one of the few Republicans interested in challenging some of Trump's nominees. He had refused to return a blue slip on one and clashed with McGahn, whose law firm had represented some political opponents of Kennedy. But Kennedy was still more cooperative than not.

The implosion of a few nominees with ties to McGahn suggested to some people the pitfalls of giving one person such power over judicial nominations. "There is good and bad," said one Republican involved in the nomination process with McGahn. "You can be swift without a committee, but there are no checks and balances."

Despite the occasional setbacks, the judicial parade marched on in 2018. Perhaps the nomination that most galled Democrats was that of Michael B. Brennan, a Milwaukee lawyer and former state judge. An active Republican and ally of then-governor Scott Walker, Brennan was first picked in August 2017 for an appeals court post that had been vacant since 2010.

When the slot first became open, Obama had nominated Victoria Nourse, a University of Wisconsin law professor and former Senate Judiciary Committee counsel, picking her from four candidates recommended by a special state review commission used by senators of both parties. Senators set up these committees in several states to eliminate some of the politics from judicial selection.

Nourse was highly regarded in Washington as one of those who had helped Biden, then a senator, write the landmark Violence Against Women Act in the 1990s. But in a decision that would turn out to be fatal for Nourse, the Senate never moved forward on her selection before the midterm elections of 2010.

Obama renominated her at the start of 2011, but the Wisconsin political landscape had changed dramatically. Democrat Russ Feingold was defeated in the midterms by the Republican businessman

Ron Johnson. Johnson was not at all interested in moving forward with the Nourse nomination or that of another Wisconsin pick: Louis Butler, an African American and former state supreme court justice put up for a district court seat. Johnson dug in against both nominees and assailed the Obama administration for not consulting with him and instead renominating both candidates on the day Johnson was sworn in.

Kathryn Ruemmler, the White House counsel, met with both Johnson and Senator Herb Kohl, the remaining Wisconsin Democrat, in an attempt to break the impasse and was treated dismissively by Johnson, who wrote an op-ed in the *Milwaukee Journal Sentinel* criticizing Nourse's thin ties to the state.

"Nourse was not even licensed to practice law in Wisconsin until December 7, 2010, almost six months after Obama first nominated her," he said. "It is true she has been a professor at the University of Wisconsin Law School since 1993, but she has spent a third of that time teaching elsewhere. Most important, she has been a visiting professor outside of Wisconsin since 2008, teaching first at Emory University in Atlanta and then at Georgetown University in Washington, DC."

Johnson refused to return a blue slip on either nominee and got some support from a group of Wisconsin lawyers who weighed in on his behalf in a rebuttal to a newspaper editorial hitting Johnson for blocking the nomination. Their view was that since Democrats had not confirmed her when they had the chance, Johnson now had the right to oppose her.

"Nourse's nomination has not garnered the broad-based support it needs, so no one has made it a priority. Some of her supporters now rush to point fingers and assign blame to a senator who just wants to be heard and fulfill his constitutional duty of 'advice and consent.' Why can't Johnson, elected by the citizens of Wisconsin, participate in the selection of a judge for a Wisconsin seat on the Seventh Circuit, as Kohl did?" the attorneys wrote. One of those signing the rebuttal was Michael Brennan, the future nominee.

Stymied by Johnson, Nourse withdrew her nomination in 2012. Obama tried again in 2016, and his new candidate, Donald Schott, actually got a blue slip from Johnson and was voted out of the Judiciary Committee. But McConnell, thoroughly uninterested in installing Obama nominees in the president's last year, never brought Schott up for a vote.

The seat remained empty into 2017, and filling it was now the responsibility of President Trump. Senator Tammy Baldwin, who had been elected to replace Kohl after his retirement in 2012, urged the new administration to allow Wisconsin's judicial recommendation commission to work its will. But it was not to be. McGahn had his eye on Brennan and was not about to wait to see what came out of the nonpartisan group, a fact that irked Baldwin, who refused to return a blue slip.

"The president instead moved forward in a partisan manner, with a nominee preselected by the White House before our state's bipartisan process had even begun," she wrote Grassley in a lengthy complaint about the stacked deck for Brennan. "It is unacceptable and it is why I could not in good conscience return a blue slip on this nomination."

No matter: Grassley was ready to move ahead without her, and for the second time an appeals court judge without two home state blue slips headed toward approval.

During his confirmation hearing in January, Brennan was asked how he could support blocking a nomination over a blue slip in Nourse's case but not his own. He replied that the circumstances were different. And indeed they were: he was now the nominee.

As a result, a lawyer who had defended a senator's right to stall a nominee by denying a blue slip was the direct beneficiary of holding that vacancy open and was being confirmed despite the absence of a blue slip—but this time it was a Democratic senator who was not cooperating. Democrats and their allies were outraged.

"Mr. Brennan's nomination makes a mockery of the blue slip process," said Leahy. "And it makes a mockery of the time-tested process that home state senators have abided by in Wisconsin for decades. That should concern all of us."

Republicans were ecstatic. May was only half over, and the Senate had confirmed Brennan and five other appeals court nominees, giving Trump twenty-one in just eighteen months in office. "That means that nearly one-eighth of the circuit judges in America have been appointed by Donald Trump and confirmed by this Republican Senate," McConnell crowed as the sixth of the month was approved. "We think we're making dramatic progress on that front."

He, McGahn, Grassley, and Senate Republicans were relentless in trying to push through nominees, easily outpacing Obama when it came to judges. The Trump nominees tended to be white and young, some in their thirties and forties, meaning they could spend decades on the bench. By the end of 2018, Trump would see a total of thirty judges placed on appeals courts and fifty-three on district courts.

A few nominees continued to go awry, but only severe problems were keeping nominees off the bench, because of Republican solidarity.

One, Ryan Bounds of Oregon, was headed for the US Court of Appeals for the Ninth Circuit despite objections from both home state Democratic senators, Ron Wyden and Jeff Merkley. Last-minute concerns raised by Senator Tim Scott of South Carolina, the only African American Republican senator, over Bounds's past writings on diversity and multiculturalism left Bounds short of the votes for confirmation. Scott scuttled another nomination as the year ended when he came out against the confirmation of Thomas Farr to a long-open district court seat in North Carolina over Farr's racially charged work on campaigns for the late Jesse Helms as well as his defense of a voter ID law seen as a way to discourage minority voting. Scott, acting as the racial conscience of his party, was one of the few remaining roadblocks to confirmation.

The Senate bypassed blue slip objections from Senator Bob Casey, Democrat of Pennsylvania, to place David Porter on the US Court of Appeals for the Third Circuit. Porter's confirmation was part of a late-summer deal struck by Democrats with McConnell to let multiple judges through to allow Senate Democrats running for reelection to return home to campaign. The Democratic compliance angered activist groups that wanted Democrats to drag out every nomination as long as possible, but their complaints didn't hold up the agreement.

It was a surrender in a war in which Democrats had already been disarmed.

The conflict over the judges was not being lost on the high court. Just a few days after McConnell's celebration, Justice Ruth Bader Ginsburg, while receiving an award, lamented the deep partisanship infecting the confirmation process and suggested that such sentiment constituted a threat to the courts by breeding distrust in their neutrality. "My hope is that one fine day Congress will return to the bipartisan spirit that prevailed for my nomination," she said. "Such a return would enable our Congress to engage in lawmaking for the good of all the people the law should exist to serve."

Her comments reflected a real naivete about what was transpiring in the judicial wars. There would be no letup with so many court vacancies remaining, and Republicans, eyeing the approaching midterms, were determined to push every nominee through in the unlikely event that Democrats would seize control of the Senate and put a stop to the Trump-McGahn-McConnell-Grassley juggernaut.

Grassley was so brazen as to encourage any of Ginsburg's colleagues who were considering retirement to do so quickly, so that Republicans could be certain to get a replacement on the bench before Election Day.

"My message to any one of the nine Supreme Court justices, if you're thinking about quitting this year, do it yesterday," Grassley told the radio host Hugh Hewitt on May 10, about a month before the court would finish its term. "If we have a Democrat Senate, you're never going to get the kind of people that are strict constructionists that Don McGahn is getting up to us."

No one immediately took Grassley up on his plea. But whether anyone would quit and provide Trump an opportunity to further remake the Supreme Court even as he was aggressively reconfiguring the lower courts was becoming a major question in Washington. The answer would not be long in coming.

25

The Kennedy Seat

THE SUPREME COURT was closing shop for the summer of 2018 on Wednesday, June 27, and nearly all of Washington was keeping a close eye on Justice Anthony M. Kennedy, the court's nearly eighty-two-year-old swing vote on social issues, most notably abortion rights.

But first the public had to absorb a final politically charged ruling for the term—the so-called *Janus* decision. Overturning four decades of precedent, the conservative majority ruled 5–4 that nonunion workers could not be compelled to pay fees to public employee unions that collectively bargain on their behalf. McConnell had said earlier that it was just the sort of case for which he had held open the Scalia seat to install someone like Gorsuch, who was part of the prevailing side. Trump cheered the ruling in a tweet.

"Big loss for the coffers of the Democrats!" he declared.

As for Kennedy, his possible retirement had been rumored, but he hadn't given any definitive public clues about whether he would leave the court. If he did, his departure would create an ideology-shifting vacancy that could be filled by President Trump. The mere prospect threw a chill into Democrats and progressive advocacy groups given the Republican hold on the Senate and Mitch McConnell's now-proven track record of getting what he wanted when it came to high court justices.

Even Trump wasn't sure what would happen. In one of his regular phone calls with McConnell that morning, the president asked Mc-Connell if he believed Kennedy would step down. McConnell, who had seen court resignation rumors come and go many times, said he doubted it.

As the day progressed, it appeared more and more likely that Kennedy was staying on the court. No pronouncements otherwise emanated from the marble temple on First Street Northeast across from the Capitol. Foes of Trump figured that if Kennedy would only stick it out, Democrats had a slim chance of winning the Senate in the upcoming midterms, giving them an opportunity to block a Trump-picked successor or, at a minimum, exert a strong influence over his choice. Democrats held their breath, crossed their fingers, and knocked on wood. As the noon hour passed and no word on Kennedy emerged from a luncheon at the court, the sense took hold in Washington that he was not retiring, that there would be no preelection Supreme Court confirmation fight. Trump would have to await another opportunity to fill his second vacancy. A sigh of relief passed in many quarters, given that the capital was already in nearly hour-by-hour turmoil and the thought of another brutal Supreme Court confirmation fight thrown into the disruptive mix seemed almost too much to bear.

Then, just before two p.m., Kennedy's retirement was announced by the court and the Trump administration. He had already been to the White House, in a visit that was kept secret, to personally inform the president.

The city shook. Trump would get the opportunity to fill a second Supreme Court vacancy in less than two years in office. And this was not just any vacancy. This was "the Kennedy Seat." Though he had been nominated in 1987 by Ronald Reagan after Bork and another nominee, Douglas Ginsburg, imploded, Kennedy had been the decisive fifth vote on a variety of contentious social issues, most recently legalizing gay marriage in 2015. He still had a generally conservative record—he had found the Affordable Care Act unconstitutional and did not side with the liberal bloc in any 5–4 cases in 2018. But his vote was pivotal on some of the issues that mattered most to a public that paid little attention to the court's more routine business.

The justice gave that most common of Washington reasons in explaining his decision to leave the bench. "It has been the greatest honor and privilege to serve our nation in the federal judiciary for 43 years, 30 of those years on the Supreme Court," he said in a statement issued by the court. The statement said he "added that while his family was willing for him to continue to serve, his decision to step aside was based on his deep desire to spend more time with them."

The struggle over the vacancy created by the death of Antonin Scalia two years earlier had been a titanic fight with immense implications. But in the strictest court terms, replacing Scalia with Gorsuch was replacing a conservative with a conservative. Now Trump, who with McConnell's help had been getting lower-court judges in place at a record pace, would be replacing the prime swing vote on the Supreme Court with a known conservative from his list of twenty-five very conservative judicial candidates.

Despite the uncertainty about whether he would leave, Kennedy's retirement could not be considered shocking and had been anticipated for years. He was nearly eighty-two and had been on the court for three decades. Being a Supreme Court justice was not a particularly taxing job, as evidenced by the fact that septuagenarians and even octogenarians were not unusual. But family and health considerations were always a factor.

As it turned out, not everyone at the White House had been in the dark about Kennedy's plans. McGahn, the White House counsel, had developed a close relationship with Kennedy and visited him in his chambers on occasion. He saw Kennedy as a sophisticated political thinker from the justice's days in California and would consult with him on nominations. McGahn had also taken care to surround himself with Kennedy clerks and see that some were placed on the federal bench and other positions of influence.

Kennedy showed some of his own capacity for political intrigue in the way he handled his retirement announcement. Kennedy was ready to leave, but wanted to set the wheels in motion discreetly, avoiding the possibility of a leak. So he went through a cutout, Steven Engel, a former Kennedy clerk who was now in the Office of Legal Counsel at the Department of Justice. Kennedy had summoned his trusted former aide to a Smithsonian museum restaurant to inform him so he could pass the word along to McGahn. What followed was a bit of Washington cloak-and-dagger to keep the city—and the country —in suspense.

McGahn told no one at the White House, notably the president, for fear the news would get out. But he couldn't resist having some fun with the secret. In a meeting with advisers to Senator Dianne Feinstein just before the Kennedy news broke, McGahn mentioned they would soon be seeing more of each other. In retrospect, the staffer realized that McGahn was in the know.

Kennedy still hadn't told McGahn directly, but they began putting in place a plan to covertly get the justice into the White House so he could personally inform Trump. On the appointed day, McGahn arranged a government car so he could travel to the court himself to pick up Kennedy and deliver him to the president. Only then did he inform John Kelly, the White House chief of staff, that Kennedy was coming down to the White House and that Trump needed to finish a scheduled lunch with the secretary of state, Mike Pompeo, on time and wait in the residence. As he met the impeccably dressed justice at the court, McGahn was struck by the import of the moment—he was bringing Tony Kennedy, carrying a resignation letter, to the president, and hardly anyone knew about it. It was thrilling for him, almost cinematic.

The final piece of the puzzle was getting Kennedy into the executive mansion without being seen. But as it turned out, it wasn't so difficult. Much of the press corps was occupied elsewhere on the grounds for the arrival of President Marcelo Rebelo de Sousa of Portugal. McGahn waltzed Kennedy, unseen, right through the front door. Kennedy was fifteen minutes into the meeting with Trump before he finally revealed his plans, and Trump graciously received the letter. He would get a chance to put a second pick on the high court. McGahn walked Kennedy to the car and headed back to his office, where he immediately called Brett Kavanaugh to convey the news and told him to prepare.

McGahn had considered it part of his role to reassure Kennedy that Trump would not nominate a wrecking ball to take his place on the court. The possibility of being succeeded by Kavanaugh was a powerful incentive to the justice.

It was all part of a subtle Trump administration effort to cultivate Kennedy and smooth his retirement decision, to make him feel comfortable stepping down while Trump was in control. The nomination of Gorsuch, a former favored Kennedy clerk, was a clear signal from the White House. The message was, in essence, "Look, we like people that you like, we like judges that you think are capable and worthy successors." Kennedy even swore in Gorsuch, making him the first former Supreme Court clerk to serve alongside his former boss. Kennedy wanted to see himself succeeded by one of his own clerks, a first in Supreme Court history.

The *New York Times* also reported that Trump had praised Kennedy's son, Justin, directly to the justice during an encounter in the Capitol. Justin Kennedy had been an executive overseeing real estate lending at Deutsche Bank when most domestic lenders wouldn't provide financing for Trump's projects because of his poor fiscal track record. "Say hello to your boy," Trump told Kennedy as he exited his first address to a joint session of Congress in February 2017, according to Adam Liptak and Maggie Haberman. "Special guy."

Trump also nominated at least three other former Kennedy clerks to the federal bench. It was a nuanced but concerted campaign. Being any more direct would be considered bad form.

Now the justice had made his decision, and Trump was presented with another vacancy to fill from his inventory of preferred candidates from his now-famous list of prospective nominees prescreened and preapproved by the conservative legal community. Notably, the list had been expanded in November 2017 from the original one Trump had finalized prior to his election in 2016. It had been padded with a few more names, giving Trump and his conservative advisers more options and some added cover for the man some had already identified as the next nominee.

Kavanaugh's name jumped off the enlarged list. The judge was a well-known Washington presence who had been confirmed to the US Court of Appeals for the District of Columbia Circuit in 2006 after a nearly three-year wait. Kavanaugh, fifty-three, was an alumnus of the George W. Bush administration, where he had himself participated in tense conflicts over judicial nominees. He was a longtime member of the Federalist Society who was popular in conservative circles and with those who had worked with him in the Bush White House.

Along with Kavanaugh, the other notable addition to the list in November 2017 was Amy Coney Barrett. Barrett, forty-five, the conservative former Notre Dame law professor, had been confirmed only a month earlier to the US Court of Appeals for the Seventh Circuit after a very contentious hearing that centered on her deep Catholicism.

"The dogma lives loudly within you, and that's of concern when you come to big issues that large numbers of people have fought for for years in this country," Dianne Feinstein, the senior Democrat on the Judiciary Committee, baldly told her at her confirmation hearing, referring to abortion rights. That comment set off charges in conservative circles of anti-Catholicism, raising Barrett's profile and elevating her popularity on the right. She was ultimately confirmed and now had worked her way onto Trump's list.

In news reports handicapping the candidates, Kavanaugh's and Barrett's names were usually the first mentioned.

Barrett wasn't a judge yet when Trump, McGahn, Leo, and others had assembled the first two lists, so her absence was not necessarily a surprise. Kavanaugh, however, was a prominent member of the second-most-important federal court in the country and an extremely well-known commodity in Washington. That was part of his problem. Brett Kavanaugh was a Republican insider's insider. Not only was he on the federal bench in the courthouse on Constitution Avenue just down from the Capitol and the high court itself, but he had been in the administrations of both George H. W. and George W. Bush. He had been part of Ken Starr's special counsel team during the investigation of Bill Clinton and had helped the Bush campaign win the infamous *Bush v. Gore* case, which had handed the presidency to Bush. To top it off, he was a local product of a prominent family who had attended exclusive Georgetown Preparatory School in suburban Maryland.

Those were usually outstanding credentials for a Republican court nominee, but not while Trump was running for president. Trump's early list of judicial prospects was intended to reflect his outsider status, and Kavanaugh would have looked jarringly out of place on that compilation. Way too Washington. But once Trump was in office, and the possibility of a second Supreme Court opening was looming. Trump's legal advisers wanted to make sure they had the right candidates lined up should an opening occur. Among McGahn and a few others in the Trump inner circle, Kavanaugh was exactly who they wanted moved onto the bench. His allies began lobbying Trump and others to make certain that his name was included.

"A lot of judges and lawyers I know made clear to, I think, various people that they thought I should at least be considered based on my record for the last twelve years," Kavanaugh told the Senate in explaining his name being added to the list at such a crucial time. "And colleagues of mine thought I should be considered." Some suggested that Kavanaugh had tailored his opinions to help his own case by underscoring his conservative streak.

Now the revised list was in play with Kennedy's retirement. And Kavanaugh and Barrett personified the Republican opportunity to shift the court to the right for decades to come. McConnell, the master of delay when it came to filling Scalia's seat, was ready to go.

"We will vote to confirm Justice Kennedy's successor this fall," Mc-

Connell declared shortly after Kennedy's retirement became public, employing a tone of certainty intended to make confirmation seem inevitable.

The pressure hit Democrats instantly. Their progressive allies—and some Democrats themselves—thought the party had not distinguished itself during Senate consideration of Gorsuch. It had come so early in the Trump administration, in the middle of such chaos, and Democratic attention had been divided.

They were determined to this time put up a more concerted campaign against the Republican drive to fill the Kennedy seat and went on the attack immediately. The opening tactic was to try to hold Republicans to the standard they had instituted in 2016 in blocking Garland—no Supreme Court nominations should be considered without giving the voters a say in looming elections.

"Senator McConnell would tell anyone who listened that the Senate had the right to advice and consent, and that was every bit as important as the president's right to nominate," said Schumer. "Millions of people are just months away from determining the senators who should vote to confirm or reject the president's nominee, and their voices deserve to be heard now, as Leader McConnell thought they deserved to be heard then. Anything but that would be the absolute height of hypocrisy."

Of course, it was lost on no one that Senate judicial fights always featured regular attempts by members of the Senate to scale the heights of hypocrisy.

The Democratic strategy may have sounded superficially powerful but did not catch on. The big difference between 2016 and 2018 was that the former was a presidential election year and the latter was not. Still, McConnell, who likes to cultivate the image of someone who couldn't care less what is said about him, was surprisingly miffed that he was being called out as a hypocrite on judges. He dispatched aides to complain that news articles weren't making clear enough that it was a midterm election year, not a presidential one.

On the floor, he pointed out that many previous Supreme Court nominations had come in midterm years as recently as the 2010 confirmation of Elena Kagan. "These aren't the final months of a second-term, constitutionally lame-duck presidency with a presidential election fast approaching. We are right in the middle of this president's first term," he retorted on the floor to Schumer and other Democrats. "To my knowledge, nobody on either side has ever suggested before yesterday that the Senate should only process Supreme Court nominations in odd-numbered years."

Still, the early stages of the fight showed how much the Garland episode would hang over the coming nomination showdown and likely color others in the years ahead. Democrats were not about to shake off their shattering experience of just two years earlier.

"The shock that the Republican majority would remove from the fourth year of the president of the United States his ability to appoint a Supreme Court justice was very high," Feinstein said as reporters chased her down a Hart Office Building hallway the day after Kennedy's retirement was announced. "For us on this side, it was a humiliation. And it is carved deep into our memory."

Their anger had been rekindled just days earlier when the Supreme Court, on a bitterly divided 5–4 decision, had upheld the Trump administration's travel ban affecting majority-Muslim countries. Like the *Janus* case decided by the same ideological margin, the decision sparked outrage and had Democrats pondering what might have been the result had Garland been on the court. Both Kennedy and Gorsuch had been in the majority.

"This is a reflection of a five-to-four decision based on a justice, Neil Gorsuch, sitting in a stolen seat," seethed Senator Jeff Merkley, the progressive Oregon Democrat, as he joined protests outside the Supreme Court on the day of the travel ban decision. "He comes by a philosophy of making decisions by and for the powerful rather than by and for the people. He has stood the Constitution on its head time and time again."

The ever-expanding Supreme Court–fight messaging machine quickly sprang into action. Trump officials, recognizing their narrow Senate majority, summoned to a White House get-together the three Democratic senators who had supported Gorsuch—Heidi Heitkamp of North Dakota, Joe Manchin III of West Virginia, and Joe Donnelly of Indiana. Trump and McGahn obviously hoped to keep them on board for the upcoming nominee to pad their margin a bit and spare the eventual nominee the taint of a straight party-line confirmation. All three of them were up for reelection in states that Trump had won easily, and crossing the president on a Supreme Court pick could spark a backlash when their seats were already in jeopardy. "It is a terrible vote," Jennifer Duffy, a nonpartisan Senate analyst for the *Cook Political Report*, said about the squeeze that was coming for the Trump-state Democrats.

The Judicial Crisis Network, the conservative advocacy group, began an initial $1 million television campaign urging backing for the president's choice. Considering the Democratic opposition to the lower-level Trump court picks—mostly unsuccessful, given the procedural power of the Republican majority—conservative leaders rightly expected an all-out assault.

"We've seen the Democrats turn the dial up to eleven on appellate court nominees, sometimes even on district court nominees," said Carrie Severino, the Judicial Crisis Network's chief counsel and policy director. Democrats, Severino added, "have gone pedal to the metal. Just imagine what they're going to do here."

On the other side, a new progressive judicial advocacy group, Demand Justice, was going to get its first real test over the Kennedy seat.

As the 2016 election had vividly demonstrated once again, liberals simply have never exhibited the same passion over Supreme Court seats as conservatives. Since the Reagan administration, Republicans have used abortion and school prayer as rallying cries to persuade evangelicals, Catholics, and other abortion opponents to focus on the federal judiciary and vote accordingly. Democrats and progressives have had some success, but the Garland episode convinced top Democrats that much more needed to be done and that Democrats should adopt some of the campaign-style practices of conservative advocacy groups like the Judicial Crisis Network.

One of those who saw the Democratic shortcoming up close was Brian Fallon, the spokesman for the Clinton campaign who was also a former spokesman for the Justice Department and Chuck Schumer. Fallon was destined for the podium at the White House briefing room had Clinton won the presidency. The Scalia vacancy and the thwarting of Garland were in no small way directly responsible for him being denied that job.

A square-jawed Harvard graduate, Fallon was known for his strategic instincts, fiery temper, and little patience for journalists he thought were dumb. As he cast about for a new endeavor in the aftermath of the Clinton defeat, John Podesta, the former campaign's chairman, suggested he should consider heading up a judicial activist group on the left.

"We have ignored this field of battle for too long," Podesta said in a *New York Times* story disclosing the existence of the emerging group. "On the progressive side," he continued, "we are a little bit old-school where you just pick qualified people and it will all work out. Obviously, we came to a rude awakening with the Garland fight."

Multiple other progressive organizations had been around for decades and were still engaged on judicial issues, but Fallon believed he could bring new digital media savvy to the judicial arena. He lined up experienced lawyers from the Obama White House and the Senate to help him out. Demand Justice was born. It would not have the money to compete with those on the right, but it was a start.

Fallon knew his ability to block nominees was limited with Trump in the White House and McConnell running the Senate. For the moment, Fallon and his sponsors—they included George Soros, but most were undisclosed under the "dark money" rules that Democrats often complained about—saw themselves as a tool to stiffen the spine of Democrats who were reluctant to reject Republican-nominated judges, particularly those senators in red states. That set up the potential for conflict between Fallon and Schumer, his old boss and mentor, who saw his role as protecting Democrats in the Senate, particularly those same red state senators. Given the liberal bent of the organization, Schumer began referring privately to his former aide—who had met his wife, Katie Beirne Fallon, while both were working for the senator—as "Lefty Brian."

With the new available seat, Fallon had a chance to demonstrate the capabilities of his new group, and he would play a role both publicly and behind the scenes as the conflict ramped up over the new Supreme Court opening.

Democrats were making clear that their opposition to this new nominee was going to reach a new level. Senator Bob Casey of Pennsylvania, a moderate Democrat not known for inciting controversy and who was up for reelection in a state carried by Trump, issued a statement saying he intended to oppose anyone nominated by Trump. Though many of his Democratic colleagues no doubt held the same view, it was unusual to go ahead and say it before the nominee was even selected. Casey didn't hold back.

"In a nation with over 700 sitting federal judges, many of whom were appointed by Republican presidents, it is outrageous that President Trump will nominate from a list of just 25 dictated to him by the Heritage Foundation," he said in a statement. "This list is the bidding of corporate special interests hell-bent on handing health care over to insurance companies, crushing unions that represent working men and women, and promoting policies that will leave the middle-class further behind. Any judge on this list is fruit of a corrupt process straight from the D.C. swamp."

Casey's colleagues were otherwise waiting to see who Trump would put forward to replace Kennedy, but this was obviously going to be an ugly fight. The confirmation was never going to be as easy as the installation of Justice Gorsuch. Trump had a record now, faced a sweeping federal inquiry, and the #MeToo movement had energized American women in entirely new ways.

26

Golden Boy

TRUMP WANTED TO waste no time in filling the Kennedy seat, and there were important reasons for the White House to hurry. The new term was going to start in a few months, and the White House and McConnell wanted a full complement on the court.

Plus, the midterm elections were coming in November. Though Republicans had a major advantage because of where the competitive races were being run, Democrats had an outside chance of winning the majority. There was no telling what could happen to a nomination if Democrats prevailed, even though Republicans would still control the Senate for a lame-duck session. Another reason existed, one that Republicans and the Trump administration didn't want to talk about. The investigation of the special counsel Robert Mueller into Russian interference in the 2016 election was forging ahead, raising the prospect that the Supreme Court could be called on to decide challenges to it. Republicans would feel more comfortable about that situation with a second Trump nominee sworn in and seated on the high court.

The list made Trump's job that much easier. The field of candidates was obvious, and McGahn quickly reached out to potential contenders. Kavanaugh was in the White House for a meeting with McGahn by Friday—two days after Kennedy's announcement—and had his first face-to-face meeting with Trump the following Monday. Things were moving very quickly as McGahn worked to carry out his original strategy.

Besides Kavanaugh, Trump met that Monday with the other top contenders—Amy Coney Barrett; Raymond Kethledge, the appeals court judge from Michigan; and Amul Thapar, the appeals court judge from Kentucky and a favorite of McConnell's.

Kavanaugh may have been the clear choice for McGahn, but many other Republicans did not hold Kavanaugh in the same regard. They saw nothing but trouble. Kavanaugh was viewed by some influential Republicans on Capitol Hill as too Washington, too closely aligned with the Bush-style Republicans that had produced Chief Justice Roberts, and too political when it came to some of his rulings, raising the possibility of unpredictability on the high court. They began to push back. But time was short.

Barrett was seen as the most likely nominee after Kavanaugh. Since the focus of the confirmation fight was likely to be abortion rights, given Kennedy's role in protecting *Roe v. Wade*, it would make sense for Trump to go with a woman and avoid the appearance of two male Trump-appointed judges joining three other conservative men on the court in overturning such a landmark decision. But Barrett, an inexperienced judge who had survived a contentious hearing nine months earlier, would be a tough sell to Susan Collins and perhaps Lisa Murkowski of Alaska, the only pro–abortion rights senators in the party. Collins was certain to make preserving *Roe* a central element of her review of any nominee, and her likely resistance made a Barrett pick highly problematic. Trump also liked his Supreme Court nominees to have sterling academic credentials, and Barrett was not an Ivy Leaguer. His interview with her was said to have not gone well.

Trump and McGahn were in regular contact with McConnell, who offered his assessment on the top candidates and definitely wasn't as interested in Kavanaugh as McGahn was. McConnell told Trump that Kethledge and Thomas Hardiman, the appeals court judge from Pennsylvania who'd met with Trump during the first vacancy, might present the least difficulty in winning confirmation. They were respected, low-key judges with solid records and few big controversies, which would make it difficult for Democrats to generate a wave of opposition to them. But steadiness and low profiles were not exactly qualities Trump was seeking in a judge. Trump liked some flash.

His nomination of Gorsuch—and his ability to keep it secret and pull off a smooth East Room ceremony—had been highlights of his first few months in office. Kethledge had his supporters and a record as a strong "originalist" in interpreting the Constitution but was lacking in pizzazz.

McConnell offered a warning about Kavanaugh: his long career in Washington and his work for both Ken Starr, the special counsel who had investigated Bill Clinton, and George W. Bush in the difficult years following the September 11, 2001, attacks would present complications. Kavanaugh had been Bush's staff secretary, funneling the flood of paper to and from the Oval Office. Democrats could conceivably demand to see hundreds of thousands of documents from his White House years, slowing the push by both Trump and McConnell to get their person on the court as quickly as possible.

Democrats were not the only potential obstacle for Kavanaugh. Some Republicans were worried that he was too much of a conventional Republican who had not fully embraced the new hyper-partisan ethos of the Trump era. Senator Rand Paul, the Kentucky Republican, was also a potential roadblock because of his dim view of the Bush administration's surveillance and antiterror policies, though Paul almost always came around to the party position in the end.

Even Trump had evidenced signs that he was lukewarm about Kavanaugh. Not only was he not on the first two iterations of the list of potential nominees, but Trump expressed some concern that he was too closely associated with George W. Bush, a man who had made clear his distaste for Trump. In many ways, Kavanaugh was a product of the Bush era. He could fairly be considered the former president's third nominee to the court after Chief Justice John Roberts and Samuel Alito.

Those trying to derail Kavanaugh tried to play on Trump's insecurities and dislike for the Bush regime. As the nation awaited the nominee, an interesting story appeared in the *Daily Caller*, a conservative news site that Trump was known to read. "Movement Conservatives Fume at Trump SCOTUS Favorite," blared the headline of a July 3 article. "This Is the Low-Energy Jeb Bush Pick." It was obviously calculated to rile Trump, who had coined the derisive Low-Energy Jeb nickname during the 2016 primary campaign. If anything was going to get Trump to reject Kavanaugh, it was the accusation that he was sending a Bush clone to the court. Another story, this one for ABC on July 2, said that antiabortion forces were lobbying the White House, worried that Kavanaugh didn't have the nerve to overturn Roe. An anti-Kavanaugh undercurrent on the right was out there.

But McGahn and Leo saw Kavanaugh as the template for the kind of justice they wanted on the court. In interviewing candidates for lower-court posts, McGahn used Kavanaugh's writing and decisions as a test. Those who expressed familiarity with them moved to the top of the pile; those who didn't found their papers shuffled down below. Kavanaugh was to join with Gorsuch in providing the one-two punch to dismantle the administrative state. Remembering the original strategy of installing Gorsuch followed by Kavanaugh, Steve Bannon, forced out of the administration in its first year, pushed back from the outside on those leery of Kavanaugh and his Bush connection.

Trump was persuaded by McGahn and let it be known that he would announce his next court pick on Monday, July 9, just twelve days after Kennedy's announcement. "Big decision will soon be made on our next Justice of the Supreme Court!" he tweeted from his weekend retreat in Bedminster, New Jersey.

As the hour of the announcement approached, it was still unclear to the public just who Trump had picked until Kavanaugh was seen at the White House—and Barrett was seen at her home in Indiana. No meandering drive toward the nation's capital for her.

It was the kind of presidential moment Trump loved, the combination of spectacle and power as he brought Kavanaugh and his family into the East Room before the assembled dignitaries and guests. They again included Maureen Scalia, the widow of Antonin Scalia, whose death two years earlier had set in motion the dramatic events that were still playing out with huge consequences for the country. Republican senators traveled over to the White House together by bus.

"I've often heard that, other than matters of war and peace, this is the most important decision a president will make," Trump said, glorying in the spotlight. "The Supreme Court is entrusted with the safeguarding of the crown jewel of our republic, the Constitution of the United States." Trump went on to praise Kavanaugh for his "impeccable credentials, unsurpassed qualifications, and a proven commitment to equal justice under the law."

The president also singled out some aspects of Kavanaugh's life that would get regular attention during the weeks ahead—his charitable work as well as his coaching of a basketball team for girls in middle school.

"Beyond his great renown as a judge, he is active in his community," Trump said. "He coaches CYO basketball, serves meals to needy families, and—having learned from his mom, who was a schoolteacher in DC—tutors children at local elementary schools.

"There is no one in America more qualified for this position, and no one more deserving," said the beaming president.

Now it was Kavanaugh's turn, a moment that he had seemingly been preparing for his entire life. Given his résumé and background, he resembled a test-tube creation of a Republican Supreme Court nominee: Georgetown Preparatory School, Yale and Yale Law School; Kennedy clerk, Bush ally and adviser; twelve years on the US Court of Appeals for the District of Columbia Circuit. He was a man who understood Washington and had cultivated the right friends and allies, even working the press behind the scenes. A golden boy in all respects.

Eyes glistening as he talked of his family, Kavanaugh promised to remain an independent judge. "I believe that an independent judiciary is the crown jewel of our constitutional republic," said Kavanaugh, who retained a bit of a frat boy, ex-jock look. "If confirmed by the Senate, I will keep an open mind in every case."

Kavanaugh began his remarks with what many saw as an odd bit of dissembling meant to ingratiate himself with Trump. "No president has ever consulted more widely or talked with more people from more backgrounds to seek input about a Supreme Court nomination," he said. Given that Trump had moved so quickly, had barely conferred with Democrats, and was working off a narrowly defined list, Kavanaugh was badly overstating his case. He had watched the Gorsuch nomination and was not going to make the mistake of failing to flatter a president who thrived on it. To Democrats, it would not be the last time Kavanaugh stretched the truth in his hunger for a spot on the Supreme Court.

Now that the decision was made, conservatives were all-in on Kavanaugh. The groaning over his nomination on Capitol Hill vanished and was converted into a commitment to do whatever it took to push the nomination through.

"Trump Hits Another Home Run with Supreme Court Pick Brett Kavanaugh," exulted the website of the Heritage Foundation.

It was an emotional and rewarding moment for Kavanaugh and his gathered friends and family, one that showed that all his work had paid off. It left them all exhilarated and glowing with happiness. The warmth would not last.

27

Advice and Dissent

KAVANAUGH WAS A shining star within Washington's Republican circles, a do-gooder who was also good at his day job of being a professional judge. He was an outgoing, personable political climber who had reached the heights of his field without walking over too many of his colleagues along the way. During his White House remarks, he noted that he considered himself personal friends with every one of the seventeen other judges he had worked with on the DC circuit court.

McGahn and other advisers rated Kavanaugh a solid and well-tested bet, someone who had been around Washington so long and had been under such scrutiny over the decades that it was impossible to think an unknown scandal could arise to bedevil him.

Senate Democrats, on the other hand, loathed him. Some of them, such as Schumer, Durbin, and Leahy, were extremely familiar with him from the Bush administration and his two previous confirmation hearings. They saw him as a smarmy, disingenuous political operative who had eagerly done the bidding of Ken Starr, Karl Rove, George W. Bush, and Dick Cheney.

Schumer once called him the "Hard Right's political lawyer." In 2004, Durbin had famously dubbed him the "Zelig or Forrest Gump of Republican politics" for his tendency to appear at all big partisan moments. "You show up at every scene of the crime."

Schumer immediately said he would oppose Kavanaugh with "everything I've got"—a line Republicans would remind him of again and again during the confirmation fight—and he laid out the new nominee's political track record.

"Judge Kavanaugh was embedded in the partisan fights of the past few decades: the notorious Starr report, the Florida recount, President Bush's secrecy and privilege claims once in office, and ideological judicial nomination fights throughout the Bush era," he said on the floor. "The Hard Right has had a goal. They can't achieve their philosophy through the elected two branches of government, try as they might, the Congress, the president. But if they get control of the one nonelected branch, the judiciary, they can turn the clock back in America decades, maybe centuries. That has been their goal, and Judge Kavanaugh when he worked in the White House helped them achieve that goal."

Dianne Feinstein, who would manage the confirmation for the Democrats as her party's senior member on the Judiciary Committee, said she had never seen such a short gap between the vacancy occurring and the nominee being announced. She questioned how closely the White House had looked at Kavanaugh, surmising that his selection had been precooked.

Republicans portrayed Kavanaugh as the most qualified nominee they had ever seen. They said Democrats had sacrificed their ability to challenge him by proclaiming their opposition before examining his record.

But Democrats didn't need to learn much more about Kavanaugh to decide they didn't like him. Not only had they had extensive previous experience in considering his record, but they and other activists had been scrubbing the backgrounds and rulings of all the top candidates before Trump formally disclosed his choice.

The question for them was more about what line of attack to take in trying to undermine his nomination. Abortion? A threat to the health care law? His days in the Bush White House, when policies on warrantless wiretapping and the torture of terror detainees were being developed? His involvement in the judicial wars?

All were being discussed and tried out as themes. Behind the scenes, another possibility was being pursued: The #MeToo movement had exploded into American culture in the aftermath of the new scrutiny of powerful men and their sexual abuse and harassment of women. Opponents of Kavanaugh thought it could play a role in this confirmation as well. It was unimaginable to many that a credible sexual harassment charge against a Supreme Court nominee would get the same dismissive treatment as did the claims by Anita Hill against Justice Clarence Thomas twenty-seven years earlier. Surely it would be considered disqualifying in the present moment.

The object of the initial scrutiny was Kavanaugh's ties to Alex Kozinski, the California appeals court judge whose own confirmation fight had helped touch off the modern era of judicial confirmation clashes more than three decades earlier.

Kavanaugh had clerked for Kozinski and had a long relationship with the judge, who had been forced to retire in 2017 after the *Washington Post* published accounts from multiple women documenting sexual harassment by Kozinski. He had shown women law clerks explicit images on his computer and also participated in an email chain of obscene and offensive jokes. His behavior was evidently well known at the highest levels of federal court circles but had been ignored for years. Both Kavanaugh and Kozinski had helped screen potential law clerks for Justice Kennedy, and Kavanaugh had also brought on Kozinski's son as one of his own clerks in 2017.

Activists digging into Kavanaugh's past thought it highly unlikely that the nominee could have had such a long-term relationship with Kozinski and neither have known nor witnessed such misbehavior. But as journalists and opposition researchers pursued leads, they could find no one who had seen Kavanaugh present when Kozinski acted inappropriately or who was willing to go public with such an account.

At the White House, administration officials wanted to put the focus on Kavanaugh's twelve years on the federal bench. They believed that service was most relevant and that it had cleansed Kavanaugh of his partisan background during his prior years in Washington.

Along with Senate Republicans, Trump officials also made it very clear that the administration was not interested in making available many of the documents from Kavanaugh's time as a lawyer for the Bush administration or as staff secretary—a position that would have made him, according to one's preferred metaphor—the president's "in-and-out-box" or a document "traffic cop." In either event, he was certainly privy to the flood of sensitive paperwork sent to the president. On some of those documents he may have weighed in with opinions of his own. This was the extensive paper trail that McConnell was worried about. Senate Republicans figured the number of documents that could potentially be sought for the new nominee was greater than the amount for the five previous nominees combined. Democrats wanted to see them all and they stepped up the pressure.

They got some help from Kavanaugh himself. In a March 2015 speech at Marquette University in Milwaukee, Kavanaugh said he was sometimes asked what prior legal experience was most useful for him in his role as judge. "I say, 'I certainly draw on all of them,' but I also say that my five and a half years at the White House and especially my three years as staff secretary for President George W. Bush were the most interesting and informative for me."

That admission provided Democrats an opening to push for Kavanaugh's records, saying he himself had described them as most relevant to his judicial service. But Republicans weren't about to expose either Kavanaugh or George W. Bush to extensive, time-consuming disclosure. Despite Democratic demands, the White House and the Grassley-led Judiciary Committee came up with a constrained process that would result in a limited release of the documents, one without the traditional participation of the National Archives.

Instead, Republicans unilaterally imposed a system with the cooperation of the Bush presidential library in which a team of lawyers led by William Burck, a former colleague and friend of Kavanaugh's, reviewed documents and decided which could be released to the committee and to the public. Republicans portrayed this as a way to speed up the process.

Grassley, ever defensive of his management, came under fierce criticism. But he portrayed it as the "most transparent process" ever because of tens of thousands of documents that would be made public. In reality, though, just a small fraction of the papers Kavanaugh handled were made public, well short of the Democratic request. It was an untried approach with no independent oversight, and Democrats were highly suspicious and skeptical. They savaged it as a partisan effort at concealment by Kavanaugh's friends and colleagues who were directly tied to his nomination and past work.

"Obviously, one might think that the lawyer who is clearly totally hooked in to the Republican appointment of the Kavanaugh mechanism would not allow things that might be controversial, that might not put Kavanaugh in such a good light," Schumer said. "And yet there is not even a standard as to which documents are made public and which are kept confidential.

"Does that sound fair to the Senate?" he asked. "Does that sound fair to the American people, who have a right to read and understand who this potential future Supreme Court justice may be?"

The handling of the documents was to become a major flash point in the confirmation hearings and a significant source of tension between Democrats and Republicans on the panel as personal relations crumbled over the Kavanaugh fight. To make matters worse, Republicans, on the night before the start of the hearing on September 4, released another tranche of 42,000 pages of documents that Democrats really had no chance to review before the start of the proceedings.

In the prelude to the hearing, clashes had erupted over the documents and other parts of Kavanaugh's record, but nothing surfaced that would shake nearly solid Republican support. With their majority power, Republicans were confident they would prevail, and it appeared likely that Kavanaugh was on his way to a seat on the court by the first Monday in October.

Susan Collins, one potential obstacle, had met with Kavanaugh for two hours on August 21 and said she was convinced that he would not join an effort to overturn *Roe*.

"I specifically asked Judge Kavanaugh if he had made any commitments or pledges to the Federalist Society, or the White House, about how he would decide any legal issues," she said in a statement. "He unequivocally assured me that he had not made any such commitments and he expressed his deep respect for the independence of the judiciary. I also was pleased to learn that Judge Kavanaugh believes, as I do, that Article III of the Constitution was intended to include the concept of precedent and that he sees precedent as much more than simply a matter of practice and tradition. In addition, he expressed agreement with Chief Justice Roberts's confirmation hearing statement that Roe is settled precedent and entitled to respect under principles of stare decisis."

Collins was clearly looking for a way to get to yes, and McGahn, seeing her as a linchpin to the nomination, kept in close touch with her.

Frustrated by their lack of weapons to combat Kavanaugh, Democrats revisited a sensitive topic: Should they have held their fire on a filibuster against Gorsuch in 2017 for the next Supreme Court nomination? Schumer and most other Democrats argued that they had needed to do all they could to stop Gorsuch and they did not question their decision, which Chris Coons and Michael Bennet still considered a mistake.

"I never understood the strategy," Bennet said after Kavanaugh was nominated. "We achieved nothing by filibustering Judge Gorsuch except giving Mitch McConnell the opportunity to strip us of our ability to filibuster a nominee who will cause a dramatic shift in the balance of the court."

But he and Coons couldn't secure an agreement with centrist Republicans that, in exchange for not filibustering Gorsuch, Republicans would then deny McConnell the necessary votes the next time. And Schumer and other Democrats said that without such a commitment, McConnell would simply change the rules on the future nominations and they didn't see the point of holding back. "Justice Gorsuch was an extreme nominee, and his recent record vindicates our decision to do everything we could to stop him," Schumer said.

McConnell had shown that he would do whatever it took to gain the upper hand over confirmations. Who knows if he would have gone first in changing the rules if Harry Reid had not beaten him to the punch? The question was irrelevant, since the sixty-vote filibuster was gone and highly unlikely to ever return.

The hearing was set to begin, and Democrats knew they could not rely on business as usual to make their point. They needed to make a stink—a big one. Committee members held a conference call with Schumer the night before to plot strategy on how they would approach the next day's proceedings in the cavernous room on the second floor of the Hart Senate Office Building, the same room where Gorsuch had breezed through his hearing. But the environment had changed. Just days after Washington had come together in a bipartisan celebration of John McCain's career at multiple memorial events for the senator, who had died on August 25, partisanship was back with a vengeance.

28

The Hearing Will Not Come to Order

Supreme Court confirmation hearings are usually contentious but staid affairs. That was not to be the case for the Kennedy seat. Protesters dressed in red *Handmaid's Tale* habits stood silently outside the hearing room in the hallways of the Hart building. Democrats were furious over the last-minute document dump by the White House. The atmosphere was tense, and conflict was anticipated. As he entered the hearing room, Durbin stopped by the press table and suggested that Democrats were not going to go quietly. He was right.

Chairman Grassley was just thirteen words into his opening statement and had not even reached Kavanaugh's name when Senator Kamala Harris, the ambitious freshman Democrat from California, interrupted and sought recognition.

"Mr. Chairman," she said as all eyes turned to her while Grassley tried to plow through. "Mr. Chairman."

In their conference call the evening before, Democrats had plotted a strategy for pushing Grassley, and it was agreed Harris would go first. She was quickly followed by Senator Richard Blumenthal, who tried to force a vote to adjourn since Democrats hadn't been given access to Kavanaugh's White House documents. Then a previously silent woman seated adjacent to the press tables in seats reserved for the general public erupted.

"This is a mockery and a travesty of justice!" she shouted to the shock and surprise of most in the room. "This is a travesty of justice. We will not go back. Cancel Brett Kavanaugh, adjourn the hearing."

The hearing was a pandemonium, and Kavanaugh and his assembled friends and family, including his two young daughters, had to sit by quietly, watching and listening as the nominee became the focus of a searing national debate that was only beginning.

Grassley seemed stunned but finally had to stop and engage the Democrats, who were peppering him with criticisms and requests for documents. "I ask that you stop so we can conduct this hearing the way we have planned it," said Grassley, who was also fighting off more shouts from protesters. "Maybe it isn't going exactly the way that the minority would like to have it go, but we have said for a long period of time that we were going to proceed on this very day. And I think we ought to give the American people the opportunity to hear whether Judge Kavanaugh should be on the Supreme Court or not."

Democrats realized they were not going to shake determined Republicans from eventually proceeding. But they had other goals in mind. First, they wanted to make a public case that Republicans were unfairly withholding documents relevant to Kavanaugh's record. Second, they wanted to show their Democratic allies and angry voters that this hearing was not going to be routine and that Democrats were going to, well, resist.

Republicans seemed caught off guard both by the strenuousness of the complaints from Democratic lawmakers and their willingness to challenge Grassley, but also by the sheer number of in-room protesters willing to be heard and removed by Capitol Police. The volume of their complaints pierced the hearing at regular but unpredictable intervals. Feinstein jumped at some of the eruptions.

Women would file in to a row of seats next to the press section, sit quietly for a bit, and then individually rise and shout for the hearing to be halted and Kavanaugh rejected. "Kavanaugh can't be trusted!" was typical. More than sixty women were arrested the first day, and Republicans were not happy. Senator John Cornyn said it was the first confirmation hearing he had participated in that was being conducted by "mob rule," and others made their objections known as well.

"I think we ought to have this loudmouth removed," Orrin Hatch complained as his opening statement was interrupted by shouting. "We shouldn't have to put up with this kind of stuff."

Republicans were already under fire for lack of transparency with Kavanaugh's document record. They weren't about to close the hearing to the public despite the constant interruptions. Plus, Republicans, sensing a new political opening, were more than happy to paint Democrats and their allies in the Kavanaugh opposition as rude and disorderly, relegated to making a scene rather than making a case against the nominee. McConnell, who was not at the hearing, said as much on the floor, accusing Democrats of "rude, disrespectful, and boorish behavior."

"I guess our Democratic friends' coordinated plan was to throw a big pot of spaghetti at the wall and see if anything stuck. Well—nothing stuck. Nothing stuck except the complete contrast between a gracious, thoughtful, patient nominee. And the hyperventilating by Senate Democrats, who are obviously not interested in giving Judge Kavanaugh the fair consideration he deserves."

Republicans also suggested certain critics were showboating to enhance their potential presidential credentials, particularly Senators Harris of California and Cory Booker of New Jersey, two rumored 2020 candidates who, not so coincidentally, were the two newest Democratic members of the committee.

But Democrats were not going to back off and repeatedly pressed Grassley for a delay to allow them to look at the new documents. In doing so, they reminded Republicans of how they had conducted themselves just two years earlier.

"Mr. Chairman, we waited for more than a year with a vacancy on the Supreme Court under the direction of your leader in the United States Senate and the republic survived," said Durbin. "I think the treatment was shabby of Merrick Garland, President Obama's nominee. The fact that we cannot take a few days or weeks to have a complete review of Judge Kavanaugh's record is unfair to the American people, it's inconsistent with our responsibility under Article Two, Section Two of the Constitution to advise and consent on Supreme Court nominees."

Grassley was cranky and perturbed with the Democrats and losing control of the first day of the hearing. He was determined to prevent Democrats from making their charge stick that he was being unfair and partisan and fought back constantly even as he gave Democrats the opportunity to challenge him.

There was no question he was doing things differently than had been done in the past when it came to documents and determining which would be considered "committee confidential." That category was being unilaterally applied by Senate Republicans and the group of Republican lawyers reviewing those from the Bush archive. Under the classification, senators and senior aides could look at the documents but they could not discuss them at the hearing without the consent of Republicans. About 150,000 documents had been placed in the "committee confidential" category at the urging of Bill Burck, the lawyer and friend of Kavanaugh's overseeing the review. Democrats hit Grassley hard for a serious break with committee practices.

"We used it in extremely rare circumstances where we would meet after this committee hearing and sit down, and it usually related to a handful of pages or a handful of document references," said Durbin, a senior member of the panel. "Instead, what we've found now is that we are seeing hundreds of thousands of documents characterized as committee confidential unilaterally. It's not done on a bipartisan basis; it's being done by the chairman." Durbin also ridiculed Burck's stunning and unusual role in the business of the Senate.

"When Judge Kavanaugh was in my office meeting with us, I asked him, 'Who is Bill Burck? By what authority can he restrict the information given to the Senate Judiciary Committee and to the American people? Is he a government employee?' No one knew this mysterious Bill Burck, who is filtering these documents," Durbin said.

"So, I figured since the nominee carries the Constitution in his pocket, there must be some reference to Bill Burck in Article Two, Section Two, but it just says, 'advice and consent of the Senate.' It doesn't include Mr. Burck. By what authority is this man holding back hundreds of thousands of documents from the American people? Who is he? Who's paying him? So committee confidential is being determined by a man, a private attorney, and we don't know who he works for or who he's accountable to."

Grassley and the Democrats went around and around. It was obvious that without the votes to overrule him and with Republicans eager to get on with the business of confirming Kavanaugh, Democrats had no chance of success—a reality that would haunt them throughout the hearing. It was time for the committee to begin hearing from Kavanaugh in public for the first time since his nomination a few months earlier.

In his own opening remarks, Kavanaugh repeated much of what he had said then about his family and upbringing, his coaching of a girl's basketball team, and of his commitment to be a fair judge. He also singled out for praise one member of the District of Columbia court of appeals, "a court now led by our superb chief judge, Merrick Garland." He closed with flowery sentiments.

"I am an optimist. I live on the sunrise side of the mountain, not the sunset side of the mountain. I see the day that is coming, not the day that is gone."

As it turned out, Kavanaugh didn't see what was coming at all.

29

The Paper Chase

DEMOCRATS WERE NOT happy with the lockdown Republicans had put on documents from Kavanaugh's service in the White House, but that didn't mean they had no paperwork at hand to pursue with the nominee. They intended to use what was available to show that Kavanaugh had not been truthful in his two previous confirmation hearings for his appeals court post about his work in the Bush White House.

As the questioning of Kavanaugh began, Democrats sought his views on abortion rights, presidential power, and gun control. But they also wanted to press him on a more obscure—but to senators much more personal—episode involving thousands of documents pilfered from the computers of Senate Democrats between 2001 and 2003. These were the same documents that emerged in 2003 after the withdrawal of Miguel Estrada from consideration for an appeals court seat that revealed Democratic concerns about Estrada being groomed as the first Hispanic nominee to the Supreme Court.

A sensation at the time, the incident had been largely forgotten in Washington. But not by Senator Leahy, then the top Democrat on the Judiciary Committee, whose computers had been rifled by Republican committee staffers who then shared the documents and insights gleaned from them with the staff at the White House overseeing judicial confirmations. Now Democrats had documentary evidence that Kavanaugh had seen some of the pilfered bounty.

Questioned about the documents obtained by the staffer, Manuel Miranda, during his 2004 and 2006 hearings, Kavanaugh was adamant that he knew nothing about their provenance.

"I did not know about any memos from the Democratic side," he had said in 2006. "I did not suspect that. Had I known or suspected that, I would have immediately told Judge Gonzales, who I'm sure would have immediately talked to Chairman Hatch about it. Did not know about it, did not suspect it."

But Democrats now had emails that showed that Kavanaugh, while handling some contentious judicial nominations during the early years of the George W. Bush administration, had been in direct communication with Miranda, who was providing sensitive information about Democratic strategy while warning Kavanaugh and other White House aides not to discuss the information outside their immediate circle.

In July 2002, for instance, Miranda had sent Kavanaugh and others an email that said: "As I mentioned on Friday, Senator Leahy's staff has distributed a confidential letter to Dem Counsel on Thursday from [redacted] who served as the attorney for Jane Doe in some or several of the Texas bypass cases. According to either the letter or the Leahy staff, Ms. [redacted] sent this letter in the strictest confidence."

To Leahy and other Democrats who had their computers infiltrated in what Leahy called a digital Watergate, this was new evidence that Kavanaugh had known Miranda possessed information he was not authorized to have and had shared it with Kavanaugh and the White House. The email did not explicitly cite the source, but it and others— including an invitation to meet in person to discuss other details— carried a clear suggestion that Miranda had inside information. This was doubly important to Leahy, Durbin, and others still in the Senate, since it was they who had been victims of the pilfering.

"I am concerned because there is evidence that Mr. Miranda provided you with materials that were stolen from me," Leahy told Kavanaugh. "And that would contradict your prior testimony. It is also clear from public emails—and I'm refraining from going into nonpublic ones—that you had reason to believe materials were obtained inappropriately at the time."

Kavanaugh disagreed. He said that such knowledge of the opposition strategy was a central part of court nomination fights, and he stuck with his denial of knowing that Miranda and a second staffer were able to access Democratic computers. "It's very common when you're in judicial selection process to determine what are all the senators interested in for an upcoming nominee or an upcoming hearing," Kavanaugh said. "That is the coin of the realm: Senator X is interested in focusing on administrative law, Senator Y is going to ask about environmental law, senator is concerned about your past work for this client.

"It's common, I think, for everyone to talk to each other at times, and share information. At least, this was my experience. This was twenty years ago, almost, where you would talk to people."

Those answers were infuriating to the Democratic aides who had worked on the Judiciary Committee at the time. They remembered a supercharged partisan atmosphere in which it would be ridiculous to think that Democrats would share confidential strategy with Republicans. "That is simply not accurate when it came to judicial nomination fights," said Kristine Lucius, a former counsel to Senator Leahy.

As more attention was focused on the old computer issue, Miranda issued a statement declaring that he had never discussed where he had gotten the information with Kavanaugh. While Democrats had their deep suspicions, there was no smoking gun on the subject.

Kavanaugh had been dishonest in declaring that he had no knowledge of the Bush administration's warrantless wiretapping program, which had been started in the aftermath of the September 11 attacks, and that he had not been involved in crafting terrorist detention policies. Democrats believed that some of the documents released by the Bush archives undermined his denials, but Kavanaugh insisted under tough questioning that he had told the truth.

Republicans, in their questioning, mainly rose to Kavanaugh's defense and helped him clean up his testimony to put to rest any suspicion that could have arisen from the Democratic grilling.

"Very directly, did you ever knowingly participate in stealing anything from Senator Leahy or any other senator?" Lindsey Graham, the South Carolina Republican, asked when his turn for questioning arrived.

"No," responded Kavanaugh.

"Did you ever know that you were dealing with anything that was stolen property?" Graham asked in a quick follow-up, getting the same one-word answer.

Orrin Hatch sought to immunize Kavanaugh on his relationship with Kozinski, and Kavanaugh attempted to paint a picture in which he did not have a close relationship with his former mentor. He said he did not see or talk to him by phone very often, though they had worked on a book on precedent together with multiple other judges. They also communicated over clerkships for Justice Kennedy.

Kavanaugh, who frequently mentioned his own record in hiring women law clerks, was adamant that he was unaware of any issues with Kozinski's conduct. "When they became public, the first thought I had was no—no woman should be subjected to sexual harassment in the workplace, ever, including in the judiciary—especially in the judiciary. And when I heard—When that became public, I think it was in December, it was a gut punch. It was a gut punch for me."

Senator Richard Blumenthal, the Connecticut Democrat, tried a different approach with Kavanaugh. Blumenthal wanted to show that the judge's dissent in a 2017 abortion case that came before the appeals court was politically motivated and intended to assure conservative leaders that the judge would overturn *Roe*, winning him a coveted spot on Trump's list for the Supreme Court in the process.

In the case, Kavanaugh dissented from a majority opinion that gave a pregnant seventeen-year-old immigrant the right to seek an abortion. Blumenthal noted that Kavanaugh referred to *Roe* as "existing"

Supreme Court precedent and also expressed reservations about "abortion on demand."

"You were telling the Trump administration if they wanted someone who would overturn *Roe v. Wade*, you would make the list," Blumenthal said. "These were your bumper stickers in that campaign—abortion on demand, existing precedent, law not as it necessarily was as you wished it now."

Kavanaugh denied the assertion and noted that he hadn't joined in an even more conservative dissent that questioned the woman's right to an abortion at all—a view that had drawn him criticism from the Far Right. But he refused to say whether he would vote to overturn *Roe*. "Senator, each of the eight justices currently on the Supreme Court, when they were in this seat, declined to answer that question," Kavanaugh said.

The hearing went through all the other usual confirmation touchstones. Kavanaugh, as others before him, gave away little. He continued to stress that the landmark abortion ruling was a well-established precedent that would be difficult to overturn.

But again, one of the documents that was released from his White House years complicated matters. One of the first that was leaked, a 2003 email obtained by the *New York Times*, showed that Kavanaugh took exception to a line in a draft op-ed that claimed legal scholars considered *Roe v. Wade* "settled law." Kavanaugh objected, saying that some would challenge the idea that it was virtually accepted as settled law. His view was challenging the assertion and didn't necessarily represent his thinking, but Democrats seized on it as evidence that he did not think *Roe* was sacrosanct.

Following that email, multiple other ones classified as "committee confidential" began to leak, and Democrats on the committee proudly said they would no longer be constrained by a process they considered a sham.

Cory Booker, as the hearings entered their third day, reveled in his decision to make public some emails that he believed undercut

Kavanaugh on racial issues. "I'm going to release the email about racial profiling, and I understand that the penalty comes with potential ousting from the Senate," he said. "And I'm releasing it to expose that, number one, the emails that are being withheld from the public have nothing to do with national security, nothing to jeopardize the sanctity of those ideals that I hold dear."

He drew a rebuke from Cornyn and other Republicans, who believed Booker was grandstanding. "Running for president is no excuse for violating the rules of the Senate or of the confidentiality of the documents that we are privy to," Cornyn said. The Senate and the determination of confidentiality and classification. That is irresponsible and conduct unbecoming a senator."

But Booker wouldn't back down and made a comment that will be remembered for the rest of his career, as he encouraged Cornyn to pursue a Senate investigation into the disclosure of the emails. "This is about the closest I'll probably ever have in my life to an 'I am Spartacus' moment," said Booker, implying with a classic movie reference that he was challenging the ruling powers.

The fight fizzled out as the main portion of the hearings came to an end and no explosive material came to light. Democrats believed they had shown Kavanaugh had lied about some aspects of his work while in the Bush White House.

"Brett Kavanaugh used materials stolen from Democratic senators to advance President Bush's judicial nominees," Feinstein said in a tweet as the hearing concluded. "He was asked about this in 2004, 2006 and this week. His answers were not true."

But they had not inflicted the type of damage that could derail the nomination. Republicans, angry over what they saw as over-the-top attacks on a highly qualified nominee many of them had known for years, were more than ready to steamroll the opposition and install Kavanaugh.

Democrats had satisfied some of their constituent groups that they were willing to go to the mat against Kavanaugh even if his confirmation was a sure thing. "Given they were forced to conduct this hearing with one hand behind their backs, they did an exceptional job in making clear how much of a threat Kavanaugh is to health care, abortion, and checks and balances," Nan Aron, the president of the liberal Alliance for Justice, said. "They fought vigorously on all fronts to get documents."

It didn't appear to be enough. Senate Republicans were moving ahead with a committee confirmation vote with the intention of getting Kavanaugh on the court for the start of the new term in early October. Little appeared to be standing in their way.

30

The Letter

KAVANAUGH WEATHERED HIS formal confirmation hearing, but an independent search was still ongoing for information that contrasted with the upstanding, altar boy image that he, Senate Republicans, and the White House tried to project in the Hart Building hearing room.

Rumors and reports persisted that Kavanaugh's youthful behavior was far from exemplary, and journalists who had done some of the #MeToo reporting, along with anti-Kavanaugh activists, continued to pursue them and reach out to potential sources. But if there were women who had had bad experiences with him, they were not willing to come forward into what would certainly be a searing public spotlight. Plus, news organizations were facing questions about how hard to press on such long-ago behavior. It seemed far different from the case of Clarence Thomas, who was an adult and a federal supervisory employee during the time Anita Hill said he sexually harassed her.

Four days of hearings concluded on September 7, and Kavanaugh's confirmation seemed inevitable, with a formal committee vote set for September 20. All that was about to change.

On September 12, Ryan Grim, an experienced Capitol Hill reporter for the *Intercept* and formerly of the *Huffington Post*, published a story alleging that Democrats on the Judiciary Committee were pressing Feinstein to share with them a letter from a female California constituent concerning Kavanaugh. Someone wanted the letter, which had been held in confidence by Feinstein and her staff, out.

Grim's story did not say what type of incident was involved but that the woman was being represented by a lawyer who had represented other women who had encountered sexual harassment. That night Democrats held a meeting at which Feinstein shared the contents of the letter, which had first been sent to Representative Anna Eshoo, a Silicon Valley Democrat, by a constituent who had asked to remain anonymous.

The next day, September 13, the *New York Times* was the first to report that the letter concerned accusations of sexual misconduct. Then, with more people becoming familiar with its contents, the details began to spill out. A woman had sent a letter dated July 30 alleging that Kavanaugh and Mark Judge, another student at the elite Georgetown Preparatory School, had assaulted her at a teenage gathering three decades earlier. She did not want to come forward.

Feinstein issued a cryptic statement, saying she had "received information from an individual concerning the nomination of Brett Kavanaugh to the Supreme Court. That individual strongly requested confidentiality, declined to come forward or press the matter further, and I have honored that decision. I have, however, referred the matter to federal investigative authorities." It was unclear what the FBI would do with the letter, if anything.

Kavanaugh, through the White House, denied the allegations, saying they never took place. But the man who had repeatedly emphasized his support for women and whose two young daughters had been at his side throughout the process—the man who had said repeatedly he had no knowledge of Judge Kozinski's behavior—was suddenly facing credible accusations of his own.

The White House, Senate Republicans, and conservative advocacy groups dismissed the disclosure as a last-minute smear as Kavanaugh was on his way to confirmation and a seat on the court. "This has all the indicators of an eleventh-hour character assassination and a desperate attempt to delay and defeat the nomination of Judge Kavanaugh, who has a sterling reputation in his community, his profession, his church, and among hundreds of friends, colleagues, and coworkers," said Carrie Severino of the Judicial Crisis Network.

It was uncertain what impact the allegations would have. This wasn't 1991, when Clarence Thomas survived his sexual misconduct accusations. This was 2018, and the #MeToo movement was having a major impact on society, forcing a reckoning with men who had abused their power and authority for years. It was hard to imagine that the confirmation march for Kavanaugh could proceed as before.

Yet even with this potential bombshell thrown into the mix, Kavanaugh remained on track. Republicans said they did not intend to pull back from the committee vote on his confirmation.

The FBI had simply taken the letter from Feinstein and returned it to Kavanaugh's background file at the Judiciary Committee, where it could be reviewed by senators who wanted to see it. Agents were not undertaking any new investigation of the accusations. Democrats did not have any investigative staff capable of pursuing it. Kavanaugh was said to be furious about the accusation arising, a disclosure that would certainly taint his reputation no matter what the outcome.

Kavanaugh's opponents conceded that they didn't think the existence of the letter, even in the changed cultural environment, could turn the nomination's tide without the woman coming forward and accusing Kavanaugh publicly. Headed into the weekend, it appeared unlikely to happen.

Then, on the afternoon of Sunday, September 16, the *Washington Post* published a detailed story saying that Christine Blasey Ford, a college professor in Palo Alto who had grown up in the suburbs of Washington, had come forward to say that she had been attacked in a bedroom at age fifteen by Kavanaugh.

"While his friend watched, she said, Kavanaugh pinned her to a bed on her back and groped her over her clothes, grinding his body against hers and clumsily attempting to pull off her one-piece bathing suit and the clothing she wore over it," the explosive *Post* story read. "When she tried to scream, she said, he put his hand over her mouth."

The story was of a magnitude to imperil the nomination. Republicans once thought they could knock out Merrick Garland with a theater review that referred favorably to a song about sexual assault. Kavanaugh was facing a serious charge of sexual assault himself.

Blindsided Republicans immediately took steps to determine what its impact would be, meeting at the White House with Kavanaugh to plot strategy. (At the same time, early Republican opponents of Kavanaugh muttered that if the accusations had only come out before his nomination, they might have been spared the whole ordeal.)

Both Mitch McConnell and Don McGahn quickly reached out to Susan Collins, the Maine swing vote, to get her impressions and perspective on what they should do. Collins was a key to the confirmation. From the beginning, she had appeared to want to back Kavanaugh, but she also was being deliberate and careful, as was her style. She would not be pushed, and she would be reluctant to move forward without an airing of the accusations or giving Ford a chance to tell her story if she indeed wanted to do so. Lisa Murkowski, the other Republican female centrist, had already raised concerns about Kavanaugh but wasn't considered as important as Collins as far as the fate of the nomination.

Collins suggested to McGahn that perhaps Kavanaugh should concede something had occurred but that it was just high school behavior that had gone too far and that he regretted it. But Kavanaugh was adamant that the incident had not happened and that he would not lie about it. McGahn also told the senator that there was no retreat for Kavanaugh, that if he lost the nomination fight he would be lucky to be working in a hardware store within weeks.

Collins and others criticized Feinstein for sitting on the letter and throwing the nomination into such turmoil when she had earlier opportunities to question the nominee about it. "What is puzzling to me is the Democrats, by not bringing this out earlier, after having had this information for more than six weeks, have managed to cast a cloud of doubt on both the professor and the judge," Collins said in an interview the evening of the story in the *Post*. "If they believed Professor Ford, why didn't they surface this information earlier so that he could be questioned about it? And if they didn't believe her and chose to withhold the information, why did they decide at the eleventh hour to release it? It is really not fair to either of them the way it was handled."

Other Republicans were more pointed, saying they suspected that Democrats held on to the letter intentionally to use as a late-stage missile if other efforts to blow up the Kavanaugh nomination failed.

President Trump himself was oddly restrained—no tweets, no sharp attacks on Ford. He had been warned that the situation was so delicate that an attack on Ford could shift the votes of Collins and others who were publicly undecided.

Collins and Jeff Flake also both suggested that if one believed Ford was telling the truth, it would necessitate a vote against Kavanaugh.

White House officials were initially hoping they could power through the revelation of the identity of Ford and the details of the accusations. But that strategy quickly unraveled, and by Monday night Republicans had agreed to another hearing—although a week of negotiations and back-and-forth would be needed to set the terms.

The situation was remarkable in its parallels to the Thomas-Hill hearings, conducted twenty-seven years earlier. Like Kavanaugh, Thomas appeared to have confirmation in his grasp when leaked accusations of sexual harassment necessitated another hearing. But there were differences as well. Democrats controlled the Senate in 1991 and were considering the nominee of a Republican, George H. W. Bush. This time, social media was driving much of the discussion. But it would be, at its heart, another case of a woman facing a skeptical Senate, and her testimony would be weighed against that of a judge who had the powerful backing of much of Washington's establishment.

There was another major difference as well. The Clarence Thomas hearings had taken place more than a year out from the next election. In this case, the hearings would play out before a politically polarized nation just weeks before a crucial midterm election, and the confrontation was certain to have some impact on the outcome in November.

McConnell, for his part, remained confident, telling a convention of Christian conservatives that Kavanaugh would be confirmed no matter what. "President Trump has nominated a stunningly successful individual," McConnell assured the gathering in a Washington ballroom. "You have watched the fight, you watched the tactics. But here's what I want to tell you: in the very near future, Judge Kavanaugh will be on the United States Supreme Court. Keep the faith. Don't get rattled by all this."

That same day, in one of their regular phone calls, McConnell told Trump that he and Senate Republicans would see the nomination through, with McConnell using a colorful colloquialism, saying he was "stronger than mule piss" when it came to Kavanaugh.

McConnell was not the only Republican who seemed to have his mind made up about the outcome.

Mike Davis, the Gorsuch adviser, had permanently joined Grassley's Judiciary Committee staff as an always-ready-for-combat committee counsel. He made his views known on Twitter as Grassley's staff sought to negotiate the parameters of a hearing with Ford's attorneys.

"Unfazed and determined. We will confirm Judge Kavanaugh. #ConfirmKavanaugh #SCOTUS," Davis said in a tweet that drew considerable attention, since he was supposedly keeping at least the appearance of an open mind on the accusations against Kavanaugh. It was a mistake by an aggressive staffer, and he quickly deleted the tweet and sought to explain it.

"To clear up any confusion, I was referring to Democrats' partisan political attacks and their refusal to take part in the committee's thorough and fair investigation," he said in a subsequent tweet. "I deleted the tweet to avoid any further misinterpretation by left wing media as so often happens on Twitter."

The hearing was set for the following Monday. Democrats wanted the FBI to investigate Ford's claims before then, but no inquiry was launched. Republicans, anxious about their all-male lineup on the Judiciary Committee grilling Ford, announced they would bring in a female sex crimes prosecutor from Arizona to handle their questioning.

Both sides tried to get the upper hand in the talks. Lawyers for Ford said she would not be ready to testify on Monday, and Grassley threatened to move ahead with the committee vote if she refused to attend. But it was so much posturing. The hearing was always going to happen; Republicans could not afford to stifle Ford and upset Collins and Flake; Ford wanted her day in court.

As Republicans feared, the delay did allow time for added allegations to surface, as various leads that journalists had been pursuing broke into the public. One, reported by *The New Yorker*, alleged that Kavanaugh exposed himself to an undergraduate classmate while a freshman at Yale. But the woman involved, Deborah Ramirez, initially questioned her own memory, undercutting the story's impact. And the *New York Times* disclosed that it had pursued the story but was unable to corroborate it, a fact that Republicans seized on. Kavanaugh adamantly denied anything had happened at Yale.

At the same time, Michael Avenatti, the spotlight-loving lawyer who was representing the adult film star Stormy Daniels in her fierce hush-money legal battle with Trump, entered the fray. He let it be known that he was in contact with yet another person aware of sexual misconduct by the nominee.

On September 26, Avenatti released a statement by the woman, Julie Swetnick, who had grown up in a far Washington suburb. She said she had attended parties at which Kavanaugh and others had engaged in egregious behavior including coercing and drugging young women into having sex with multiple teenagers. "I have a firm recollection of seeing boys lined up outside rooms at many of these parties waiting for their 'turn' with a girl inside the room. These boys included Mark Judge and Brett Kavanaugh," she alleged in the statement.

Republicans considered Avenatti's involvement a blessing in disguise. They saw him as a publicity-hungry partisan—he had already made noise about running for president in 2020—who would go too far in pressing accusations against Kavanaugh, undermining all the other claims in the process. Kavanaugh said the statement from Avenatti's client struck him as something from the *Twilight Zone*, and he dismissed it.

Other outlandish and uncorroborated reports of sexual misconduct filtered in to the Judiciary Committee but were not considered credible and did not become a serious part of the public inquiry. When things did pop up, Grassley had the advantage of an experienced investigative staff from his oversight work to quickly run them down, an option the Democrats did not have.

With the accusations swirling around Kavanaugh reaching a fevered intensity, the nominee and the White House decided to take some bold action. The White House arranged for an interview of the nominee on the friendly venue of Fox News. Nominees and their handlers typically eschew these kinds of tactics. Democrats had rejected the idea of letting Merrick Garland do interviews to build support, for example. The fear is multifold—that it can lead to revelations that could hurt the nominee, but also that it demeans the process and makes the nominee look more like a political candidate than he or she already does.

Republicans believed that Kavanaugh was in enough trouble to justify the risk. They initially considered having Jan Crawford, a veteran Supreme Court reporter at CBS, conduct the interview but quickly quashed that idea. They instead turned to Fox News as more accommodating terrain, though the interviewer, Martha MacCallum, turned out to be no pushover.

Asked why he was doing the interview, Kavanaugh responded with a wonky answer. "I am looking for a fair process, a process where I can defend my integrity and clear my name," Kavanaugh said as the interview began. "And all I'm asking for is fairness and that I'd be heard in this process."

That went over like a lead balloon at the White House, where Trump and McGahn wanted Kavanaugh to be forceful, assailing the accusations as outrageous and unfounded. Trump was not impressed.

"Trump needs to see people fight for themselves," said one White House aide. Like the case of Gorsuch and his clerks, Kavanaugh had turned for strategic guidance to old and comfortable Bush-era allies, including two former Bush counselors, Dan Bartlett and Ed Gillespie. Trump insiders believed the nominee had gotten faulty advice to tone down his remarks—the opposite of what Trump and his team wanted.

Kavanaugh repeated his denials when asked why Ford would come forward with a false accusation. "What I know is the truth," he said. "And the truth is, I've never sexually assaulted anyone in high school or otherwise. I am not questioning and have not questioned that perhaps Dr. Ford at some point in her life was sexually assaulted by someone in some place. But what I know is I've never sexually assaulted anyone in high school or at any time in my life." As for the Yale incident reported by *The New Yorker*, he adamantly denied that happened and said if it had, "it would've been the talk of campus." Kavanaugh even went so far as to reveal that he had been a virgin in high school and for many years after.

The interview and Kavanaugh's passive showing would have implications later.

The day of the hearing brought a tense atmosphere to Capitol Hill. The testimony was not going to be in the cavernous room where the initial hearing was conducted but instead was in the committee's cramped regular meeting room. Capitol police cordoned off much of the Dirksen Senate Office Building hallway for security.

How much had the #MeToo moment and movement changed America? Would Ford be believed despite a lack of corroborating evidence? Could this woman from out of Kavanaugh's distant past emerge from Northern California and sink the court nomination he had so carefully pursued?

Ford was first to testify, and her entrance gave the nation its initial glimpse at the unassuming professor and psychologist who was understandably nervous as she confronted some of the most powerful politicians in the world.

"I am here today not because I want to be," she said. "I am terrified. I am here because I believe it is my civic duty to tell you what happened to me while Brett Kavanaugh and I were in high school."

Ford quietly related the now-familiar story of going with a small group of friends from a country club swimming pool to a party, at which, while going upstairs to a bathroom, she was forced into a bedroom by an obviously drunk Kavanaugh and Judge. Kavanaugh jumped on her, she said, put his hand over her mouth, and tried to get her clothes off. Judge eventually jumped on the bed and they all tumbled off, giving Ford a chance to escape. She left the party and barely mentioned a word about it until meeting with a therapist in 2012. Ford said she initially hoped that her providing the information confidentially to the Senate would be enough for senators to weigh it and reject Kavanaugh—a thought that showed her naivete about the process.

The questioning proceeded, but Republicans had made a miscalculation. Grassley had decided to allow questions to proceed in five-minute increments. So the prosecutor Republicans had engaged to prevent an all-male GOP inquisition—Rachel Mitchell—could not build momentum in her examination of Ford, and the situation was awkward at best.

Ford said her most searing memory from that night was Kavanaugh and Judge laughing at the assault and that she was "100 percent" certain that it was Kavanaugh who assaulted her. McGahn, watching from a nearby Senate office, thought her answer about the laughter was a mistake. He believed Ford should have focused on memories of Kavanaugh's physical appearance, driving home with a description that it was him.

Mitchell also attempted to undermine claims by Ford's attorney that she had a fear of flying—hence her inability to agree to an earlier hearing—and throw doubt on a polygraph exam she had taken. But Ford's overall testimony overshadowed those attempts to chip away at her credibility.

It was a remarkable and emotional performance that seemed to convince both Republicans and Democrats. Even Trump, watching from the White House, wondered if Kavanaugh was finished. He called McConnell to get his thoughts.

"We are only at halftime," McConnell replied.

The nomination appeared severely endangered if not completely dead, done in by Ford's calm and credible recitation of an event that clearly appeared to have haunted her through her adult life.

McGahn watched the riveting testimony in the office of Senator Thom Tillis, the North Carolina Republican who, as a member of the Judiciary Committee, was in the hearing room listening to Ford. McGahn had started out in a conference room but relocated because the TV wasn't working correctly. Kavanaugh had been readying himself at home and said he didn't watch. McGahn believed him.

As Ford's testimony unfolded, McGahn started receiving worried texts from his circle. But he remained confident. After the Fox interview, McGahn had taken steps to prepare Kavanaugh for this moment. In his White House office with the help of experienced litigators, McGahn had Kavanaugh practice aggressive responses to questions and questioners. He wanted to see the nominee push back, cut off his interrogators, and turn their questions back on them. The idea had come from Hatch, who said that at some point Kavanaugh would have to show his mettle. McGahn also plotted strategy with Lindsey Graham about how to maintain Republican support in the committee by presenting a choice to colleagues between supporting an unfairly accused Kavanaugh or joining Democrats in tearing him down.

Kavanaugh arrived with his wife, Ashley. McGahn and others, including some of Kavanaugh's former law clerks, began discussing last-minute strategy in the committee anteroom. One clerk suggested that Kavanaugh should consider a conciliatory approach, given Ford's compelling testimony.

McGahn was furious. "Did I tell you you could say that?" he asked in an acid tone. He demanded that the room be cleared. When Ashley

Kavanaugh started to follow the others out, McGahn said he had not meant her.

"What do I need to know?" the nominee asked.

"You need to reboot the room," McGahn told him. He urged Kavanaugh to approach the moment as if Ford had not even testified, that he needed to defend his character, family, and reputation. Speak from the heart. This, McGahn told the anxious nominee, was the culmination of his life's work, all those nights of extra homework had boiled down to this moment. "If you do your job," McGahn said, "I will get the votes."

Kavanaugh heeded the advice. Entering the hearing room, he assumed a fierce, take-no-prisoners stance from the start, eager to display his anger at what he and his family had been put through.

"This confirmation process has become a national disgrace," a visibly upset Kavanaugh began. "The Constitution gives the Senate an important role in the confirmation process, but you have replaced advice and consent with search and destroy."

He called the Democrats an embarrassment and then said that when their first effort at an "old-fashioned attempt at Borking" hadn't worked, they had lain in wait with the secret accusations from Ford. He blamed the episode on Democrats out to get him for a multitude of reasons.

"This whole two-week effort has been a calculated and orchestrated political hit, fueled with apparent pent-up anger about President Trump and the 2016 election. Fear that has been unfairly stoked about my judicial record. Revenge on behalf of the Clintons, and millions of dollars in money from outside left-wing opposition groups," he said.

The Clinton line was especially striking, since it seemed to refer to his work for Kenneth Starr in pursuing the impeachment of Bill Clinton. The suggestion being that Democratic members of the panel were carrying out a vendetta based on his work twenty years earlier—an idea that probably hadn't occurred to most of the Democrats. It felt like Kavanaugh, fighting for his judicial life, was embracing a conspiracy theory. He also left out the fact that millions of dollars had been spent on his behalf by conservative advocacy organizations.

"This has destroyed my family and my good name. A good name built up through decades of very hard work and public service at the highest levels of the American government," Kavanaugh steamed.

As they prepared for the hearing, Democrats had divvied up the areas of questioning they wanted to pursue. They pressed him on everything from his drinking to whether he had attacked Ford to curious and suggestive entries in his high school yearbook and his meticulously kept and preserved high school calendars. Kavanaugh fought back forcefully and at many times rudely, his facial expressions reflecting clear disgust. Asked by Senator Amy Klobuchar if he had ever blacked out from drinking, Kavanaugh snapped back in an utter breach of decorum.

"You're asking about, you know, blackout. I don't know. Have you?" he said.

"Could you answer the question, Judge?" said an obviously surprised Klobuchar. "I just—So you—That's not happened. Is that your answer?"

"Yeah, and I'm curious if you have," he responded.

"I have no drinking problem, Judge," she said.

"Yea," he said, ending the remarkable exchange. "Nor do I."

With the hearing reaching such a toxic level, Grassley called a recess, and upon returning, Kavanaugh apologized to Klobuchar. But the exchange raised the issue both sides would have to address: Was Kavanaugh's Trumpian combativeness winning him backers or finally costing him the nomination?

The answer depended on the political perspective of the audience. Democrats and Kavanaugh's critics believed he had gone too far. But this was the era of Trump. Verbal pugilism had become ingrained and common and could be a plus. The sense among Republicans that Kavanaugh was doomed and that his nomination would have to be withdrawn began to shift with his defiant rebuttal of the accusations against him.

As he walked through the Capitol, Representative Tom Cole, an Oklahoma Republican and a former national party official considered a reasonable voice in the party, was asked what he thought of Kavanaugh's performance.

"Home run!" Cole answered. "How can you vote against him after that?"

As Democrats pursued their punishing questions, Republicans allowed Mitchell, the outside prosecutor, to question Kavanaugh on their behalf on the details of his activities in his teenage days and his calendars, gathering information in bits as a prosecutor would in a courtroom. The effort, confined to the five-minute segments allowed by Grassley, was still proving ineffective in a proceeding that was essentially a political trial, not a courtroom affair. Her questioning did produce one of the more comedic moments as Mitchell queried him about his high school drinking.

"Yes, we drank beer," an irritated Kavanaugh said as he readily admitted to imbibing. "My friends and I, the boys and girls. Yes, we drank beer. I liked beer. Still like beer. We drank beer."

The atmosphere was about to undergo a drastic change when the questioning reached Senator Lindsey Graham, the South Carolina Republican.

Graham's closest friend in the Senate, John McCain, had died just weeks earlier after a brutal struggle with brain cancer. McCain's death was understandably going to have an impact on Graham, who had basked in his mentor's aura. McCain had tended to treat Graham as a beloved junior partner. The death had shaken Graham, and his increasingly strident conservative tone was drawing attention in Washington, as was his growing defense of and alliance with Trump, a former presidential rival whom Graham had condemned during the campaign. Trump had also belittled McCain's military service and resented his vote against health care repeal, and the relationship between the men had been poisonous even after McCain's death.

And court fights had a special way of driving Graham to distraction.

He incessantly noted that, at great risk to his standing among Republicans in South Carolina, he had voted for President Obama's two nominees—Sonia Sotomayor and Elena Kagan. Though he didn't share their judicial philosophy, Graham said he believed that a president was entitled to qualified nominees. (He also liked to note that Obama himself had joined the unsuccessful filibuster of Samuel Alito.)

During the first round of hearings on Kavanaugh, Graham ridiculed Democrats for being so outraged at Trump picking a former Republican operative like Kavanaugh when Democrats had done so in the past. To the political winners, he said, go the judicial spoils.

"You had a chance and you lost," he reminded them. "If you want to pick judges from your way of thinking, then you better win an election. I voted for two of your choices, Sotomayor and Kagan, got a lot of crap.

"You can't lose the election and pick judges," he reiterated. "If you want to pick judges, you better win."

Graham's anger at the treatment of Kavanaugh had built to a climax by the time his turn came around, and he did not cede his moment to the outside attorney.

He started with an assault on the Democrats.

"If you wanted an FBI investigation, you could have come to us," he told them. "What you want to do is destroy this guy's life, hold this seat open, and hope you win in 2020. You've said that, not me. You've got nothing to apologize for.

"When you see Sotomayor and Kagan, tell them that Lindsey said hello, because I voted for them," Graham said. "I would never do to them what you've done to this guy. This is the most unethical sham since I've been in politics. And if you really wanted to know the truth, you sure as hell wouldn't have done what you've done to this guy."

Graham turned to Kavanaugh and asked if he were a "gang rapist," which drew a one-word response: no. Graham then unleashed comments meant to shame fellow Republicans still weighing voting against Kavanaugh. His huddle with McGahn had borne fruit.

"To my Republican colleagues, if you vote no, you're legitimizing the most despicable thing I have seen in my time in politics," Graham declared. He angrily challenged the Democrats as well. "You want this seat? I hope you never get it."

Kavanaugh and the Republicans, through Graham's diatribe, seemed to have regained the offensive and rescued the nomination.

Democrats pressed their case against Kavanaugh, peppering him with inquiries about his drinking and yearbook entries while Kavanaugh heatedly belittled their questioning as ridiculous and harmful to innocent friends and acquaintances. The main demand of the Democrats was to win a new FBI investigation into the accusations not only by Ford, but by Deborah Ramirez, the Yale classmate, and possibly other accounts that had been offered—an idea that Republicans adamantly rejected.

Again, one of the unexpected allies in their argument against the Democrats was Joe Biden. As in the case of Merrick Garland, when Republicans kept referring to Biden's 1992 speech warning the president against a court nomination in an election year, Republicans had unearthed another set of Biden remarks damaging to the Democratic cause. In 1991, Biden, the then-chairman of the Judiciary Committee, had pushed back against calls for the FBI to investigate Anita Hill's claims.

Senator Mike Lee, the Utah Republican, took the opportunity to remind Democrats of Biden's position that an inquiry would be pointless.

"During the Clarence Thomas hearings, nearly three decades ago, Chairman Biden made some interesting observations about FBI reports and their role in this process," said Lee. "Here's what he said. 'The next person who refers to an FBI report as being worth anything obviously doesn't understand anything. The FBI explicitly does not, in this, or any other case, reach a conclusion. Period. Period.' Those are his dual periods, not mine."

The hearing was drawing to a close, but not before a last bit of drama at the hands of Senator John Kennedy, the junior Louisiana Republican developing a reputation for folksy and highly quotable statements in the grand tradition of previous senators from the state.

"Do you believe in God?" Kennedy asked the nominee.

"I do," he answered.

"I'm going to give you a last opportunity, right here, right in front of God and country. I want you to look me in the eye," Kennedy said. "Are Dr. Ford's allegations true?"

"They are not as to me," said Kavanaugh. "I have not questioned that she might have been sexually assaulted at some point in her life by someone, someplace. But as to me, I've never done this; never done this to her or to anyone else. And I've talked to you about what I was doing that summer of 1982. But I'm telling you I've never done this to anyone, including her."

The nearly eight-hour hearing concluded. Kavanaugh's nomination was in the hands of six senators—three Republicans and three Democrats—who remained publicly undecided.

But the president's view was clear.

"Judge Kavanaugh showed America exactly why I nominated him," Trump tweeted. "His testimony was powerful, honest, and riveting. Democrats' search and destroy strategy is disgraceful and this process has been a total sham and effort to delay, obstruct, and resist. The Senate must vote!"

31

"Forever Change the Senate and Our Nation's Highest Court"

REPUBLICANS HAD HAD enough. Less than twenty-four hours after the conclusion of the mesmerizing testimony by Ford and Kavanaugh, Grassley and the Republican members of the Judiciary Committee were more than ready to move ahead, approve Kavanaugh's nomination, and send it to the floor for confirmation—a little bit later than planned, but headed for approval nonetheless.

As the committee convened, the results seemed preordained, since Flake, obviously torn over what to do, ended the suspense by announcing just before the pivotal meeting that he would vote to confirm Kavanaugh.

"Our system of justice affords a presumption of innocence to the accused, absent corroborating evidence," Flake said. "That is what binds us to the rule of law. While some may argue that a different standard should apply regarding the Senate's advice and consent responsibilities, I believe that the Constitution's provisions of fairness and due process apply here as well."

With Flake's vote assured, Republicans felt no compunction to delay action any longer, and they quickly dismissed Democratic efforts to subpoena Mark Judge or to require more FBI investigation into the accusations against Kavanaugh.

"Here's where I stand," said Hatch, veteran of three decades of judicial fights. "We can't allow more time for new smears to damage Judge Kavanaugh. His family, his reputation, the reputation of the court, and, of course, the reputation of the country. We can't allow more time for partisans on the left to try to beat Judge Kavanaugh into submission."

The new momentum behind Kavanaugh made one fact clear— Republicans, by agreeing to the Ford testimony, had been mainly trying to make Jeff Flake, Susan Collins, and Lisa Murkowsi comfortable in voting for Kavanaugh. With Flake's vote now in their pocket, it was past time to move on and try to bring Collins and Murkowski on board along with Democrats such as Manchin, Heitkamp, and Donnelly.

Democrats were frustrated but had absolutely no power to slow the committee vote on their own. Feinstein, however, expressed a new reservation about Kavanaugh—his angry and contemptuous tone of the day before. To Democrats, Kavanaugh's political persona had revealed itself anew.

"Candidly, on the twenty-five years on this committee, I have never seen a nominee for any position behave in that manner," Feinstein said. "Judge Kavanaugh used as much political rhetoric as my Republican colleagues. And what's more, he went on the attack. He yelled at Democrats for having the temerity to express our frustration for not having access to over ninety percent of his record and said that some Democratic members were, quote, an embarrassment, end quote."

Leahy, a former chairman of the once august committee, tore into Grassley and Republicans for their handling of the confirmation, suggesting it would cast an expansive shadow over the Senate and the court. "The Senate is supposed to be an independent, equal branch of government," Leahy said. "We're no longer that, we're an arm, a very weak arm, of the Trump White House. Every semblance of independence has just disappeared. It's gone. And I think that is something historians will look at and they'll call it a turning point in the United States Senate."

Leahy said the Democrats wanted answers to questions surrounding Kavanaugh and weren't simply trying to stall until after the election, though he couldn't resist adding that "we have that precedent when the Republicans did that with Merrick Garland. This is about doing our job.

"Voting to advance and ultimately confirm Judge Kavanaugh while he's under this dark cloud of suspicion will forever change the Senate and our nation's highest court.

But Republicans were done. Grassley set a vote on the nomination for 1:30 p.m. and opened the floor to allow Democrats to rant. The outcome seemed assured. Most Republicans left the cramped room, intending to return after other business and lunch to finish their deliberations and vote on Kavanaugh. To do so, they had to make their way through very aggressive anti-Kavanaugh protesters.

While special permission was typically needed to be in the Capitol building itself, the Senate office buildings were a different story. Members of the public could generally roam freely and approach senators if they encountered them. Security was intensified during the Kavanaugh hearings, but police did not typically interrupt protesters if they did not touch or impede the lawmakers.

Flake had an emotional encounter as he went to join the Judiciary Committee proceedings. Just after he announced his vote, he was in an elevator when he was approached by two women who said they were sexual assault survivors outraged at his decision.

"What you are doing is allowing someone who actually violated a woman to sit on the Supreme Court," Ana Maria Archila scolded him in an encounter aired on television. "This is not tolerable. You have children in your family. Think about them."

Flake stood glumly in the corner of the elevator, looking at the floor as he listened to the women. While other Republicans testily dismissed the protesters, Flake felt differently. Though he voted with his fellow Republicans to reject Democratic demands to call more witnesses, Flake seemed uncertain. As the committee session continued, he went to the Democratic side of the dais and tapped his friend, Senator Chris Coons, Democrat of Delaware, on the shoulder to arrange a meeting in the hearing room's private antechamber.

Coons, a divinity school graduate, had won his Senate seat in 2010 after his Tea Party challenger, Christine O'Donnell, had to famously declare in a television ad that she was not a witch despite some youthful dabbling in the occult. Coons could have faced a much tougher challenger but O'Donnell had knocked off Representative Mike Castle, a popular Republican, in the primary. Now Coons had a very secure Senate seat.

Coons had emphasized trying to work across the aisle and had built a few Republican friendships, including with Flake. They had a shared interest in Africa from their time there as young men, Flake as a Mormon missionary and Coons as a student. As the committee moved toward a vote, Coons urged that a relatively straightforward inquiry take place.

"I have conveyed to my friends and colleagues I wished we would take a one-week pause, one week only, not to spread it out across the next election but to allow a professional FBI interview with everyone who might have information," Coons said. He had provided Flake a copy of his remarks but didn't anticipate they would have much impact.

As they met in the crowded anteroom, Coons expected Flake to explain his vote for Kavanaugh and express a hope that the bitter process wouldn't hurt their friendship. Instead Flake, stung by the elevator encounter, wanted to pursue Coons's idea for a one-week delay to allow an FBI inquiry. As the two engaged in negotiations over how to proceed, members of both parties filtered in and out of the discussions, with Democrats offering encouragement and some Republicans, including Cornyn and Thom Tillis, trying to dissuade Flake, saying the issue was settled and that the inquiry was simply another Democratic delaying tactic. Staff pushed in as well to monitor what was going on.

To escape the kibitzing, Flake and Coons crammed together into an old telephone booth in the room to make cell phone calls. It was a cozy and awkward scene as Flake checked in with leaders of the FBI and Coons called Murkowski to get buy-in on the new plan.

In the hearing room, it gradually became clear that something was afoot. Grassley and Hatch, the two veterans of the Clarence Thomas hearings, shared a private conversation as they sat downcast at their seats.

The time for the vote came and went. Finally, a visibly nervous Flake entered the room, quietly asked Grassley if he could have consent to speak for a minute, and took his seat. Then the Arizonan dropped a bombshell.

"I have been speaking with people on the other side; we have had conversations ongoing for a while with regard to making sure that we do due diligence here," he said. "I think it would be proper to delay the vote for up to but not more than one week in order to let the FBI continue to do an investigation limited in time and scope to the current allegations that are there."

Confusion briefly reigned as Grassley quickly called the vote on the nomination to forestall efforts by the Democrats to postpone it or incorporate an understanding of just what Flake's proposal entailed. Some Democrats appeared to think that Flake's call for the investigation would be included in the committee vote for Kavanaugh, but it was not. Still, if Flake—as well as the other undeclared Republicans— would not vote for Kavanaugh on the floor without a new investigation, they would get an investigation or Kavanaugh's nomination would go down.

Though Flake's gambit certainly wasn't what Republicans wanted, it wasn't as bad for them as first appeared. Notably, with Flake's help, they had advanced Kavanaugh out of committee. Flake could have pushed for a postponement of the committee vote, but he didn't. And once the inquiry was complete, McConnell could take the nomination straight to a floor vote. Flake had given up his leverage over the committee action.

Plus, beyond the vague stipulation that the investigation could take no longer than a week and address the "current allegations," no firm conditions on who or what the FBI should investigate were put in place. Republicans and the White House could shape the parameters of the inquiry.

Flake had done his Republican colleagues a big favor—they just didn't realize it at the time. Provided the new investigation didn't turn up damaging information, the inquiry would ultimately make it easier for uncertain Republicans to back Judge Kavanaugh. It would also temper the perception that Republicans were much more interested in getting Judge Kavanaugh onto the court as quickly as they could rather than determining the validity of sexual misconduct accusations against him.

"It is reassuring to the public," Senator Susan Collins, a Maine Republican and an ally of Mr. Flake, said about the delay. "It shows that Republicans want to make sure that we have all the facts to make an informed decision."

Wavering Republicans wanted to show they were not part of a rush job to seat Kavanaugh without following up on the sexual misconduct accusations. But a damning new FBI inquiry would require one of the key witnesses—Mark Judge or Leland Ingham Keyser, a close friend who Ford said was at the fateful party—to change their story, and that seemed unlikely.

Still, the news of another investigation did not go over well in the leadership suite of Senate Republicans or at the White House. McConnell was unhappy and warned Flake, Collins, and others that the delay would only allow more misconduct accusations to surface and that Kavanaugh's family would continue to suffer. He was certain that Democrats would not be satisfied with whatever the new investigation produced.

McConnell and the president really had no choice. Without the week's delay and the FBI's questioning of players in Ford's account,

Kavanaugh could not win Senate approval. And that was the whole point.

"I've ordered the FBI to conduct a supplemental investigation to update Judge Kavanaugh's file," Mr. Trump said in the statement. "As the Senate has requested, this update must be limited in scope and completed in less than one week."

32

Endgame

FLAKE AND COONS were feted for their rare bipartisan achievement, but the celebration would not last long for Democrats. They soon complained that the FBI was being constrained in its ability to pursue any and all leads. But the fact was that Flake and his fellow undecided Republicans—who essentially controlled the inquiry—had not asked for an open-ended investigation.

To them, exploring "current allegations" meant talking to those who might have firsthand knowledge of Ford's accusations as well as the claim that he exposed himself to his fellow undergraduate at Yale. The story brought forward by Avenatti would get no attention, and Republicans continued to use those claims as evidence of how outrageous the attacks on Kavanaugh had become. "Dems Embrace Avenatti Circus Allegations," screamed the headline of one roundup of news from McConnell's office.

It quickly became clear that the FBI report would produce no new evidence against Kavanaugh or a change in testimony by any witnesses. In the end, agents interviewed less than a dozen people, including those who Ford said were at the gathering where she was assaulted, as well as Deborah Ramirez, who said Kavanaugh exposed himself, and some of those who were said to be present then. No corroboration emerged.

Republicans were also seeing rising anger over the Kavanaugh showdown among their voters, a welcome development since they were worried heading into the midterms that Democrats were outpacing Republicans in terms of voter enthusiasm. The Republican anger freed them to take a harder line against Ford and other Kavanaugh accusers instead of worrying that they were going to alienate women and independent voters who felt Republicans were not taking the charges seriously.

Trump led the way. At a rally in Mississippi on October 2, the president mocked Ford after weeks of restraint, accusing Kavanaugh's critics of pursuing a standard of "guilty until proven innocent. That's very dangerous for our country."

Noting his own record of being accused of sexual misconduct, Trump said for him it was part of the job description but that it shouldn't have happened to Kavanaugh. He gave this portrayal of the testimony by Ford, who had said she consumed one beer on the night in question.

"What he's going through: thirty-six years ago, this happened. 'I had one beer.' Right? 'I had one beer.' 'Well, you think it was . . .' 'Nope, it was one beer.' 'Oh, good. How did you get home?' 'I don't remember.' 'How did you get there?' 'I don't remember.' 'Where is the place?' 'I don't remember.' 'How many years ago was it?' 'I don't know. I don't know. I don't know.'" The crowd clapped and cheered.

"'What neighborhood was it in?' 'I don't know.' 'Where's the house?' 'I don't know.'" More applause.

"'Upstairs, downstairs, where was it?' 'I don't know. But I had one beer, that's the only thing I remember.'

"And a man's life is in tatters. A man's life is shattered. His wife is shattered. His daughters, who are beautiful, incredible young kids— they destroy people. They want to destroy people. These are really evil people."

It was a classic Trump teardown and played to the grievances of his base. Though it rankled Flake and Collins, it was also a message to the party that it was okay to favor Kavanaugh over Ford and to move ahead with the nomination.

On October 4 the FBI submitted its report and the Senate headed for its vote as the undecided senators finally needed to make their positions known.

Joe Donnelly, the Indiana Democrat, had already said he would oppose the confirmation just before Flake won the one-week reprieve, possibly jumping the gun. His announcement left Heidi Heitkamp, the endangered North Dakota Democrat, and Joe Manchin of West Virginia as the only two Democrats who could potentially back Kavanaugh and put a thin bipartisan veneer on his approval.

One day before the first floor vote on Kavanaugh, Heitkamp, who had backed Gorsuch, announced she could not do the same for Kavanaugh. The decision represented a grave political risk and probably ended any chance she had of being reelected. But she said she could not support him considering Ford's accusations and his behavior at the emotional hearing.

"I voted for Justice Gorsuch because I felt his legal ability and temperament qualified him to serve on the Supreme Court," her statement read. "Judge Kavanaugh is different. When considering a lifetime appointment to the Supreme Court, we must evaluate the totality of the circumstances and record before us. In addition to the concerns about his past conduct, last Thursday's hearing called into question Judge Kavanaugh's current temperament, honesty, and impartiality. These are critical traits for any nominee to serve on the highest court in our country."

Heitkamp's Senate career was likely over, but she would vote her conscience.

Now all eyes turned to Collins, the quintessential Senate swing vote, and Murkowski. They controlled the outcome. The two women sat next to each other on the Senate floor and consulted frequently on how they would approach certain votes. Together they had been the key to blocking Senate Republicans from overturning the Affordable Care Act in 2017. They had also worked in tandem on the Kavanaugh vote along with Manchin, Heitkamp, and Donnelly, though the latter two were no longer part of the discussions.

Murkowski had her own, parochial reasons for moving carefully on Kavanaugh. Questioning by Senator Hirono at his initial hearing exposed Kavanaugh's relatively narrow views on the rights of Native Americans, and his position was noticed in Alaska. Native Alaskan groups opposed his nomination, and top state officials weighed in against him as well, not just on native concerns but also the possibility he might unravel the health care law that was increasingly popular in Alaska. Murkowski, who in 2010 had won on a write-in campaign after losing her primary to a Tea Party–backed challenger, relied heavily on native Alaskan support and wasn't in a hurry to antagonize that group, even though she would not be on the ballot again until 2022.

The first vote on the morning of October 5 was a procedural vote but a meaningful one to force a final vote on the confirmation. Formerly, this so-called cloture motion would have required sixty votes. But under the changes on Supreme Court nominations imposed by Republicans in 2017, only a simple majority was necessary. In some cases in the past, senators would support cloture to bring a nomination to a final vote and then oppose confirmation, but that made little sense under the new rules. The test vote was looming large.

Republicans remained on edge as the vote started, since it was still publicly unclear what Collins and Murkowski would do. Democrats would need both to vote no if they were to have a chance to stop Kavanaugh. Collins arrived first and Murkowski soon joined her at their adjoining desks. They shared a smile and a few quiet words. When it came to her place in the alphabetic roll call, Collins gave a strong aye vote. A few moments later, Murkowski, barely audible in the chamber, voted no. The two women had split. But Republicans still had the votes to advance. Aware of the vote count, Manchin entered the chamber late and cast his vote for Kavanaugh with the Republicans. Weeks of uncertainty were ending.

It still was not finished. Collins said she would announce her final position in a speech later in the day before the Senate took up the confirmation itself.

Collins was no fan of Trump, put off by his style and insults. To her, Kavanaugh was more a product of Bush-style Republicanism than Trumpism. The Bushes still maintained a home in Maine and were well liked in the state. Collins, like most of the Bush family, was an establishment Republican who believed government could be a force for good. George W. Bush lobbied her personally by phone twice on behalf of Kavanaugh, his former aide. The former president attested to Kavanaugh's character and promised she would not be sorry for her support. She also made a quiet visit to Kennebunkport to see the ailing George H. W. Bush.

Collins had been *the* target of Republican leaders throughout the confirmation fight. She was the linchpin. The confirmation had been very rough on her and her husband, Tom Daffron, as they had been subject to constant protests in Washington and Maine alike by both strangers and neighbors. A crowdfunding campaign had already raised millions of dollars for an opponent should she vote for Kavanaugh and choose to run again in two years.

Now it was finally time for her to have her say. During a meeting in the members' dining room of the Senate, she let the leadership know her plans. Grassley cried when he learned her position.

Just after three p.m. on October 5, Collins took the floor. Over nearly forty-five minutes, she made a well-researched case for Kavanaugh, one that infuriated Kavanaugh's opponents but was possibly the best-reasoned argument for Kavanaugh that Republicans had presented so far.

She attacked the grueling, partisan process that had led to this moment and said she saw Kavanaugh as a qualified judge who respected precedent when it came to such issues as abortion and gay marriage.

"As the judge asserted to me, a long-established precedent is not something to be trimmed, narrowed, discarded, or overlooked," she said. "Its roots in the Constitution give the concept of stare decisis greater weight simply because a judge might want to rule on a whim. In short, his views on honoring precedent would preclude attempts to do by stealth that which one has committed not to do overtly."

As for Ford, Collins said she found her testimony to be "sincere, painful, and compelling," and that Collins believed Ford experienced a sexual assault. But the lack of corroboration left the Ford account short of the standard Collins believed needed to be met in the case of such a major confirmation.

"Fairness would dictate that the claims at least should meet a threshold of 'more likely than not' as our standard. The facts presented do not mean that professor Ford was not sexually assaulted that night or at some other time. But they do lead me to conclude that the allegations fail to meet the 'more likely than not' standard. Therefore I do not believe that these charges can fairly prevent Kavanaugh from serving on the court."

It was over. Almost as soon as Collins finished, Manchin announced he too would support Kavanaugh. The votes were there. Kavanaugh, after one of the most divisive episodes in a confirmation history full of divisive episodes, would join the Supreme Court. Trump, in less than two years, had placed two conservative judicial stalwarts on the nation's highest court and created a clear 5–4 conservative majority. McGahn had gotten his men.

Kavanaugh was formally confirmed the following day as protesters ringed the Capitol and occupied the steps before police forced them off the plaza over to the Supreme Court. A few hours after the vote, Kavanaugh was taken to the Supreme Court, where he was sworn in by Chief Justice John Roberts, a longtime acquaintance.

At a White House ceremony a few days later, Trump was beaming as he celebrated his win. But he also offered a rare sentiment not usually seen at such events. "I want to apologize to Brett and the entire Kavanaugh family for the terrible pain and suffering you have been forced to endure," said Trump, who also offered a kind word to McConnell for the "incredible and wonderful job" he had done.

Kavanaugh was sworn in again by the retiring Kennedy, the man who had stepped aside to make way for his former clerk to take his place. That was a Supreme Court first.

In his remarks, Kavanaugh again cited his record on hiring women clerks and spoke of his other good works—a favorite theme. And he promised that the confirmation process had not changed him when it came to the administration of justice, scarring though it had to be.

"Although the Senate confirmation process tested me, as it has tested others, it did not change me," he said. "My approach to judging remains the same. A good judge must be an umpire, a neutral and impartial decider who favors no litigant or policy. A judge must be independent and must interpret the law, not make the law. A judge must interpret statutes as written. And a judge must interpret the Constitution as written, informed by history and tradition and precedent.

"I am optimistic about the future of America and the future of our independent judiciary, the crown jewel of our constitutional republic," Kavanaugh said.

If it was a crown jewel, it was one that, like the Senate, had been badly tarnished by partisanship over the preceding two years.

Benefitting from the Scalia seat held open by McConnell, Trump won the election and the ability to shape the courts, but at a steep cost to all three branches of the government in terms of public respect and confidence.

33

Repercussions

THE VOTE BY Collins infuriated Democrats and led to immediate promises that she would face a serious challenge in 2020 should she decide to run again. It also took some of the shine off her centrist standing in the capital. She faced angry comments from the public in Washington and furious constituents back home.

She was also condemned by abortion rights advocacy groups.

"In the midst of a national dialogue about sexual assault, Senator Collins sided with those who disbelieved, disrespected, and even mocked survivors of sexual assault," said Dawn Laguens, an official at Planned Parenthood. "No senator who votes to confirm Brett Kavanaugh to the Supreme Court can count themselves as a champion of *Roe v. Wade* and women's health and rights."

Collins didn't help herself when she appeared on CNN the Sunday following the vote and said that while she believed Ford was assaulted, she did not think Kavanaugh had done so, despite testimony by Ford that she was "100 percent" certain Kavanaugh was her attacker. "I do not believe that Brett Kavanaugh was her assailant," Collins said. Critics saw that as a cop-out.

As for her contentious vote, "I have to do what I think is right," Collins said. "Over the years the people of Maine have trusted me to exercise my best judgment, and that's what I did in this case."

Throughout the battle, Collins was angry that she was under attack from groups such as Planned Parenthood after she had for years championed the abortion rights cause at political risk and helped guarantee continued funding for such efforts. Her vote—and her speech—did win her plaudits from Republicans and a promise from McConnell that protecting her would be a top party priority in 2020.

She also won a rare favorable shout-out from Trump as Kavanaugh was sworn in.

"We are indebted to Senator Susan Collins for her brave and eloquent speech, and her declaration that 'when passions are most inflamed . . . fairness is most in jeopardy.' How true. How true," the president said.

Collins had carried the day for Trump and his nominee. Now critics would hold her accountable for every decision he rendered from the court. There were rewards as well. Money poured into her campaign account in the aftermath of her vote, and she set a personal best with just under $2 million raised in the final quarter of 2018. She was preparing for what could be the most difficult race of her career.

Murkowski faced backlash of her own from angry Republicans in Alaska. But she would not face the voters until 2022 and had already proved her ability to run in difficult circumstances and prevail in a state where hers is a well-known name.

Republicans also breathed a retrospective sigh of relief that the filibuster rules over the Supreme Court had been changed during the Gorsuch nomination. With the amount of acrimony surrounding Kavanaugh, they conceded that it probably would have been impossible to make the procedural change to advance him, leaving themselves open to charges of bending the process to install a flawed nominee.

Lindsey Graham, incensed over the treatment of Kavanaugh, headed out on the campaign trail to rail against his Democratic colleagues for their opposition. Even in the overheated political environment, it was an unusual move. But Graham reveled in his newly won celebrity treatment on the road.

As a newly hard-core Trump devotee and fire-breathing conservative, he found a much better reception than he ever did as a presidential candidate. He also went a long way toward securing support from both Trump and conservatives in the event of a Republican primary against him in South Carolina in 2020. In the past, he had been unsteady with the Far Right at home due to his alliance with John McCain, but those days were over.

He really stepped up the volume as he traveled the country urging the defeat of Senate Democrats with whom he had served. Graham had completed his evolution from an independent-minded Republican willing to challenge party orthodoxy and work with Democrats to someone committed to obstructing and railing against them.

"If we win here, it will be the most visible sign that Kavanaugh did matter," Graham said as he urged cheering Missourians to support Josh Hawley, the Republican rival to Democrat Claire McCaskill. "If you want to pay them back, elect Josh Hawley."

The conflict did seem to drive up Republican enthusiasm in such Trump strongholds as Indiana, where Donnelly, the Democrat, voted against Kavanaugh, though he had little to say during the fight.

"The thing that took the whole energy level up was Judge Kavanaugh," said Mike Braun, the Republican Senate contender in Indiana, talking about the tone of the conflict. "I think that was so appalling to most Hoosiers, independents, and even conservative Democrats it boosted all races across the country, especially here. Kavanaugh showed how they litigate their point of view, which is ugly."

While Republicans were crowing about their gains in voter energy, Democrats believed that the Kavanaugh fight was simultaneously helping them in the suburbs, where they were closing in on control of the House of Representatives.

As the election season headed toward its climax, the intensity of the sentiment over the Supreme Court showdown seemed to diminish a bit. Trump, on an unprecedented presidential blitz, focused much of his attention on immigration—a wedge issue that had often served him well—and a so-called caravan of refugees from Central America walking up through Guatemala and Mexico toward the border. He sent US Army troops to contain them in one of the more politicized uses of America's military in recent memory. In the final days of the election, polls showed Democrats with much of the momentum.

Returns on November 6 were a Democratic triumph in the House, with the Nancy Pelosi–led forces gaining forty seats and ousting the Republican majority. The takeover meant that Trump would confront an empowered opposition eager to hold him and his administration accountable. Democrats also did well in the state house races, installing Democratic governors in swing states that had been key to Trump's victory in 2016, notably Wisconsin, Michigan, and Pennsylvania.

The Senate was a different story. Democrats had always faced an uphill struggle in 2018, with ten seats up for election in states won by Trump in 2016 and the party defending twenty-six overall to nine for the Republicans. Democrats went down hard in Indiana, Missouri, North Dakota, and Florida, states where the incumbent Democrats had opposed Kavanaugh.

Graham believed the proof was at hand.

"Virtually all Senate Democrats running in Trump states who voted against Brett Kavanaugh were defeated," he said after the election. "Their constituents held them responsible for being part of a despicable smear campaign orchestrated by the Left."

Graham's use of the word "virtually" was instructive. In fact, more Democrats running in Trump-won states who voted against Kavanaugh were reelected, most notably Jon Tester, who survived a very difficult race in Montana. Trump visited the state four times in a personal drive to defeat Tester after Tester derailed the nomination of White House physician Ronny Jackson for secretary of the Department of Veterans Affairs. The other Trump-state winners were Bob Casey in Pennsylvania, Sherrod Brown in Ohio, Tammy Baldwin in Wisconsin, and Debbie Stabenow in Michigan.

Democrats took some lumps in the Senate contests, and Kavanaugh could have been a factor. But it was likely that the North Dakota,

Indiana, and Missouri Senate seats would have been lost even had the Kavanaugh fight not erupted. Overall, the damage was far less than what it might have been and what had been predicted early in the election cycle.

Schumer, the Democratic leader and a senator at the center of many judicial fights, saw the intensity surrounding the Kavanaugh nomination as a net plus for Democrats. "Kavanaugh's nomination hurt the Republicans significantly in the election, harming them greatly in the House and doing very little damage in the Senate," Schumer said.

One thing was not in dispute in light of the success of Republicans in holding and slightly expanding their majority in the 2018 midterms—McConnell and his fellow Republicans would continue to install judicial nominees sent up from the White House and now had more cushion to do so. With the threshold for confirmation still set at a simple majority, Democrats remained without tools to stop the onslaught, ensuring that the parade of conservative nominees would persist. Republicans, in fact, began plotting how to accelerate the assembly line to prevent Democrats from using what little procedural recourse they had to drag nominations out.

"You know what my top priority is. I've made it very clear," McConnell told reporters the day after the elections. "It's the judiciary, the two Supreme Court appointments, the twenty-nine circuit judges, the eighty-four overall number of judges." His goal remained, he said, "to keep confirming as many as we possibly can for as long as we are in a position to do so."

McConnell also began setting the stage for the Senate to consider a Supreme Court nominee in the 2020 presidential election year should an opening occur. He did not want to be hamstrung by his own "let the American people decide" standard. Given the age and health risks of some of the current members, that unwritten rule could be a little more binding than McConnell would like.

"The tradition going back to the 1880s has been if a vacancy occurs in a presidential election year, and there is a different party in control of the Senate than the presidency, it is not filled," McConnell said at a news conference.

That was another new standard—and a blatant shift by McConnell to give Republicans the cover to fill any vacancy that should occur during the remainder of Trump's term. During 2016, there had been scant talk of which party controlled the Senate as a determining factor. It had been all about letting the voters decide. Evidently, if the voters had decided to put the same party in control of the White House and Senate four years earlier, that was good enough for McConnell.

The switch was too much for Grassley, whose reputation for fairness and integrity had suffered so much over the previous two years. He said that if he were in charge, the committee would not move forward with a Supreme Court nominee in 2020.

But Grassley would not be in charge. Instead, the committee was taken over by Lindsey Graham, the new pro-Trump firebrand. The man who turned the tide for Kavanaugh at his hearing. Graham, saying he remained outraged by the Democratic tactics against Kavanaugh, promised an aggressive posture as chairman.

"I promise you this as chairman of the Judiciary Committee," Graham told a crowd in Greenville, South Carolina, in February 2019, "we are going to start over and we are going to get as many conservative judges in the system as I possibly can."

McConnell is more convinced than ever that his solitary decision made in a hotel room in the tropics during a Senate recess in February 2016 is the most important move of his political life, one that has led to a transformation of the federal courts. (Not to mentioning making him a hero among conservatives, who were in the past suspicious of his commitment.)

"The most consequential decision I've made in my career is not to do something," McConnell told a cheering evangelical audience in Washington as Kavanaugh's nomination ran into trouble. "That was to not fill the vacancy created by the death of Justice Scalia in the middle of the presidential election. Let the American people decide who they want to make this lifetime appointment. Well, it turns out that one of the most consequential decisions I ever made led to the appointment of Neil Gorsuch."

In the end, both sides believed that the warfare over the courts and Kavanaugh played to their immediate benefit—probably the worst possible outcome for the Senate, the Supreme Court, and the badly broken confirmation process. The nation's governing institutions were left facing severe challenges to both their credibility and their ability to assure the public they were acting on behalf of all Americans.

34

Polarized

IT WAS A straightforward order from the Supreme Court issued on January 22, 2019. But to anyone worried about the rightward direction of the reconstituted court, it was ominous. The five Republican appointees, their ranks bolstered in the past two years with the arrival of Justices Gorsuch and Kavanaugh, lifted an injunction prohibiting the Pentagon from carrying out President Trump's ban on transgender people serving in the military. The 5–4 ruling allowed the military, which had been reluctant to enforce the ban, to move ahead with a new policy while the merits were fought out in the lower courts.

A few weeks later, on February 7, the court again ruled 5–4, this time to block a Louisiana antiabortion law that would limit access to abortion providers from being put into force. Chief Justice Roberts joined the liberal bloc in delaying the law in what appeared to be another effort by him to prevent the court from so abruptly lurching right. But the more notable aspect of the ruling was that Kavanaugh felt so strongly about backing the Louisiana law that he was the sole justice to issue a dissent. He argued that the law—like a Texas version that had already been found unconstitutional—should not be delayed and that it was up to doctors who performed abortions to try to meet the new standard for approval to determine if a legal issue existed.

The final verdict wasn't delivered in either case, but progressives saw the rulings as a bad portent of the future. In the Pentagon case, they worried that the decision reflected a court newly insensitive to transgender rights. Kavanaugh's critics exploded over the abortion case, saying his dissent showed that he would move quickly to unravel abortion rights despite his many declarations during his confirmation battle that he would follow precedent.

Susan Collins also quickly came under attack, with progressive groups arguing that she was responsible since she had dismissed concerns about Kavanaugh undoing *Roe*. The group Demand Justice was quickly up with an ad in Maine. "Collins promised to protect women's rights," said the ad, which showed her shaking hands with the then-nominee. "It was all a sham. We won't forget."

Collins said the decision was being misinterpreted and that she still had faith in Kavanaugh.

Democrats and those on the left blamed Trump and McConnell for having "dragged the Supreme Court dramatically to the right" as the Democratic Senatorial Campaign Committee (DSCC) put it. The group said the transgender order handed down without any comment from the court was a powerful "reminder of how easily the Supreme Court can protect or undermine our most basic rights."

"When he ran for president, Trump promised to appoint Supreme Court justices who would appease his base," the group said. "And the proof is in the pudding: Brett Kavanaugh's presence on the court has already led to devastating decisions like today's allowing discrimination against transgender service members."

Of course, the DSCC was trying to raise money off the court decision, doubly underscoring just how politicized the atmosphere around the court had become. Its warning of a "right-wing takeover" of the court was issued to generate donations in support of Democratic Senate candidates who could block Trump's picks or help a Democratic president put nominees on the court over the objections of Republicans.

Clearly, the courts were now an extension of and an arena for the partisan politics that had engulfed the other two branches—the legislative and the executive. A cascading series of conflicts over three decades had culminated in an incendiary clash over three Supreme Court nominations in two years, tearing the Senate and the nation apart.

The 5–4 division had the potential to become very familiar as the court reviewed social and government policy. The justices like to say they don't wear party identification on their robes, but it was becoming increasingly clear that in the major cases arising out of the political and cultural divisions of the moment, the party label on the man who had made the appointment was a dependable indicator of how a justice would rule.

"Today's partisan split is anything but a flash in the pan," the legal scholars Neal Devins and Lawrence Baum wrote in their book, *The Company They Keep*, arguing that the justices are heavily influenced not only by who appoints them, but also by their own elite social networks. "It now defines the Court and will likely play a key role in Court decision making for the foreseeable future.

"More than ever before, the future of Court decision making is therefore tied to presidential and Senate elections."

This was a risky moment for the court, an institution held in higher esteem than the other two branches but one that saw its approval slipping. The secrecy of the court and the lack of transparency around its proceedings kept most of the public in the dark about its activities, probably one reason Americans still viewed it more favorably than the other two branches.

In the abortion ruling and in navigating a way to uphold the Affordable Care Act a few years earlier, Roberts had given every indication that he was aware of and worried about the court's image. He appeared to be taking steps to lower the partisan temperature. In public remarks, Roberts has sought to emphasize the nonpartisan role of judges. "People need to know that we are not doing politics," he said in an early 2019 speech at Belmont University College of Law in Nashville. "They need to know that we're doing something different, that we're applying the law."

But big social issues can be kept off the docket only for so long. Questions also swirled about Roberts's own power within the court. The four other conservatives—Thomas, Alito, Gorsuch, and Kavanaugh—represented a power center of their own, one that would be cemented were Trump able to replace one of the more liberal justices before leaving office.

The authority of the Supreme Court comes from the willingness of the public and the other branches of government to accept its decisions. As has long been noted, the court has no army to enforce its rulings and is reliant on Congress and the executive branch to hold up their end of the constitutional bargain when it comes to complying with court rulings. As the desegregation of schools showed, sometimes the state needed to use its police power to ensure that the court's edicts were followed.

A court that comes to be seen by a significant segment of the public as illegitimate because of the way its justices were installed—or because the court has an ideology far out of balance with that of a changing nation—runs a grave risk of losing both its moral and legal authority. To many on the left, both Gorsuch and Kavanaugh have asterisks attached to their confirmations and they will always be pretenders.

If the court moves forward and overturns precedent—particularly in the case of abortion rights—the pressure to enact major changes will mount and become part of the political dialogue in congressional and presidential races, as candidates are pressed on their opinions about overhauling the court. All recent nominees have stood by the principle of stare decisis during their confirmation hearings, but once on the court they can do as they please, and the conservative court showed no hesitation in overruling precedent in the 2018 union contributions case.

Proposals for court reform are being examined and debated with new seriousness. The basic ideas are establishing term limits of varying lengths for justices to dilute the influence of individual presidents, adding seats to the court, or establishing a rotating banc of justices similar to how an appeals court functions. The number of justices on the court has fluctuated in the past, so it would not be unprecedented to change its size, though it would require legislation. House Democrats have also proposed enacting new ethics rules for the high court, since its justices are exempt from a judicial code of conduct that applies to other federal courts.

The political winds that have always swirled around the Supreme Court have become much stronger, and its justices are going to find it difficult to ignore the outside clamor even from the privileged seclusion of their well-appointed chambers.

Directly across First Street from the court, the Senate sits wounded from its confirmation battles. The conflicts have exacted a serious toll on the institution, the relationships of those who serve in it, and its public image. The fights over Garland and Kavanaugh showed the public a dark side of a storied institution engaged in all-out political warfare rather than an attempt to find some common ground.

The filibusters of Miguel Estrada and other George W. Bush nominees, the nuclear option of 2013, the blockade of Garland, the changing of the rules to install Gorsuch, the diluting of the blue slip and the poisonous Kavanaugh hearings combined to demonstrate that the Senate's famed power of advice and consent has been corrupted to what appears to be the point of no return. Gone are the days when presidents would truly consult with senators of the opposition party in picking nominees to generate consensus or the times when senators would give deference to a president in considering the White House's nominees. "I'm not going to play it the old way if the old way is dead," said Lindsey Graham after he took over the Judiciary Committee at the beginning of 2019.

Under current rules, and at the current levels of vitriol and distrust, a future president of one party could easily be thwarted from getting essential nominees through a Senate controlled by the other. With both parties responding to their political bases, voting against the nominee of a president from the opposing party has become the norm rather than the rare occurrence. It is a prescription for a badly dysfunctional government.

As the result of the 2013 rules change eliminating the sixty-vote threshold for most nominees and the 2017 extension of that standard to the Supreme Court, a Republican president abetted by a Republican Senate will have had years to fill the courts without the need of a single Democratic vote, negating the need for any kind of compromise, consensus, or negotiation. "That is the collateral damage that is going to flow over time from abandoning the sixty-vote requirement," Graham told his Democratic colleagues. "Right now we don't need any of you all, and there will come a day when you don't need any of us.

"Judges are going to be more ideological because you don't have to reach across the aisle to get anybody's input, and it is going to have an effect over time on the judiciary that I very much regret," he said.

Regret, perhaps, but Graham appears undeterred in taking full advantage and he has made clear that he anticipates even more contentious fights ahead.

"The worst is yet to come," Graham warned Democratic Judiciary Committee members in March 2019 as he again ignored Democratic complaints about Republicans refusing to honor the blue slip as the GOP majority pushed through appeals court nominees over objections from home-state Democrats.

A handful of Democrats and Republicans have suggested that restoring the sixty-vote threshold on nominees would be a path to regaining a sense of fairness and repairing some of the partisan damage. But that seems unlikely.

As Carl Levin warned in 2013, the nuclear option initiated by Democrats demonstrated that a majority of senators can change the rules of the Senate anytime they please. Why would the Senate go back to its old rules when one party or the other could just dismantle them again at an advantageous moment?

The Senate seems more likely to be headed in the other direction: eliminating the filibuster entirely for legislation as well as nominations.

Support for the concept is rising among Democrats, who say that gutting the filibuster when they return to power would be the only way to move through the sweeping social legislation they seek—single-payer health care, required reductions in greenhouse gases to combat climate change, and immigration reforms—not to mention changes in the makeup of the Supreme Court. Democrats remain stung by the way Republicans obstructed the Obama agenda for six years only to capture the Senate in 2014 and prevent the president from placing his pick on the Supreme Court. Should they return to power, Democrats will face immense pressure from their progressive wing to dump the filibuster entirely.

The end of the filibuster might make it much easier to pass bills through the Senate, but it would also remove any incentive for the party in power to try to find bipartisan solutions. Huge policy and program changes could be enacted by one party on its own. Democrats pushed through the health care law, and Republicans spent intense effort to unravel it in court and in Congress when they regained power. Republicans pushed through sweeping tax changes. Democrats promise to undo them when they regain power.

The cycle means more policy fights thrown into the federal courts for a final decision at a time when the courts themselves are more marked by partisanship. The courts are used to mediate policy feuds because of partisan conflicts in the other two branches, throwing into question the supposed objectivity and neutrality of the third branch. It is a cycle that threatens the effectiveness of the federal government.

Activism won't only be on the Democratic and progressive side. New conservative groups will spring up to counter the assault on the conservative court, to defend its members against accusations of illegitimacy and to protect the gains Republicans made with Trump.

Recognizing the rising determinative role of the courts in interpreting federal policy, the combination of McGahn, McConnell, and Grassley—with a big assist from Trump, of course—made remarkable strides in placing deeply ideological conservatives backed and groomed by the Federalist Society on the federal appellate and district courts.

The Trump parade of judges flipped the ideological balance of at least one appellate circuit, increased the conservative bent of others, and narrowed the advantage of Democratic appointees on liberal courts such as the Ninth Circuit, based in San Francisco. More significantly, the Trump judges are younger on average than those appointed by his predecessors, meaning they could still be on the courts into the 2050s and beyond. Even when they replace judges picked by previous Republican presidents, the Trump appointees are typically more conservative than the ones they replace. The only thing standing in the way of even greater gains by Republicans is the reluctance of some judges nominated by Democrats from stepping down in the current environment and allowing the Trump administration and Republican-led Senate to install their successors.

On a single day in February 2019, the Judiciary Committee sent forty judicial nominees to the floor—six appellate court judges and thirty-four district court judges. Many were holdovers from the previous Congress, but it was still a veritable flood of nominees. Later that month, the Senate for the first time ever confirmed an appeals court judge, Eric Miller of the Ninth Circuit, to a court without the support of either of his home state senators—Washington Democrats Patty Murray and Maria Cantwell.

"Court packing is proceeding apace," declared Senator Hirono, decrying the background and records of multiple nominees who were being rapidly ushered through to the federal bench. One of the forty had called Obama an un-American imposter. Another had refused to say that *Brown v. Board of Education* had been properly decided. Four of the appellate judges had not received blue slips from their home state senators.

Durbin said that multiple nominees lacked suitable qualifications and had shown judgment far outside the judicial mainstream. "We are all diminished when we barrel through these nominations," he said.

The Republican response: "Too bad." They had the votes. In a Senate where nominations are determined by a simple majority, that is all that is necessary. They had no problem with the records or views of the nominees. The Republican position was that Democrats would do the same to them if the situation were reversed. They were right in one respect—Democrats will almost certainly act similarly or even more aggressively if they get the chance in the future. History shows that the most recently wronged party steps it up a notch as soon as the occasion arises.

The forty judges approved by the Judiciary Committee in one sense represented the end of an era. Most had been nominated during the tenure of McGahn, the force behind the Trump administration's drive to remake the federal judiciary. McGahn left the White House after the Kavanaugh confirmation, his departure first announced by Trump, as usual, on Twitter at the end of August.

"White House Counsel Don McGahn will be leaving his position in the fall, shortly after the confirmation (hopefully) of Judge Brett Kavanaugh to the United States Supreme Court," Trump tweeted. "I have worked with Don for a long time and truly appreciate his service!"

Trump had neglected to tell McGahn he was going to make the pronouncement. The president had grown tired of reports about McGahn's looming departure and had never really forgiven him for failing to stop Attorney General Jeff Sessions from recusing himself from the Russia inquiry, a failing that Trump and his allies believed left the president badly exposed. McGahn had also given extensive testimony to the special counsel, a fact that alarmed Trump and White House insiders, including his daughter Ivanka and son-in-law Jared Kushner. They were no fans of McGahn.

Trump might have been ready to see McGahn go, but that was not the reaction on Capitol Hill. McConnell called him "the best White House counsel I've seen on the job" as well as "one of the most successful and consequential aides to any president in recent memory." Grassley was upset and tried to catch Trump's attention with his own tweet. "I hope it's not true McGahn is leaving WhiteHouse Counsel. U can't let that happen."

But McGahn was out, though he still had to see his way through the Kavanaugh crucible. It would be a challenge for any successor to replicate the determination and willingness to bludgeon Democrats that McGahn had shown in the judicial fights.

Grassley himself was moving on as well. His time as a nonlawyer heading the Judiciary Committee was at an end, and he finished it on a successful note, finally gathering the overwhelming support needed to convince McConnell to bring up a bipartisan criminal justice measure he had labored on for years. After all he had done for McConnell on judges, it still took a tremendous push from Grassley to get the majority leader to bring up the overhaul for a vote, though it passed overwhelmingly. McConnell feared that reducing sentences for felons hurt his party's law-and-order image, despite the concept having deep conservative support.

Grassley became chairman of the Finance Committee, a panel without the searing partisanship of the Judiciary Committee. He quickly took a more bipartisan stance on several issues, but Democrats will never forget or forgive his role in the blockade of Garland, the weakening of the blue slip, or his handling of the Kavanaugh hearing.

McConnell will forever be credited by Republicans and condemned by Democrats for his resistance to Obama that culminated with obstruction of Garland for nearly a year. But the biggest beneficiary of that effort was not McConnell or even Gorsuch, the man ultimately named to the seat so suddenly vacated by Scalia on that holiday weekend in February 2016. The biggest winner was undoubtedly Donald Trump.

Trump would almost certainly not have won the presidency without that open court seat to entice Republican voters and keep them supporting him despite personal failings of the sort that were on vivid display in the now infamous *Access Hollywood* tape. The opening also led to the creation of Trump's list, which allowed him to identify the specific people he intended to place on the court, adding another level of insurance for conservative leaders, who were able to rally their followers behind Trump.

With McGahn as chief architect, the strategy of pushing movement conservatives onto the courts also helped Trump sustain the support of his core voters even as his administration struggled with incompetence and failures, such as the inability to repeal the health care law—a major conservative disappointment. The success in naming judges was the signal achievement of Trump's first two years.

In the coming years, those judges will be among the members of the federal bench called to rule on Trump's policies and practices in cases arising from challenges initiated by increasingly confrontational Democrats and other legal adversaries around the nation.

Mitch McConnell made a snap decision one night in 2016. The consequences will reverberate for decades.

Afterword

As THE US House of Representatives closed in on the impeachment of President Donald J. Trump in November 2019, Trump and top Senate Republicans assembled in the East Room of the White House for a celebration. Trump was about to suffer the ignominious fate of becoming only the third US president to be impeached by a vote of the full House. Yet he and his steadfast Senate allies were downright ebullient.

"Thank you all for being here as we celebrate a profoundly historic milestone and a truly momentous achievement," Trump told the cheerful audience, none beaming so broadly as Senator Mitch McConnell, the ruthless Senate majority leader.

The occasion was to mark the confirmation of the forty-fifth federal appeals court judge nominated by the president and enthusiastically confirmed by the McConnell-led Senate since early 2017. One quarter of all federal appellate judges in the nation were now hard-right appointees thoroughly vetted by the conservative Federalist Society in advance of their lifetime appointments. They were younger, whiter, and more ideologically predictable than even those put forward by previous Republican presidents, and they would serve for decades.

A plan set in motion three years earlier to remake the federal judiciary by seizing the unexpected opportunity afforded by the astonishing election of Trump had succeeded beyond anything McConnell could have imagined when he set out to do it. And he was not shy about highlighting his essential role in the top-to-bottom remaking of the federal judiciary that had taken place. Even with the White House occupied by a man who did not appreciate it when others claimed credit Trump thought his due, McConnell was willing to trumpet how his own machinations had benefited the president.

"You had been helped enormously by a decision that I made, and these guys backed me up, not to let President Obama fill that Scalia vacancy on his way out the door," McConnell said when summoned to the podium by Trump. McConnell was referring, of course, to his norm-shattering move in February 2016 to block any attempt by Barack Obama to replace Antonin Scalia on the court though Obama still had eleven months in office. That decision led Senate Republicans to ignore the nomination of Judge Merrick B. Garland and helped seal Trump's election that November by attracting conservative voters and evangelicals who set aside their doubts about Trump and his character in favor of the prospect of another Republican nominee to the Supreme Court.

That led to Trump putting at least two new justices on the high court, empaneling a dependable conservative majority with the possibility of more to come. But that was hardly all of it. By the end of 2019, almost 190 new federal judges had been seated on the bench through the intense Republican focus on filling court vacancies. Thirteen district court judges alone were confirmed during the Senate's last week of 2019 and Democrats, due to rules changes by both parties, were essentially helpless to impede the onslaught. Republicans took full advantage of the more than one hundred vacancies Trump inherited because of Republican obstructionism during the final two years of the Obama era and then some.

McConnell was quick to correct Fox's Sean Hannity in a December interview when Hannity professed amazement at all the vacancies Obama left behind.

"I'll tell you why," McConnell interjected. "I was in charge of what we did the last two years of the Obama administration."

Those final district court judges of 2019 were just icing on the cake. The real prize was the fifty judges named to the thirteen circuit courts around the nation, the judicial settings where most of the binding decisions are made. It was twice as many as Obama had seen confirmed in his first three years and nearly as many as Trump's immediate predecessor had put on the bench over eight years.

At the start of Trump's tenure, some analysts had predicted his stamp on the courts would not be so overpowering because it would be difficult to influence the overall tilt of the circuit courts.

No one was saying that at the end of 2019. Republicans had shifted three circuits—the Second, Third, and Eleventh—from a majority of judges nominated by Democrats to a majority of judges put on by Republicans. Even the famously liberal Ninth Circuit based in San Francisco—a court seen as a reliable impediment to Trump policies—was nearing parity.

All the appeals court nominees were certifiably conservative. Some had the type of backgrounds—Supreme Court clerkships, elite law schools, prosecutorial careers—that would have brought them to the attention of any Republican president and landed them on the bench. But others had little to no actual trial experience. Their nominations rested on their conservative bona fides, contacts in the conservative judicial movement, and backing of the Federalist Society. At least two were rated unqualified by the American Bar Association, a finding that in the past would have scuttled any hope of confirmation.

The parade of conservatives to the courts had so alarmed progressives that they were openly urging sitting federal judges who had been nominated by Democrats to hold off on any retirement plans until after the 2020 elections, hoping to limit the number of vacancies McConnell and Trump would be able to fill. With the president facing impeachment, progressive groups called for the Senate to halt confirmations entirely—a plea that McConnell would definitely not heed.

Democrats were aghast at both the pace and the quality of the nominees.

"As a senator, I have now worked with four separate administrations, Democrat and Republican, on the appointment of federal judges," said Senator Chuck Schumer, the Democratic leader from New York who has a long history in judicial confirmation fights. "I can say with perfect confidence that over the last three years, President Trump has nominated—and Senate Republicans have approved—the most unqualified and radical nominees in my time in this body."

The legal results were already being felt with Trump-nominated judges weighing in with conservative rulings in a number of cases concerning federal policy, including abortion rights, immigration, and health care. Trump, enmeshed in impeachment and unpopular with most Americans according to the polls, knew he had one man to thank for an element of his legacy that could not be taken from him no matter what happened in the months ahead.

"Mitch, great job," the president told him that day at the White House. "We are going to be, I think, just about number one by the time we finish—number one of any president, any administration," the president exulted. Number one was always number one with this president.

McConnell had his issues with Trump. The majority leader was a man who would say something only when it suited his interests while the president was a man who always had to say something—much of it angry and nasty toward his critics and opponents. Trump was vengeful. Donald F. McGahn II, who as White House counsel engineered the judicial assembly line in close coordination with McConnell, didn't attend the White House event celebrating the accomplishment, nor was his name even mentioned. McGahn was persona non grata after Trump pushed him out over his cooperation with the special investigation into Russian election interference. Excluding McGahn was an egregious oversight that underscored Trump's pettiness.

McConnell's relentless push for judges came at a cost to the Senate. The legislative activity in the "world's greatest deliberative body" virtually dried up, frustrating both Democrats and Republicans who grew increasingly bored simply processing nominees rather than doing the policy work some of them came to Washington to do. The frustration was spilling out.

"I have this sense," said Senator Lamar Alexander, a close McConnell ally who is leaving the Senate at the end of 2020, "that there is going to be a collective feeling around here—and I'm not sure when it will come—that there is more to life than judges and impeachment." Alexander had several major bipartisan pieces of legislation that had not seen the light of day despite broad support.

But to McConnell, Senate life was judges. And more judges. With his own name on the ballot in November 2020, he was eager both to show conservatives that he was doing all he could to stack the courts while avoiding legislative votes that could divide his party and cause him problems with the White House. No Republican could survive an election battle if Donald Trump turned on them—the party had become an extension of the president.

At the Supreme Court, 2019 had delivered a divided verdict on the impact of the new conservative majority, mainly through the careful management by Chief Justice John G. Roberts Jr., of both the cases and the outcomes. One of the most politically charged rulings of the year, whether to add a citizenship question to the 2020 Census, went against the administration on a 5–4 outcome, with Roberts being the decisive vote in joining the liberal bloc. Both Justices Neil M. Gorsuch and Brett M. Kavanaugh—the two justices added to the court by Trump—sided with their fellow Republican-nominated justices.

Roberts joined with them on other high-profile decisions, such as taking the court out of partisan gerrymandering cases. Other decisions walked right up to the edge of "deconstructing the administrative state"—ending the power of the federal bureaucracy. It was clear that the next time a relevant case came along that the high court would rein in the power of federal agencies—a main priority of the new justices.

More immediately, the court faced multiple decisions on the reach of executive power and legal immunity sought by the White House as House Democrats pressed their investigations into the president and his administration. The court was being watched closely to see if Trump would prevail despite ample precedent that he should not.

The high court faced a testing year that would challenge its credibility anew.

On the campaign trail, Democratic presidential candidates were under increasing pressure to detail how they would counter Trump and McConnell's assault on the courts as progressives demanded answers that were hard to deliver. No clear strategy emerged, though Democrats recognized that a second Trump term with a Senate Republican majority would mean an even more profound transformation of the lower courts and likely the Supreme Court as well.

As for the evangelical support that helped deliver the presidency to Trump, it remained solid despite some breaks as a few leading Christians questioned the movement's unwavering allegiance to a president whose constant falsehoods, bitter personal attacks, lack of compassion, and profane comments ran counter to conventional Christian beliefs.

Lindsey Graham, the South Carolinian who had taken over the Judiciary Committee and the confirmation assembly line in 2019, thought he knew the reason why.

"When you run and get reelected a year from now," he told Trump at the White House judicial celebration, "one of the main reasons is that people in the conservative world believe that you fight for judges."

It wasn't possible to predict Trump's future despite Graham's best effort. But in one respect at least, his legacy—and McConnell's—is firmly established. They had steamrolled Democrats on judges, succeeding beyond their wildest dreams in reshaping the courts and influencing the interpretation of federal law for generations to come.

Even after their personal influence is long gone from the capital, Trump and McConnell—two political figures reviled by their opponents as well as large segments of the American public—will still have their say through scores of jurists they installed through hardball political tactics and a willingness to press their advantage to the fullest extent. To them, that was more than enough reason for an exuberant White House celebration in the middle of an impeachment fight.

January 2020

Acknowledgments

MANY PEOPLE DESERVE my deep gratitude for their help and support in writing this book.

I want to first thank my ever-patient wife, Kim, for her regular morale boosts, and my two sons, Nicholas and Benjamin, for agreeing to still occasionally be seen with me. I want to express appreciation to my siblings for their regular expressions of surprise that I could write a book. Also many thanks to my friend and fellow cruise ship lecturer Maureen Dowd for her encouragement and confidence in me over many years.

The impetus for this book came from Matt Latimer and Keith Urbahn at the Javelin literary agency, and they should share in any credit and none of the blame. I also want to thank Jonathan Jao, my very understanding editor at HarperCollins, for guiding and putting up with a first-time author, and to HarperCollins for publishing this book.

Thank you also to the *New York Times* and the Sulzberger family for allowing me a thirty-three-year opportunity to view important events up close and convey my impressions of them to the knowing audience of the *Times*. I want to thank the management of the *Times*, including executive editor Dean Baquet, Washington bureau chief Elisabeth Bumiller, and Washington editor Bill Hamilton, for their indulgence. Thanks also to former executive editor Jill Abramson for taking a chance on me way back when.

I owe a particular debt of gratitude to Adam Liptak, the crack SCOTUS reporter of the *Times*, for his patience and generosity in sharing his deep expertise with me. His guidance was essential. Fellow

Cubs fan and *Times* legal expert Charlie Savage deserves a shout-out as well.

To my office podmates and esteemed authors who share a section of the Washington bureau with me—Helene Cooper, Mark Mazzetti, Mark Landler, Matt Rosenberg, Scott Shane, and Mike Schmidt—I say thanks for sharing all your book advice, friendship, and particularly the laughter we need in our stressful jobs. Mark Leibovich doesn't sit with us but he deserves thanks as well. David Corn gets credit for curbside writing advice.

Thanks also to Jared and Andrew for their companionship, and to Mikayla Bouchard, my podcast partner, for her constructive advice.

Also my deep appreciation to all the politicians, staff members, and operatives who agreed to talk to me so I could offer a comprehensive account of what I believe to be a vital and unappreciated story about the state of our government, how we got here, and where we might be headed. Some of you now probably regret talking to me.

As a longtime resident of Capitol Hill, I find the Capitol to be a constant beacon of inspiration and national pride. I hope the people working inside it find a way to overcome their deepening divisions for the good of us all.

Notes on Sources

Chapter 1: Based on interviews by the author with Trump administration principals with firsthand knowledge of White House strategy regarding the Supreme Court.

Chapter 2: Accounts of Justice Scalia's death are taken from public records and news reporting at the time. Mitch McConnell was interviewed by the author, with some of his views and perceptions of President Obama taken from McConnell's own memoir, *The Long Game*.

Chapter 3: Leonard Leo was interviewed by the author. His interaction with the Scalia family came from a source familiar with events. Josh Holmes, the McConnell strategist, was interviewed by the author.

Chapter 4: Denis McDonough and Susan Collins were interviewed by the author. Events in California came from White House aides present at the time. David Krone's comments were from contemporaneous emails to the author. The conversation between Don McGahn and Donald Trump came from a source with direct knowledge. The exchanges from the debate came from transcripts. Remarks by Chuck Schumer and Mike Lee came from interviews on February 14, 2016, with the *New York Times*. Harry Reid's remarks came from a transcript as well as an interview with the author.

Chapter 5: Ron Klain was interviewed by the author. The sense of President Obama's view of the chances of filling the vacancy came from top White House officials. McConnell's comments were taken from an interview with the author.

Chapter 6: The exchange between Harry Reid and Chuck Grassley on the Senate floor was witnessed by the author with their remarks drawn from the Congressional Record. The White House reaction came from administration officials.

Chapter 7: Patrick Leahy was interviewed by the author. Other accounts of the Oval Office meeting were drawn from news stories at the time and transcripts of remarks to the press. Shailagh Murray was interviewed by the author.

Chapter 8: Leonard Leo was interviewed by the author. Trump's activities were taken from contemporaneous news accounts and people with direct knowledge. His press conference remarks are from a video and transcript.

Chapter 9: Most of the information in this chapter was taken from the historical record via transcripts, video, and contemporaneous news accounts. Leonard Leo was interviewed by the author.

Chapter 10: Information was taken from news accounts and Senate hearing transcripts. Harry Reid was interviewed by the author.

Chapter 11: Material came from the author's own news coverage at the time, transcripts of news reports, and the author's interview in 2018 with Tom Daschle.

Chapter 12: Ben Nelson was interviewed by the author. Other material came from news accounts, previously unseen documents from the

Gang of Fourteen negotiations, and the author's own coverage of the events, including the conversation with John Warner.

Chapter 13: Information was drawn from the Congressional Record, transcripts of news events, public statements, and the author's own coverage at the time on the Democratic strategy to overcome the Republican filibusters. Kathryn Ruemmler was interviewed by the author.

Chapter 14: Quotes were taken from the Congressional Record as well as the author's interviews with Harry Reid and Carl Levin.

Chapter 15: The account of the selection of Merrick Garland is based on interviews with multiple White House officials and outside advisers involved in the process. Obama's remarks were taken from transcripts. The *Harvard Gazette* published a full account of Garland's August 2016 speech.

Chapter 16: The Democratic strategy was outlined in a previously undisclosed document obtained by the author. Chuck Grassley and Orrin Hatch were interviewed by the author. Obama's remarks in Chicago came from White House transcripts. Exchanges between Grassley and fellow senators were taken from the Congressional Record. The email from the Republican strategist was to the author.

Chapter 17: Based on multiple interviews with sources directly familiar with the interactions between Trump and McGahn on the release of the list of potential nominees as well as public statements and press releases.

Chapter 18: Accounts were provided by White House and congressional officials directly involved in the campaign for Garland. Convention speeches were from transcripts, and Trump's remarks in Iowa were taken from a video of the event. The account of the post-convention White House meeting was provided by attendees. The description of the Republican election-night gathering came from those at the event, and McConnell's assessment was provided in an interview.

Chapter 19: The comments of Tony Perkins were taken from a C-SPAN video. The author interviewed Leonard Leo, Nan Aron, Eric Schultz, Mitch McConnell, and John Podesta for their perspectives.

Chapter 20: Based on interviews with Trump administration officials who had firsthand knowledge of the selection process, a previously confidential planning memo obtained by the author, biographical information of Neil M. Gorsuch, White House transcripts, public statements, and interviews with those involved in Gorsuch's meetings with senators and his hearing preparation.

Chapter 21: Drawn from transcripts of the Gorsuch confirmation hearing, the author's own reporting during the hearing, and sources with direct knowledge of the Supreme Court's decision to issue a ruling that would embarrass Gorsuch during his hearing.

Chapter 22: Based on the author's own reporting and interviews with Michael Bennet, Chris Coons, and Leonard Leo.

Chapter 23: The author interviewed Mitch McConnell for *The New Washington* podcast of the *New York Times* and also interviewed Chuck Grassley and Richard Durbin. Other information was taken from news accounts and public statements.

Chapter 24: Based on White House transcripts, senatorial correspondence, Judiciary Committee proceedings, and interviews with those involved in the Senate vetting and confirmation process.

Chapter 25: Based on multiple interviews with those with firsthand knowledge of the run-up to Anthony Kennedy's retirement and Don McGahn's role in it. Dianne Feinstein, Jeff Merkley, Jennifer Duffy, Brian Fallon, and John Podesta were interviewed by the author.

Chapter 26: Accounts provided by those with firsthand knowledge of the deliberations over the Kavanaugh nomination and the resistance to it by some conservatives on Capitol Hill and in the advocacy community as well as the author's own reporting on Kavanaugh's credentials.

Chapter 27: Drawn from public statements by senators in advance of the confirmation hearing and interviews with congressional and administration sources.

Chapter 28: Based on the author's coverage of the confirmation hearings as well as transcripts of the proceedings.

Chapter 29: Drawn from the author's coverage of the hearings and related transcripts and documents.

Chapter 30: Much of the information came from multiple interviews with Republicans deeply involved in the confirmation process both at the White House and the Senate and who were present for the non-public events described. Those accounts were supplemented by independent reporting by the author and news accounts credited in the chapter. Susan Collins and Tom Cole were interviewed by the author.

Chapter 31: Drawn from Judiciary Committee proceedings and separate interviews with various members of the committee.

Chapter 32: Based on public events and statements and media appearances by senators.

Chapter 33: Chuck Schumer was interviewed by the author. Mike Braun was interviewed by Michael Tackett of the *New York Times*. Other information was drawn from public appearances of the speakers.

Chapter 34: Based on the author's own reporting and analysis along with Judiciary Committee proceedings.

Index